MORE TRAILS,
MORE TALES

MORE TRAILS, MORE TALES

Exploring Canada's Travel Heritage

BOB HENDERSON

DUNDURN
TORONTO

Project Editor: Jennifer McKnight
Copy-Editor: Andrea Waters
Design: Laura Boyle
Cover Design: Laura Boyle
Front cover: Bob at Burnside River Canyon. *Photo courtesy of Morten Asfeldt.*
Back cover: Bob and Takako Takano on the Mara-Burnside river system. *Photo courtesy of Hans Gelter.*
Unless otherwise noted, all images are from the author's collection.
All maps produced by Chrismar Mapping Services.
Printer: Webcom

Library and Archives Canada Cataloguing in Publication

Henderson, Bob, 1956-, author
      More trails, more tales : exploring Canada's travel heritage / Bob Henderson.

Includes bibliographical references and index. Issued in print and electronic formats.

ISBN 978-1-4597-2180-7 (pbk.).--ISBN 978-1-4597-2181-4 (pdf).-- ISBN 978-1-4597-2182-1 (epub)

1. Canada--Historical geography. 2. Canada--History. 3. Canada--Description and travel.
4. Trails--Canada. I. Title.

FC76.H453 2014   971   C2014-906755-0
                                    C2014-906756-9

1 2 3 4 5   18 17 16 15 14

  Canada

ONTARIO ARTS COUNCIL
CONSEIL DES ARTS DE L'ONTARIO
an Ontario government agency
un organisme du gouvernement de l'Ontario

We acknowledge the support of the **Canada Council for the Arts** and the **Ontario Arts Council** for our publishing program. We also acknowledge the financial support of the **Government of Canada** through the **Canada Book Fund** and **Livres Canada Books**, and the **Government of Ontario** through the **Ontario Book Publishing Tax Credit** and the **Ontario Media Development Corporation.**

VISIT US AT

Dundurn.com | @dundurnpress | Facebook.com/dundurnpress | Pinterest.com/dundurnpress

DUNDURN
3 Church Street, Suite 500
Toronto, Ontario, Canada
M5E 1M2

CONTENTS

Acknowledgements   7

Introduction: Following Blazed Trails   12

PART ONE   **19**

Introduction: Peregrinations   **21**

  1   A Mara-Burnside Trip/Conference and the First   24
Franklin Expedition

  2   Remote Persons and Remote Places: Wendell   41
Beckwith, Nirivia, and Others

  3   Finding Cabins: Stories from the Horton and   53
Nahanni Rivers and George Douglas's Northcote Farm

  4   The French River and Georgian Bay: 69
Big Eddies and Ice Fields in Spring Waters

  5   Deep Time and Deep Reflection: 81
Baffin Island Ski Touring

PART TWO   **93**

Introduction: Perspectives   **95**

  6   Historical Anomalies: To Deny It or Rely On It,   98
That Is the Question

7   The Delights of Local Trails   113

8   Significant Trees: Touchstones to Other   131
    Times of Living and Travel

9   Big Canoes and Their Builders   149

PART THREE   **167**

Introduction: Personalities   **169**

10 Morten Asfeldt: Educator   171

11 Linda Leckie: Place Dweller   178

12 André-François Bourbeau: 183
    Scientist and Historical Re-Enactor

13 Adrienne Blattel: Community Worker   189

14 Mark Smith and Christine Kennedy: Map-Makers   194

15 Mike Beedell: Photographer and Adventurer   199

16 Diane Gribbin: River Guide   206

Epilogue   **212**

Notes   **218**

ACKNOWLEDGEMENTS

Writing the acknowledgements spells the end of the trail for a book. I write this aspect last. In so doing, there is a celebratory quality to the moment and a feeling of gratitude to the many people who have had a role, major and minor, in putting the book together.

First there are friends from the trail who have been inspirational and have shared campfire stories. Then there are friends who have provided ideas for the content within. Then there are primary researchers whose work I have pursued with great curiosity in the library and in the field. Finally, there is the publishing crew. These are folks who have encouraged me to write and helped in the process as readers, editors, and computer-savvy people (I'm happy to share my learning needs). I need lots of help from this final category of people. Heck, I need and get help from many along the trails of the book writing process on all fronts. I'm just a guy who *really* likes a good story or a useful theory, and who loves to share both. After that, I seek help as a writer for details and for writing cues. It really is a team process.

So let's name them. I likely will not get *all* those listed who should be acknowledged. As the terrain I cover, geographically and thematically, expands in these pages, so too does the number of helpers along the way. I'm happy to be all over the map here. These acknowledgements recognize this fact.

First, there have been many friends who have helped with a suggested reference, a trip route, the openness to share their story or their connections to a story, and the willingness to listen to my versions and contribute ideas. Thanks go out to friends Mandy Heyninck, Al Pace and Lin Ward, Miranda McKeen, Joe Milligan, Ryan Howard, Bruce Hyer, Alice Casselman, Sean Collins, Deb Diebel, Jim Pearson, Tracee Chambers, Cindy McKenna, Bob Ross, Kathy Hooke, William Gastle, Zabe MacEachren, Eleanor Bell, Chris Blythe, Christina Ruddy, and Cameron Deeth.

In the "My Studies" section of this book, I consider myself a secondary researcher, which means I am delving into the stories of friends who are primary researchers. Their books, articles, and websites have sent me out to explore on the trails. Thanks to Robert Burcher and Gérard Leduc as guiding lights in considering historical anomalies. Robert Burcher and Scott Cameron were central to my enthusiasm for the John Muir local trail story in Meaford. Local historian extraordinaire Allan McGillivray has been an inspiration though his commitment to the local stories of Uxbridge, Ontario, and its region. Paul O'Hara has been most generous in sharing his research into marker trees. Dave Standfield and Svend Ulstrup were instrumental to my knowledge of big canoes. Emily Root has helped me for many years to appreciate the decolonization work involved in rethinking Canadian canoe heritage. Finally, from the "My Travels" section of More Trails, More Tales, I am grateful for the assistance of Morten Asfeldt, Mike Beedell, and André-François Bourbeau for input from their vast knowledge of their specialities: Arctic travel, historical re-enactments, and northern wildlife encounters.

The Chrismar Mapping Services team of Mark Smith and Christine Kennedy have produced the informative and attractive maps so important to my travels and studies. What fun it is to work with them.

I had a proofreading party close to my looming deadline. Thanks to my readers, Heather Jordon, Tom Hawks, David Taylor, Liz Calvin, Patti Blair, Christine Kennedy, Mark Smith, and Margot Peck, for their careful individual readings of chapters. Barry Penhale and Jane Gibson have been major supporters of my work and have helped me in all aspects of publishing, from idea sharing, to editing, to promotion. It has been a pleasure to have worked with them now for over a decade. They along with the rest of the Dundurn team, particularly Jennifer McKnight and copy-editor Andrea Waters, have made this a pleasurable experience all along the trail. I am grateful to their attention to detail, a skill I left on a portage trail somewhere long ago.

To Greer Gordon, I owe special thanks. Since 2003, Greer and I have worked as a team. I write with pencil and paper. Greer types and formats and tells me what sucks early on. Hey, she isn't always right, but she always demands I never get too relaxed as a writer. Together from start to finish, I so value the team approach we bring to this book. Thanks, Greer!

Finally, Margot Peck has been my partner supporting me throughout this writing process, as well as a travel partner on a number of the trips and outings within. We have shared the joys of the trail and many friendships. What a special feeling to share life together purposefully and passionately. Most mornings we open the day with promise, surrounded by our cats and with a cup of coffee and conversation. This writing experience never felt like a lonely one. Wait, that's not because of the cats. Thanks, Margot! Love you!

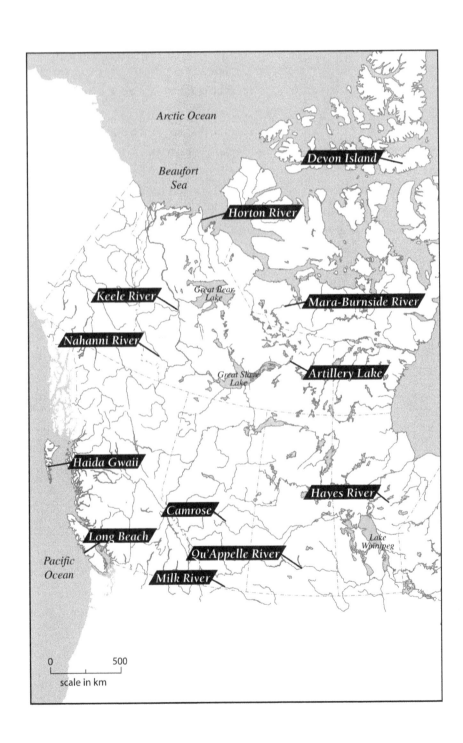

Arctic Ocean

Beaufort
Sea

Devon Island

Horton River

Keele River

Great Bear
Lake

Mara-Burnside River

Nahanni River

Great Slave
Lake

Artillery Lake

Haida Gwaii

Hayes River

Camrose

Long Beach

Lake
Winnipeg

Qu'Appelle River

Pacific
Ocean

Milk River

0   500

scale in km

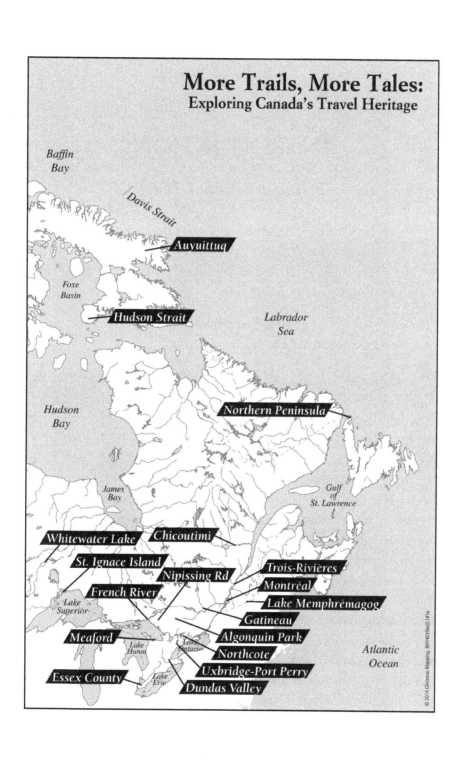

More Trails, More Tales:
Exploring Canada's Travel Heritage

Baffin
Bay

Davis Strait

Auyuittuq

Foxe
Basin

Hudson Strait

Labrador
Sea

Northern Peninsula

Hudson
Bay

James
Bay

Gulf
of
St. Lawrence

Whitewater Lake

Chicoutimi

St. Ignace Island

Nipissing Rd

Trois-Rivières

Montréal

French River

Lake Memphrémagog

Lake
Superior

Gatineau

Meaford

Lake
Huron

Lake
Ontario

Algonquin Park

Northcote

Atlantic
Ocean

Essex County

Lake
Erie

Uxbridge-Port Perry

Dundas Valley

INTRODUCTION

Following Blazed Trails

"The many become one and are increased by one."[1]
— Alfred North Whitehead

I cut a blaze — an axe-cut wedge — out of a prominent tree to mark a portage trail at a tricky canoe portage takeout. It was 1980. Little did I know then that I would be returning to this same blaze every year from 1982 to 2010. Blazed trees as trail markers have always symbolized for me the proud old ways of the bush: ways tried, tested, and true. Each time I return, eight students and I pause in canoes at the portage takeout to consider where the trail begins. Usually they opt for an open band of rock, a rising boulder field that inspired my decision to cut a new trail in the first place thirty years ago. I point out the blaze on an aging white birch. Now a faint trail heading obliquely up from the lake becomes more evident.

I mentioned the long tradition of cutting blazes to mark and follow trails. The white birch decayed and fell to the ground in 2009. This is how portage routes were traditionally opened up, that is by fire rangers, trappers, and early summer camp groups here, north of Sudbury, and throughout the woodlands of Canada. Likely the first survey crew through this particular route in 1900 followed Native blaze markings.

Reading blazes is a good observational skill to learn. "Perhaps you'll need to follow the blazes later on the trip," I suggest to the students.

The skill already proves useful at this first portage. We unload the canoes for our portage, carrying all our supplies and our canoes. Here, I often muse, students might be thinking, "I'm a long way from home." I often wonder, "Does this adventure of the inner spirit and the outer physical body feel like a strange homecoming? In other words, despite being a new experience for many students, does this feel strangely natural?" I also pause to acknowledge the satisfaction I feel in returning to that same blaze and that heritage-laden pedagogical moment year after year. Some things are changing and some things stay the same.

A blazed tree marking a trail in the Skoki Lodge area.

Finding one's way by following blazed trails: I have much enthusiasm for such an experience. Each axe cut is a thing of beauty to me. I feel like an old-timer (and I'm not even sixty) when I consider all facets of the art of marking a trail by blazing axe marks on both sides of a prominent tree. Is following a blazed trail a dying skill?

Recently, on a Skoki Lodge cross-country ski outing just east of Lake Louise, Alberta, our group came to an abrupt stop: a fork in the trail. The more used trail went straight, but the less used trail (of the last few days, anyway) went off to the left. There were pink streamers marking the route to the left. I scouted ahead and saw glorious blazes on trees on the left route. As it turned out, the straight fork was only short-lived and joined the main trail. There is a reason to pause here. Why the streamers? The well-blazed trail offered plenty of directional guidance for a ski trail. The fork represented a few groups getting off track but rejoining the correct trail around a knoll and down a hill. Today, perhaps we need pink ribbon because old school blazes are not enough. I imagine Ken Jones and Lizzie Rummel, early guides for the 1930s–40s lodge, rolling in their graves at this need for more navigational aid. Or am I becoming a crotchety, even arrogant old-timer (hmm, more a mid-timer with old-timer sensibilities, I think)? But these old-timers I'm thinking about are mostly gone now, and the blazed trees they left are slowly coming down too. Heck, Ken Jones likely cut out those axe wedges in the 1940s when working at Skoki.[2]

There is a lesson in following blazed trails. The pink streamers certainly added a practical quality to that forked trail decision, but it irked my aesthetic sensibility in the woods that day. Those streamers took something away. If we lose the ability to follow blazed trails, we lose certain wisdom of the old ways of the bush. We lose knowledge of a time when more people lived, worked, and travelled in the bush. New materials can change, even improve, some things, but there is something lost in not being able to identify old blazes and not knowing something of the type of folks who cut them and of their times on the land and water.

This book is about following blazed trails back in time, mostly to gain that special wisdom of feeling connected to and energized by places, stories, people, and practices. And why is feeling connected to and energized by old ways, old times, and old-timers valuable? Well, as Canadian ecologist John Livingston used to say about ecology: it is possible to feel "part of a greater enterprise of life."[3] Or, as educator Peter Higgins has asked, "Is it better to be a small person in a large landscape, or a large person in a small landscape?"[4] Knowing the stories of past travellers and dwellers helps us put ourselves in perspective and find our place in the place, so to speak. As we gain perspective this way, we gain an understanding of this greater enterprise. We enter a larger landscape as a richer self. It is a worthy goal, and one central to this story. The working premise here is that it is very good to be a small person in a large landscape. Thanks for that, Pete.

For over forty years now, I have been travelling, reading, and writing about Canada's travel heritage. This life passion found a healthy home in *Every Trail Has a Story: Heritage Travel in Canada* (2005), a book I had dreamed of writing for about twenty years.[5] The dream continues, or perhaps old habits die hard. Since 2005, I have continued to travel, read, and write on Canadian heritage travel themes. I would like to write a sequel, even a series following up on *Every Trail Has a Story*. While *Every Trail* focused on the three themes of places, practices, and people, *More Trails, More Tales* has shifted in focus toward peregrinations, perspectives, and personalities. In all cases, I am following blazed trails back in time, be it the trails of explorers, primary researchers, or energetic friends.

Peregrinations: I have not been a leader of northern extreme expeditions and adventures. Rather, I have travelled readily accessible northern routes and terrain more local to my Ontario home. It has been more wandering with historical curiosity as a major factor: day trips close to home and friendship trips with a "then and now" historical spark of imagination. My trips are friendly, playful outings with a heritage focus. Hardships and big challenges aren't central. In this regard, whether in the far country or close to home, they are accessible in an "I can do that" way. Some trips here may get expensive, but high-end skills and taking out special insurance policies isn't my game. Pleasure and gaining insights and comfort in a place are my game.

Perspectives: I have not been a research scholar in one or more narrow domains as historian or anthropologist. Rather, I have explored widely for the intriguing story that is little known. My attractions move me toward the stories that widen people's perspectives and give us a bigger view of the land in time and space. There is mystery here — could it be that we are ignoring evidence that would rewrite our history? Why do we so readily avoid knowledge of our early settlement trails in our schools and communities? My studies that I wish to share here push conventional thinking to new levels of insight and inquiry. Largely, they involve an inquiry followed by a connection with the scholar or expert who broke the story. I perhaps serve as their storyteller, not that they need my help. Relationship building is a big part of my studies.

Personalities: I have never been a solitary traveller or thinker. Rather, I have learned from a wealth of friends who share in the varied passions of self-propelled travel with trails and tales. Whether it is around the campfire or over coffee at Tim Hortons, like-minded friends with their own specific attentions have informed my experiences and writing. My friends' stories, with their heritage travel highlights, will be shared with that same "then and now" quality expressed in the peregrinations and perspectives sections.

More Trails, More Tales is a storytelling book. It draws widely from Canadian exploration travel literature and the following academic disciplines: history, geography, anthropology, literature, and philosophy. It is a suitable sequel to *Every Trail Has a Story: Heritage Travel in Canada*, with new content supported by a shift in terms of its themes.

Why? Why travel to places? Why explore one's home terrain? Why write about all this? What is the compelling reason to want to be engaged in places and then share this feeling and knowledge? The Swedes have a word that helps, *hemmeblind*, meaning "home ignorant."[6] This seems among the greatest travesties. In contrast, what this book does is feel the excitement of following those blazed trails and celebrate the imaginative connection to old ways that inspire and inform the present. The best I have ever heard these qualities captured is by my friend Dave Oleson, who lives with his family at the mouth of the Hoarfrost River in the East Arm of Great Slave Lake (where George Back started upriver to get onto the barrens in 1833). Dave eloquently writes:

> I crave a history. I want to weave myself and my own story into the ongoing terse narrative of this place, a narrative I can only dimly discern … the country is full of vague leavings. Old camps in ruin, traps hung in trees, rock cairns on tundra hilltops … things surface … to move through a wild land and know nothing of its human history would be an impoverishment. An

understanding of the past enables a clearer appreciation of the present. In a time of rapid change, historical perspective can help to place that change in context.[7]

I share the thesis that we need a historical perspective to help us understand both what we gain and what we lose with change. That small person in a large landscape is really an ever more humbled small person in an ever-expanding landscape. A big part of a historical perspective is an expanding humility. This is to say, a shrinking ego but a widening soul. There is nothing more ludicrous than a humble author, perhaps. Sure, I have something important to share, I think. But the humbling of spirit on the land leaves us with a clearer appreciation. The widening of the soul is that connectedness. Call it belonging, call it being part of the greater enterprise of the Canadian historical experience and being humbled by it.

Finally, following blazed trails is practical and metaphorical. It will keep you on track and keep you imagining the grander track you share in. How did Lawrence Durrell put it? "All landscape ask the same question in the same whisper. I am watching you — are you watching yourself in me."[8] Those blazed trails on the land and the ones we will travel on together on paper really do whisper. That is, if we really do listen. I hope this book will help humble those who listen. Certainly I am compelled to write as I think about my trips, my studies, and my friends against the backdrop of the grandness of belonging: peregrinations so humble by comparison, perspectives so grateful to those primary researchers, and personalities — a mere sample here — so accomplished with a story to share.

PART ONE

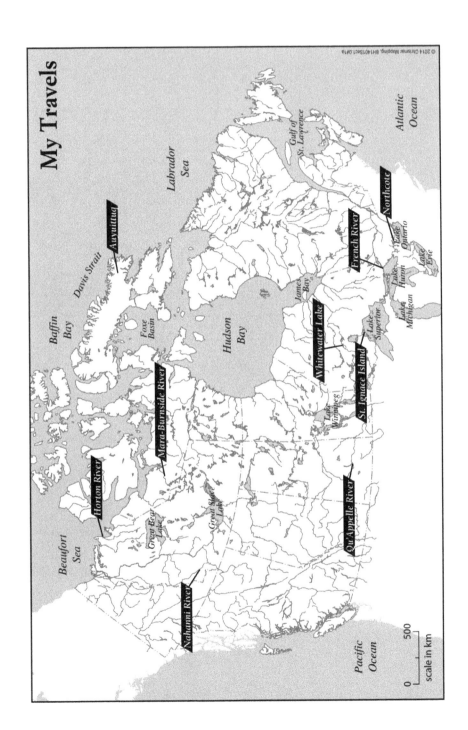

My Travels

INTRODUCTION

Peregrinations

"Not all those who wander are lost."[1]
— J.R.R. Tolkien, *The Fellowship of the Ring*

There is no grand logic to my recreational travels. It is fair to say that my self-propelled travels (mostly by canoe in these pages) are wanderings largely based on wonderings. I follow the whim of a good story, such as Wendell Beckwith at Whitewater Lake. I follow the excitement of friends for a route, such as the Mara and Burnside rivers or Lake Superior's northern shore. The story might be a pleasant surprise discovered when on the trail and researched later, such as Franklin's knowing about the Burnside River as a choice route to return to Fort Enterprise, or Francis Simpson's comments on a near canoe swamping at Recollect Falls. However, the most common scenario is that imaginative spark of a story leading to a trip. I had wanted to hunt for Vilhjalmur Stefansson's cabin at Coal Creek on the Horton River long before the conception of that trip.

The stories are usually heritage stories, the ways of earlier travellers or dwellers in a remote environment well-suited to outdoor travel. Here the integrity of the land and the water is often something to revel in. What a country we live in! The stories in some cases are more dream-like than concrete heritage finds. A concrete find is seeking out Raymond Patterson's wood stove on the Wheatsheaf Creek of the Nahanni River.

A dream-like story is pondering the Penny Ice Cap, vestige of the last ice age, while ski-touring on Baffin Island, or contemplating all those who have struggled in spring's semi-ice-covered lakes throughout the north.

But there is never a sense of being aimless or lost. What is sought and often found is the joy of entering a story. I, like many, seek to be a participant in the story and in the evolving, ever-emerging landscape, which is enlarged with each new story added. When I have travelled with a good story, I become a livelier storyteller. And, like Thomas King said so eloquently, "The truth about stories is that that's all we are."[2]

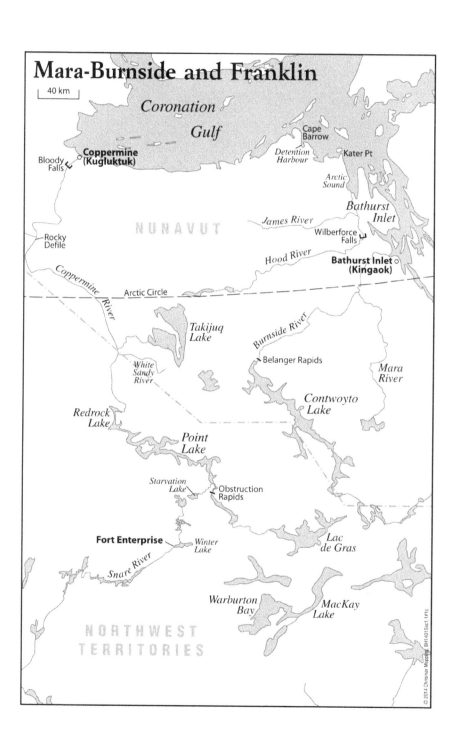

Mara-Burnside and Franklin

40 km

Coronation
Gulf

Cape
Barrow

Coppermine
(Kugluktuk)

Bloody
Falls

Detention
Harbour

Kater Pt

Arctic
Sound

Bathurst
Inlet

Rocky
Defile

N U N A V U T

James River

Wilberforce
Falls

Hood River

Bathurst Inlet ○
(Kingaok)

Coppermine River

Arctic Circle

Takijuq
Lake

Burnside River

Belanger Rapids

Mara
River

White
Sandy
River

Contwoyto
Lake

Redrock
Lake

Point
Lake

Starvation
Lake

Obstruction
Rapids

Fort Enterprise

Winter
Lake

Lac
de Gras

Snare River

Warburton
Bay

MacKay
Lake

N O R T H W E S T
T E R R I T O R I E S

1

A Mara-Burnside Trip/Conference and the First Franklin Expedition

"And would we have survived, too, if given a chance? Kept peace and sanity and most of our toes? Kept hope when cell phone, wristwatch, and film advance failed and borealis was the only electric thing within range?"[1]
— Elizabeth Bradfield

Is it a canoe trip or is it a conference? Can it be both at once? How will fourteen professional educators and travel guides all used to leading trips work together? What about differences in terms of practice and philosophy between the six countries represented, not to mention fourteen dynamic personalities? These were certainly questions on everyone's mind as we gathered in Yellowknife in 2010 for what we all thought was a first of its kind: a wilderness educators' conference and canoe trip.[2] We would paddle the Mara Burnside rivers to the Arctic coast at Bathurst Inlet.

We were tired of meeting at conferences in Sheraton Hotels around the world. Personally, it always feels disingenuous as an outdoor educator to gather in Ballroom A anywhere in North America and discuss issues such as, Can the "no trace" camping philosophy fit with a "you can be home in the wilds" philosophy? For the record, the conference with keynote speakers and concurrent sessions isn't the only way (or the best way) for professionals to meet. Here was my chance to test this theory! It was also the closest I have come to the specific landscapes of the first Franklin expedition, 1819–22.

The canoe trip/conference was the idea of the eminently qualified Morten Asfeldt, who cut his teeth guiding for Nahanni River Adventures in the 1980s before travelling to many (dare I say most) Arctic rivers with students at the Augustana Campus of the University of Alberta in Camrose, Alberta (see Chapter 10). This would be Morten's fourth time down the Mara-Burnside river system. Along with Morten, the co-organizer was Simon Beames, a Canadian outdoor education scholar teaching at the University of Edinburgh. The two of them made fishing for lunch; regular sightings of wolves, grizzlies, muskox, and the Bathurst Inlet caribou migration; not to mention days of runnable whitewater and esker camping all a reality for those who responded to the invite. Together, Morten and Simon saw this canoe trip/conference to completion. Why the Mara-Burnside? It offers a bit of everything that Arctic rivers can offer. Of course, I would focus on the history.

But first, the conference idea.

Here's how it worked. Thirty invitations were sent out, and twelve folks signed on. Morten and Simon would have their canoe trip/conference. Delegates came from Canada, the United Kingdom, Denmark, Norway, Sweden, and Japan. We were to write two papers to be distributed to delegates before the canoe trip. These papers served as conference sessions: one a curricular item of practice, the other an important theory to us as individuals. English would be our common language, though Scandinavian dialects were often more practical at times. Sessions included rethinking how we use metaphors to teach, how to use a group writing journal, understanding the body on a canoe trip, the importance of water for life, nature interpretation, how to wisely engage students, finding tools on the land, generating group discussion on environmental lifestyle, and peppering ritual and heritage into the experience.[3] We discussed our personal views of our carbon footprint in coming here, learned of local political issues (the possible coastal shipping port at Bathurst Inlet), and argued the merits of journey-based and local outdoor education. I have just scratched the surface here. Suffice it to say, I only remember dozing off once (or twice) during evening sessions after a full day on the water and my turn on dinner detail.

Certainly there was tension between life on the trail and the need to fulfill our interest in a successful professional conference. That said, it worked! We learned together. We had time for follow-up discussions on esker walks, around (or inside) the bug tent, or in canoes. We had time to expand our practices and ideas with much input from respected and non-distracted colleagues. A canoe partner on the mostly portage-free, lining-free Mara and Burnside rivers affords ample opportunity for the thoughtful dialogue and critique academics love. Though, critique led to an overly wet rapids run for a bowswoman when an enthusiastic conversation distractingly led canoes into the standing waves. The stern paddlers continued the dialogue over the roar of robust waves: the wrong line through the rapid. Such is the way of outdoor educator paddling academics.

As for the overall route, we started just downstream from the usual launch at Nose Lake. As hoped, the lake ice was a minor factor, but early season paddling ensured we would have reasonable headwater levels. By day two we had encountered our first of six grizzlies. By day three, the long, shallow rapids (not an easy go in rubber-bottomed Pakboats) gave way to kilometre after kilometre of easily runnable rapids. By day four on the Mara we were in the midst of the region's annual caribou migration, travelling a dominant esker beside which we camped on two occasions. In total we had two portages to the Arctic Ocean, one being the infamous five-kilometre carry around the final river gorge. We also had several wind-bound days — good for conferencing, bad for paddling.

The Mara-Burnside river system trip is a classic Arctic River run. There is good fishing, great wildlife encounters, opportunities for long esker walks, few people, lots of bugs, and runnable rapids. We all had our special interests. For some, it was fishing, for others, wildlife sightings or paddling rapids. For me, I'm a happy generalist, with a special interest in the area's history. The Mara-Burnside is not a historic river corridor like the Coppermine, Thelon, or Back rivers.[4] It is not a primary heritage river route, but it does have an interesting secondary role. Yes, there is a story to tell, and I had the opportunity then to share in some of the connection between the Mara-Burnside and the first Franklin expedition, but some of the story I learned following the trip. I will start with the ending. Sometimes it is the best way to begin.

Bob and Takako Takano on the Mara-Burnside river system.
Photo courtesy of Hans Gelter.

Liftoff! The winds were strong. Our Twin Otter airplane would travel from Bathurst Inlet on the Arctic coast to Yellowknife on the shores of Great Slave Lake. That's the length of the barren lands of Canada. We would fly low, affording an easy view of the lower Bathurst Inlet; the Mara, Burnside, and Coppermine rivers; eskers aplenty; barrens to tree-line transition; waterways as a corridor for easy travel; and a mass of lakes messing up any notion of water as a useful navigational aid. In the air with this excellent visibility, I was thinking of navigation, not because I would ever walk the long distance across the barrens but because the first Franklin Arctic land expedition did so in 1819–22.[5] Might I see Belanger Rapids and Obstruction Rapids, where river crossings by canoe and hastily made cockleshell canoe respectively exacted so much time and energy from the crew?[6] Might I see some dominant eskers as linear features that might have helped Franklin and company once they headed overland from the Hood River just to my northwest? I was flying over the country these men had walked through 193 years ago. This flight, along with the visceral experience of canoeing and walking in similar terrain, one river to the east of their Coppermine River, not to mention our travels in and viewing of Bathurst Inlet, helped put the first arctic

Flying back to Yellowknife from Bathurst Inlet, imagining Franklin's men's march.

land expedition closer to my mind.[7] (Although it was second to Samuel Hearne's two-year tramp with Chipewyan families thirty-five years earlier.) I know the stories. Specific days had long since been etched in my head. These two weeks on the Mara-Burnside rivers were the closest I'd come to being there, and the low-level flight was a great gift.

Who else was thinking this way as the flights began? I was rendering a human story of the past into a felt experience on the land. I was mulling over our trip with its "harsh" summer conditions compared to Franklin's men's truly harsh October conditions, (read: early winter) and our viewing of animals for pleasure rather than on desperate survival-focused hunting excursions.[8]

There are many ways to frame the country, and perhaps the best way is no way at all. That would be to sit back and stare with no references to the terrain; to just be with it. Others might be doing that, although I'm not sure it is possible for most humans. Some certainly are naturalists first. They are looking for animals: the land as a laboratory for genetic diversity, perhaps. The geographer or land scientist watches for glacial features. The theologian might explore the possibility of sacred sites or ponder the land as cathedral. The paddler watches for waterways: the land as gymnasium. Some do all of this to some degree simultaneously. I suppose I do, but the land as a storied place is how I primarily tend to look at it. Did I find it, this way of seeing, or did it find me? In other words, did I first have the theory of place-responsive pedagogy whereby as a place becomes imbued with story it becomes meaningful and then bring it to my practice? Or did I see the land as a storied place and then discover a corresponding theory? I believe the latter is true in my case. It was a matter of imaginative spark. Educators Brian Wattchow and Mike Brown discuss the varied privileged interpretations from which outdoor educators see the land: "... nature as an *arena* where students experience personal development through challenging activity; or nature as a *venue* or *landscape* that can be appreciated and encountered aesthetically and for which we should develop some affinity; or nature as an *environment* in need of sustainable management practices by humans."[9] William Godfrey-Smith in the 1970s explored ways of seeing nature: as a gymnasium (for recreation), as a cathedral (for spiritual growth), as a lab (for scientific study), and as a silo (for genetic storing and coding of materials).[10] It appears that from these environmental educators' perceptions that nature is always a resource. It is always to be used. But as we bring personal meaning and an ever wider understanding to nature — simply put, as we bring nature inside — nature shifts toward being home. It provides study and recreation, yes, but as a home place for dwellers, not a visitor's space for strangers. I was sure the naturalists, scientists, adventurers, and historians among our group all had some desire to move toward this Arctic place as a core place, rather than as a peripheral space. Indeed, we talked of such themes often.

Finally, and adding further to Godfrey-Smith's list, Warwick Fox in 1995 wisely suggested that our culture's nature awareness and perceptions have shifted with time. Culture moves. We are more aware of nature as a life support system ("which holds that a diverse non-human world benefits humans by performing functions necessary for our healthy survival, including the recycling of nutrients, the production of oxygen from carbon dioxide, and so on"); we are also moving toward seeing nature as psychologically necessary. This position acknowledges wild places are

A wilderness expedition conference session while windbound.

a needed refuge from human-designed places. While Godfrey-Smith's position stresses that we like the non-human, the ecopsychology position suggests that we ought to have diverse non-human places for our mental growth and, indeed, our sanity.[11] These two positions (the life support and the eco-psychological) along with nature as a home place were amplified educational directions for our travels on the Mara-Burnside. Paddler/delegate Pete Higgins asked us to seek a "global intimacy" in our lives by living directly with an understanding of basic ecological principles such as the water cycle and photosynthesis. Deb Schrader and Robbie Nicol helped us explore nature as an ingrained part of our psyche through narrative appreciation and exercises of deeper questioning. Remember that intriguing tension between a river camping trip and an educators' conference: there were heady times in the bug shelter or under the storm tarps.

For me, the flight back to Yellowknife was among the strongest moments of the trip for feeling the storied place. We had travelled together within a place-responsive pedagogy. Now we were leaving, and the place was coming alive before me with stories. That remained my frame of reference; that nature is a resource I must admit, but not a resource for us to use for our gain only, rather one for us to imaginatively dream into and enlarge our being. The difference in thinking of nature as resource is a matter of relationship and connectivity: nature as subject (home) or object (other). These questions were with me while on the land with our thoughtful group and on our visually stunning low-level return flight to Yellowknife. There was also a more specific set of questions. There was a historical storied way of seeing that was my mandate to share with my colleagues.

But first, a brief introduction is needed for the first Franklin Arctic land expedition.

John Franklin, with his four navy men and fifteen Native interpreters and voyageurs, travelled from York Factor on Hudson Bay to Great Slave Lake (the end of Europeans' geographical knowledge at the time) in 1819. Franklin was gone from home for forty-two months. From Fort Providence they ascended the Yellowknife River to Winter Lake, where they built Fort Enterprise from which to descend the Coppermine River and travel east on the Arctic coast, surveying it as far as Bathurst Inlet. Then they retreated late in the season, walking without food stores and Native support from the Hood River, crossing the Burnside and Coppermine rivers without proper ferrying to return to Fort Enterprise and fresh supplies. The supplies were not there for the starving men, the strongest of whom had barely had enough strength to make their way to the fort. They pressed on until Yellowknife families were found to come to their aid. Before it was all over, there were murders, cannibalism, attempted mutinies, and epic snowshoe walks of twelve hundred miles to resupply. They were hoping to add significantly to the quest of the Northwest Passage to the Pacific Ocean. Suffice it to say, there are many stories embedded in this epic canoe trip turned hiking trip turned starvation march in the central Arctic.

I had wondered before our canoe trip why Franklin had decided to commence the walking retreat off the barren lands from the Hood River. The Hood River mouth is further north down the Bathurst Inlet coast from the Burnside and has a more formidable canyon to negotiate (though he didn't know that last point). Perhaps he simply did not know about the Burnside River? When you are at the mouth of the Burnside River you look across the inlet to a long row of islands and Elliot Point. If you are travelling down the east shore of Bathurst Inlet as Franklin did, the river mouth is easily obscured from view. Despite the grandeur of the Burnside River sandbars, the river was not observed even with Franklin's detailed survey work in the Inlet. This becomes clear on site, on the ground, and from the air. I had a partial answer. The Burnside River, though a better walking route inland, was never found.

On returning from our summer 2010 travels, I went back to the books. In all, there are four accounts of various aspects of the Franklin expedition of 1819–22: Hood, Back, Richardson, and Franklin. I had wondered if the Mara and Burnside rivers were known to the Franklin party, and I had assumed not, a point significant to their overall fate. A March 20, 1820, entry in Franklin's journal, at Fort Chipewyan, provided the full answer. There, the infamous Métis Francois Beaulieu,[12] along with a Chipewyan named Black Meat, provided a rough map with distances and directions to the mouth of the Coppermine and Anatessy (now Burnside) rivers.[13] Franklin had been looking for this Anatessy River as a direct waterway to Contwoyto Lake, a significant landmark to return to Fort Enterprise. Indeed, the Hood and Western rivers were at first confused as the Burnside by Franklin. So conventional wisdom prevails: indigenous knowledge provided the explorers with the best options, but they failed to find it. Also, Franklin had wanted to complete the survey of the eastern shore of Bathurst Inlet. Had I known all this while our group was at the Burnside, I would have taken great delight in bringing our river of travel more directly into the Franklin story. I agree with the main expeditions editor, C. Stuart Houston: "had they found and recognized the mouth of the Burnside they might possibly have chosen this river as their return route as far as Contwoyto Lake."[14] I'd add, if they had found the river when in the area (August 4, 1821) and identified it as the suggested best option to return, then the death march across the barren grounds that forever defines this expedition might not have happened. The decision was made to ascend the Hood River out of Bathurst Inlet on August 15. The tired men then paddled to the more northern mouth of the Hood River and began to walk with supplies on August 31 (twenty-seven critical days later).

At our trip's end, further along in the low-level flight path, I was scouting for river crossings. At what is now known as Belanger Rapids, on the upper Burnside, their fragile canoe upset. Belanger was left stranded in the middle of the river. Franklin (with a second canoe swamping) reached the far shore, but Pierre St. Germain was swept downstream. It was mid-September. Snow was on the ground. Eventually a rope was secured across the two riverbanks and all got across. Imagine the scene: at Obstruction Rapids on the Coppermine, by October 4, 1821, the travellers were now without a canoe. Here St. Germain, with a piece of canvas and river willows, fashioned a "little cockleshell canoe." Others were hunting or preserving energy. This river crossing was a spirit breaker. Following this nine-day delay with many failed crossing attempts, the large group is forced to separate into stronger and weaker parties for a last push to Fort Enterprise.

But one must pause every once in a while when reading history like this; Pierre St. Germain did what? The pause is needed so as not to gloss over the facts and to afford time to imagine the scene and the effort. What about St. Germain's building of a cockleshell to cross the rapids? While this skilled hunter and interpreter had his request to abandon the expedition denied at the mouth of the Coppermine, he soon became its most indispensable member. One would be right to marvel at Pierre St. Germain's determination on the return overland walk with two major river crossings. First at the Burnside River crossing, St. Germain was prominent in ferrying the party across at great hardship to himself. But the big story was at Obstruction Rapids on the Coppermine. Here, without any watercraft to cross, St. Germain spent four days searching unsuccessfully for wood to make a raft. He did scrounge enough river willow to fashion a cockleshell out of the fragments of canvas available. All relied completely on the ingenuity and stamina of the starving St. Germain. This crossing was the critical moment of failure or success for the already wretched return to Fort Enterprise. St. Germain had found the way.

But how did he do it? How can one man build a craft to cross a wide river with a strong current with such meagre resources? And what exactly is a cockleshell canoe anyway? Enter my friend André-François Bourbeau. He too was caught by this moment. He too was forced to pause in his reading to ponder. Then, unlike me, he set about duplicating the life-saving canoe building endeavour.[15] (See Chapter 12.)

Reading all four officers' accounts — Franklin's, Richardson's, Back's, and Hood's — I was impressed less with the role of these men

and more with the role of interpreters, voyageurs, and Yellowknife hunters (Akaicho's Indians, as they were sometimes called). In particular,
Pierre St. Germain stands out. While St. Germain was at times a "ring-
leader of discontent" (looking back, who could blame him for that — I'm
reminded of Yossarian's plea in the novel *Catch-22*, "the enemy is anyone
who is going to get me killed"). How could St. Germain not voice concern
about Franklin's obsession with pressing on beyond the reaches of food
and Native hunter support while travelling in ever more leaky birchbark
canoes further along the stormy September Arctic Coast? Taking in personal views of the Arctic Coast from the mouths of the Burnside and
Horton rivers provides a bit of perspective on what the coast might have
been like to paddle in a stormy September season. I, for one, will stick
to the rivers, particularly as the early autumn season kicks in. Pierre St.
Germain remains my go-to guy when I contemplate that land expedition.

Back in the Twin Otter float plane, I followed water and land from
the air with a keenness to see the Burnside River crossing and then the
Coppermine. The picture I imagined of these men dealing with the river
crossings sent a chill down my spine. And while I can't claim to have
crossed paths with either rapid, the big rivers and lakes evident from the
air showcased the extreme challenges faced by starving men between
September and November 1821.

Then, as we flew south, we passed the site where a near mutiny took
place. On August 13, 1819, at Reindeer Lake (now called Descension Lake)
at the Yellowknife River headwater after days of gruelling upriver travel and
frequent portaging, a mutinous spirit broke out. The disgruntled voyageurs
requested more rations. The trip leader, Franklin, wrote of this incident:

> … whilst this meal was preparing, our Canadian Voyageurs,
> who had been for some days past murmuring at their
> meagre diet, and striving to get the whole of our little
> provisions to consume at once, broke out into open dis-
> content, and several of them threatened they would not
> proceed forward unless more food was given to them.
> This conduct was the more unpardonable, as they saw
> we were rapidly approaching the fires of the hunters, and

that provision might soon be expected. I therefore felt the duty incumbent on me, to address them in the strongest manner on the danger of insubordination, and to assure them of my determination to inflict the heaviest punishment on any that should persist in their refusal to go on, or in any other way attempt to retard the Expedition.[16]

The officer George Back wrote on the same day:

... about 10 a.m. a mutinous spirit displayed itself amongst the men — they refused to carry the goods any farther alleging a scarcity of provisions as a reason for their conduct — Mr. Franklin told them we were too far removed from justice to treat them as they merited — but if such a thing occurred again — he would not hesitate to make an example of the first person who should come forward — by "blowing out his brains" — this Salutary speech had a weighty effect on the weather cock minds of the Canadians — who without further animadeversion returned quietly their duty.[17]

I have always taken great delight in these two passages. Franklin is proper in tone. Back, I cannot help think, is more truthful. I shared this story on our trip and discussed how travel literature must always be interpreted and how having more than one account adds fuel to the imaginative fire.

Hours into our return flight to Yellowknife and we were still flying at an unusually low altitude. Somewhere below me in a mess of lakes and undistinguished terrain was their Reindeer Lake. When we hit the treeline, the patches of trees reminded me of Warburton Pike's 1892 barren ground travels to the east of us.[18] Such patches of trees provided great relief. Here, a fire could finally be had again. Often food and even a canoe would be cached in such locations to aid the return trip off the barrens back to Great Slave Lake. Franklin and his men were too far gone to enjoy any celebratory spirit in returning to the trees, and caches of food were not to be found. The Yellowknife families who had supported the expedition down the Coppermine River before returning home simply assumed the obsessed/confused travellers would perish. The stories of Hearne, Pike, and mostly Franklin lay below me as our flight advanced into the trees.

And what of the scenery I so enjoyed while on the river and on walks from campsites? As one might expect, there was for Franklin's men, who wrote published journals, a range from desolate to grand. Richardson, while on an advance exploration party, wrote in a letter on June 9, 1821, to send back to Fort Enterprise: "Amongst these hills you may observe some curious basins, but nowhere did I see anything worthy of your pencil. So much for the country; it is a barren subject, and deserves to be thus briefly dismissed."[19]

To the contrary, George Back wrote in his journal, later that same month:

> ... the scene was interesting and novel — a lake bounded on each side with high and almost perpendicular rocks, whose green summits were capped with large stones — and whose valleys displayed at certain distances a few solitary clumps of pines — claimed the first attention — whilst the continued ranges of receding blue hills — which the eye lost ultimately in the grey dimness of the atmosphere — was scarcely less attractive — our own cavalcade possessed the centre, and what with the total innovation of transporting canoes in such a manner — the singular appearance of the men and sledges — the positions and dress of the officers as well as the deep contrast between the perpetual silence of the place, and the animation of the party — afforded a most perfect view of a voyage of discovery.[20]

For me and, I trust, my enthusiastic comrades, the scenery was awesome. One person's bleak or "barren subject" is another person's "interesting and novel ... perfect view." Despite the fact that our summer travels did not correspond with the wintery conditions on the barren grounds for the Arctic land expedition, I could regularly place the men in certain aspects of the scenery slowly working their way south as I flew by. Once we landed in Yellowknife, I felt the relaxed calm of having exercised my imagination well.

I had enjoyed two weeks of a collegial canoe trip/conference. Our supplies were plenty, our time lengthy, the land welcoming with animals to view (not seen as our only food source), our purpose personal (not driven by the full force of the British Empire), and our ambitions modest. We had come together to learn from the land and share the varied attentions we each brought to the trip. Our story is a good one. It was a successful first wilderness expedition conference. Still, I cannot stop thinking about that darn Franklin story with characters such as Pierre St. Germain.

Returning home after his distressing trip, Lieutenant Back told the North West Company's representative, Willard Wentzel, at Fort Chipewyan, "To tell the truth, Wentzel, things have taken place which must not be known." Wentzel already suspected as much. He had a year earlier written to his superiors, "It is doubtful whether, from the distant scene of their transactions, an authentic account of their operations will ever meet the public eye in England."[21]

Conference delegates at Bathurst Inlet Lodge.
Photo courtesy of Burt Page.

I hope our 2010 trip is promoted widely as an example of a success-ful idea, perhaps redefining outdoor education conferencing. That first Franklin expedition was to be promoted, but how truthfully? And that is why we need to pause and ponder when reading our Canadian travel literature. Often the truth has to be gleaned from the imagination.

The American poet Wallace Stevens in 1942 wrote: "Imagination is a liberty of the mind, a power of the mind and over the possibilities of things … we have it, because we don't have enough without it."[22] To imagine, we become open to ideas. It starts with a spark of possibility. The possibility is that the stories of the place, and indeed the stories we create in the present, become alive and bring meaning to time. The his-torical muse is a solid part of place-responsive pedagogy; a storied land-scape leads beyond meaning to caring and perhaps acting on behalf of the place. All this is a sincere step towards cultivating ecological con-sciousness — part of an educative process. That is the theory.

The practice is to pepper the trail with stories that, for those who grab onto the imaginative spark of possibility, will render the past as a felt experience. It is not romanticism, but rather a widening of reality. The practice can lead to what novelist James David Duncan explores in *The River Why*. He writes of characters with "native intelligence."

> … it evolves as a native involves himself in his region. A non-native awakes in the morning in a body in a bed in a room in a building on a street in a country in a state in a nation. A native awakes in the center of a little cos-mos — or a big one, if his intelligence is vast — and he wears this cosmos like a robe, senses the barely percep-tible shifting migrations, moods and machinations of its creatures, its growing green things, its earth and sky.[23]

The big cosmos storied landscape I aspired to develop and share was that of the barren grounds. Franklin's Arctic land expedition of 1819–22 was a primary source. Some might have felt that imaginative spark. Others were always more imaginatively driven towards the animals, the landforms, and the body in motion. All of these attentions were shared amongst our group in organized sessions and informal moments. There was a happy air of eclecticism as we bounced off one another's primary interests. Much talent, much knowledge, much to share by way of theory and practice. We were on a canoe trip and at a professional conference. It worked! We were, in the words of educator David Orr, "re-educating people [ourselves] in the art of living well where they are."[24]

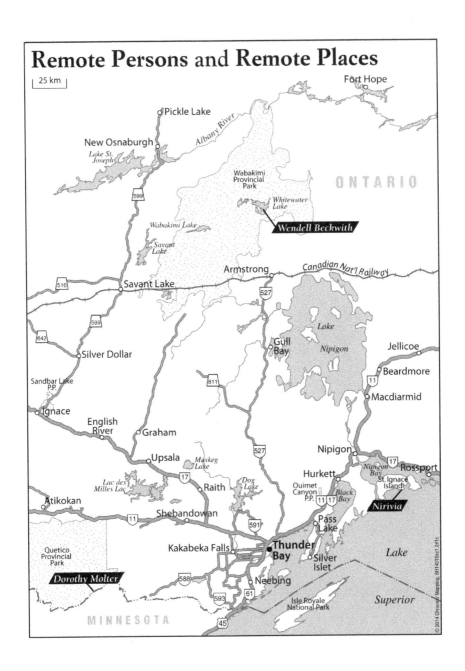

Remote Persons and Remote Places

25 km

Fort Hope

Pickle Lake

Albany River

New Osnaburgh

Lake St. Joseph

599

Wabakimi Provincial Park

Whitewater Lake

ONTARIO

Wabakimi Lake

Savant Lake

Wendell Beckwith

Armstrong

Canadian Nat'l Railway

516

Savant Lake

527

599

642

Silver Dollar

Lake Nipigon

Gull Bay

Jellicoe

Beardmore

Sandbar Lake P.P.

811

11

Macdiarmid

Ignace

English River

Graham

527

Nipigon

17

Rossport

Upsala

Muskeg Lake

Hurkett

Nipigon Bay

St. Ignace Island

Lac des Milles Lac

17

Raith

Dog Lake

Ouimet Canyon P.P.

Black Bay

11 17

Nirivia

Atikokan

11

Shebandowan

591

Pass Lake

Quetico Provincial Park

Kakabeka Falls

Thunder Bay

Silver Islet

Lake

Dorothy Molter

588

Neebing

593

61

Isle Royale National Park

Superior

MINNESOTA

45

© 2014 Chrismar Mapping, BH14015sc12rfc

2

Remote Persons and Remote Places:
Wendell Beckwith, Nirivia, and Others

"What is a hobby anyway? Where is the line of demarcation between hobbies and ordinary normal pursuits? A hobby is a defiance of the contemporary. It is an assertion of those permanent values which the momentary eddies of social evolution have contravened or overlooked. If this is true, then we may also say that every hobbyist is inherently a radical, and that his tribe is inherently a minority. To find reasons why it is useful or beneficial converts it at once from an avocation into an industry — lowers it at once to the ignominious category of an "exercise" undertaken for health, power, or profit. Lifting dumbbells is not a hobby. It is a confession of subservience, not an assertion of liberty."[1]
— Aldo Leopold

Dorothy Molter, the Root Beer Lady of Knife Lake; Alex Mathius on the Obabika River in Temagami; the "ruling elders" of Nirivia; and Wendell Beckwith at Whitewater Lake — these are all remote persons dwelling in remote places. In each case there is a strong assertion of liberty.[2]

I have always had enthusiasm for the relationship of person and place. The two must go together, and therefore I had to go to the place to really get to know the person. Recently I have visited Whitewater Lake and Nirivia, so I will deal with these remote places and their charmed people: people who are brilliant hobbyists in Aldo Leopold's meaning of the word.

I think this allure started with my 1970s university days, when in the winter I would visit my summer camp friend and canoe tripping guide Joss Haiblen. Joss had built a cabin in the tall pines on a quiet pond set apart from the active summer canoe routes of Lake Temagami. It was an idyllic place for cross-country ski touring. We would travel over to Gull Lake and hook onto the abandoned logging road network. Beyond Joss's cabin, we set up a base camp in an abandoned logging cabin. It still had a wood stove. For me, between 1976 and 1979, these two cabins were magical. Joss was my Grey Owl, my Beckwith. He was living many peoples' dream: liberty, independent, and intimate with winter. My beloved hobbies seemed to be his normal life. He worked as a canoe tripper in the summer and did his own trip in the spring. In the fall, he visited his parents in Manhattan — the juxtaposition is not lost on me there. The Temagami cabin was home through the winter and its shoulder seasons — ice freeze-up and breakup.

From Joss, I saw the best of remote living, and my hobbies turned to "an assertion of liberty." There might be another side to the story, but I didn't see it. Joss had a comfortable lifestyle of winter chores and outings. Guests were more than welcome and all thrived on day trips out from the cabin. Mostly, though, Joss was comfortable with himself. I learned many things from my visits. If I had to condense this down to a few central ideas, they would be the joy of simple, efficient technologies and of staying put somewhere where one can pursue one's central interests.

Joss, the squatter, was eventually found out when logging moved in on those tall pines. He was forced to take down the cabin, but given he had been there over five years, he was allowed to stay there under canvas. A teepee did the trick, but the logging encroachment, the loss of the cozy cabin, and mostly a new partner (Trish MacDonald from Australia) sent Joss packing to Australia to work in its parks services. Joss and I have kept up regular contact with trips here and there, every five years or so. However, I've kept hunting out remote people in remote places. I attribute my enthusiasm for this to those still evenings warmed by the wood stove in Joss's cozy cabin. I will always be content to be a part of his tribe, and many others, too, as I've travelled with friends in Canada.

Wendell Beckwith in Wabakimi is one fine example of remoteness. "We came, we saw, we sawed." That's how veteran canoe guide

Phil Cotton describes Wabakimi canoe tripping. Portages aplenty have fallen spruce that make a day's pre-planned destination dubious at best. Wendy Kipp, Deb Diebel, Margot Peck, and I had experienced one such late afternoon portage and therefore arrived at Best Island on Whitewater Lake too late to visit the much-anticipated Wendell Beckwith cabins. Saddened, we camped nearby, excited for a full day of exploration to follow. The next day, August 16, 2005, we paused to start our tour of the cabins with a reading from a healthy volume of Beckwith literature penned mostly after his death. Surprisingly, we read that Wendell Beckwith had died at this site on August 16, 1980, twenty-five years earlier to the day. This fact added a haunting aura of his presence to our quest — a quest to understand the man in part by the wondrous cabins he has left behind. Here one can really feel the remote peace, but also a remote, radical person.

A friend, Alice Casselman, who had visited Wendell in the summer and winter several times while working with Outward Bound in the late 1970s, told me there were three central pillars to Wendell's life at Best Island: environment, science, and humanitarianism. Environment was our main interest.[3]

Wendell learned over time how to live comfortably alone through the seasons of northwestern Ontario. Two of his cabins, The Workshop (later called Rose's cabin) and The Snail, are packed with environmentally wise designs to maximize comfort in six months of cold weather. There is a thirty-five-ton parabola-shaped fireplace in The Museum, his first cabin (which didn't work out as a year-round dwelling despite the fireplace). The Hobbit-like Snail faces south and is built into a sand hill as a semi-subterranean dwelling to maximize the thermal mass of the earth. In The Snail, Wendell figured he used twenty times less wood per day than in his conventionally shaped and sized Museum cabin. The Snail's ingenious teepee-like central fire had a ceiling opening and an underpad of rock to maintain heat. How Wendell evolved his understanding of living comfortably through the seasons is a detailed study on its own. A 2005 *Globe and Mail* column called the buildings "one of the country's most inaccessible architectural treasures."[4] Ironically for the canoe tripper, the fairy-tale setting, rather than being inaccessible, is in a choice location, easy to plan

Wendell's snail cabin built to maximize winter warmth.

into most Wabakimi canoe routes. I suggest you keep in mind my friend
Jon Berger's sentiments for the environmentally intriguing cabins: "They
do not fit the main patterns of the land but have their own intrinsic story
and value." Wendell established his own unique patterns with this landscape, and his story now is part of the place and deserves to stay with us.

The cabins are still a showcase of Wendell's environmental design
even now after thirty years of minimum care. Though all signs point to
the need for regular maintenance to preserve this gem in the bush, little
has been done.

While the hexagonal wooden tile flooring, the wooden crank/pulley
drop fridge (into a pit), the remarkable drying racks, and The Snail's struc-
tural shape all speak to legendary architectural abilities, Wendell the scientist is equally compelling. The patented inventor arrived in Canada as an
illegal alien, cutting the roadblock lock at a border crossing on the Pigeon
River (between Minnesota and Ontario) and leaving his wife and five kids
while he pursued pure research in a remote setting. He had a financial
backer who wanted a wilderness retreat property that Wendell and the
local Slipperjack family would build. Pure research means, in Wendell's

Wendell Beckwith at Best Island.
Photo courtesy of Moon Joyce.

own words, "You start from scratch and live in a primitive way until your mind clears." You sit with a blank sheet of paper and pencil. Again in Wendell's words: "Simplicity comes from depth ... from deep penetrating views and the simpler you get, the broader your concepts are going to become and that's what's necessary in basic research."

Wendell was interested in many subjects. He was a wizard with trigonometry. His calculations dominate his journals: thousands of pages concerning the importance of the number pi; the alignment of the pyramids, Stonehenge, and Best Island (he once built a cedar log replica of Stonehenge on the lake ice); the measurement of local ice and spring breakup; eclipse studies; and plate tectonics. You might say celestial and global mapping captured his main interests. These interests led to the following theories: the distance around the world is within a quarter of a mile of the square root of pi; the moon was more important than the sun for pyramid builders; northwestern Ontario is a geophysical keystone oddly connected, given calculations of latitude (measured with a slide rule), to Greenwich, Stonehenge, and the pyramids. Finally, pre-1980, he determined a returning ice age would ultimately solve our global population explosion and related issues. All this from a man who was involved in the invention of the ballpoint pen, became the caretaker of a wilderness retreat on Best Island, and left a warm legacy after touching the lives of many canoe trippers with his welcoming presence and curious and compelling buildings. Did I mention that the Dutch doors to The Museum are carved to show specific measures of gravity?

Wendell Beckwith's humanitarian side suggests he was far from a hermit. Alice Casselman told me Wendell was part of an elaborate scheme to help the region's Native peoples financially with an arguably ahead-of-its-time ecotourism project. A canoe trip guided by the Slipperjack family would bring tourists from the rail line to an upscale Whitewater Lake fishing lodge. En route, canoe trippers would stay in pre-established camps progressing from rustic lean-tos to canvas wall tents to cabins and finally to the main lodge. Sadly (and typically), only the upscale Ogoki Lodge was built.

Alice told me Wendell had shared his humanitarian vision for what to do with Best Island following his death: he wanted to form a northern studies institute. A series of single-dwelling snail structures would be spread over the island for invited individuals to engage in pure research. Once a week, they would get together at The Museum for a major think tank. This plan is in sharp contrast to what others who also claim to have known Wendell believe, which is that Wendell would have wanted the cabins to return to the earth naturally with time. Having read much of the available literature, conducted some interviews with folks who knew Wendell, and pondered the man and the much-revered cabins, I am confident Alice's knowledge reflects his true wishes. That said, the cabins are returning to the earth slowly. I believe the humanitarian Wendell Beckwith, who called himself a "citizen of the world" when encouraged to seek Canadian citizenship, saw a legacy in continuing to support sustainable initiatives with the local people and furthering the virtues of pure science and environmentally sound living via his northern studies bush institute. What a destination such a research centre would have become for Wabakimi trippers. Certainly all would have been welcome in Wendell's vision. In the 1970s summer heyday of Wendell's years at Best Island, up to three hundred visitors per summer were noted. He was a hermit, yes, but not in the summer canoe tripping season. We were excited to read the cabin's guest book. Not long before us in 2005, members of Wendell's family, including grandchildren, visited Best Island. One granddaughter, age five, as I remember, commented: "Now I know where I got my brains from." Long overdue guests, perhaps, but certainly it was a treat to see that a family visit was a part of the overall story.

Wendell's vision for Best Island is now important to consider. In the early part of the summer of 2005, Wilderness Connection Outfitting operator Jim Pearson arranged for the Ministry of Natural Resources to cover the roof of The Museum with a large Fabrene plastic tarp. Two separate trees have fallen, destroying sections of the roof. Time to save the buildings is dwindling! Responsibility for the buildings is uncertain. A group was established in the 1980s. Energies were later channelled for a short while through Wilderness Connections operating out of Armstrong in the summer months. Wabakimi Park staff appear uncertain as to which course to take: serious investment towards permanent repairs, modest upkeep, or turning a blind eye, defended by a local view (that appears unsubstantiated) that Wendell would have wanted the cabins to return to the earth. Frankly, I don't buy it! Perhaps some home refurbishing TV show should be brought into play.

Seriously, though, a canoe trip in the heart of the Wabakimi boreal forest, accented with a lingering tour of the Best Island cabins while being informed about the life and three pillars of Wendell Beckwith, is a rewarding and imaginative journey into how we dwell or might dwell in the Canadian north woods.

Wendell Beckwith was a true hobbyist. He expressed a committed "defiance of the contemporary." He expressed strong values toward the development of ideas and personal development. He sought out his own brand of liberty. Aldo Leopold might have called him the ultimate hobbyist. This doesn't sound right, given how the word *hobby* has come to be understood. But Wendell did exercise many of the hobbies of others with his environmental, scientific, and humanitarian work. I missed meeting Wendell Beckwith with a last-minute route choice change on a 1977 canoe trip. Too bad for me. I have only seen two pictures of Wendell. He has a big smile in both of them.

It would be a shame to lose the cabins, the critical link to the man and his story, because of short-sightedness at this crucial time. On August 16, 2005, twenty-five years to the day since Wendell's departure, I sat and thought of my own dwelling on the earth amidst the aura of the Beckwith story. It was time well spent. I was grateful to Wendell and I am certain I am not alone in drawing energy from the site. Perhaps this is Wendell's legacy: pure reflection for those canoe trippers who continue to travel and think in more primal ways.

Wendell's way is not the only way to dwell well in remote places. Enlightened Nirivians will tell you that a touch too much Scotch, a crazy idea well played, and a commitment to encouraging the natural integrity of the place can go a long way towards dwelling well and inspiring a great story.

We were on Lake Superior, sea kayaking in 2013, out for over a week travelling from Silver Islet to Gravel River (near Rossport). We had known about Nirivia from a fine area guidebook.[5] When Beth Foster paddled over to a nearby cottage and was greeted with "Welcome to Nirivia," we knew that not only were we in the right place, we were in for a fine time as well.

Now Nirivia isn't a cottage or camp name. It is rather a secluded self-styled nation state with its own commercial activity, national flag,

Nirivia's main cabin.

national anthem, titled members, and certificates of citizenship. Russell Evans, a founding member and King of Nirivia, with his partner, Sharon Manitowabi, would be our host for the afternoon. We had a lot of questions, and lucky for us, Russ was the man.

First, the Nirivia story. In 1977, four Nipigon residents, including, Russ Evans, were camped on Lake Superior near present-day Nirivia. They had learned that the Robinson Superior Treaty — Lake Superior Native bands' land claim between Michipicoten and Thunder Bay — did not include the many off-shore islands that had been their childhood playground. Russ at age thirteen had camped solo on the islands to get his Pathfinder badge. As the Scotch flowed, an older Russ and friends decided the group should claim a portion of the islands. Some loophole in the treaty allowed this process a degree of formality. Nirivia: what a name. Apparently the four may have been trying to say Nirvana, but it came out Nirivia, which, you have to admit, does have an exotic feel to it. They thought so too. Nirivians will tell you that Nirivia is more a state of mind than any serious sovereignty bid. That said, they do have an honourable declaration of intent for their fifty-nine islands (St. Ignace Island, at 132 square miles, is the largest among them).[6]

All the fun nationhood stuff — a flag, anthem, awarding of titles (Official Scribe, Commander of the Navy, and Cosmos Inspector, for example) — isn't simply a joke. And the declaration is not just political theatre or fun. The Nirivian state held for decades an active licensed tourist establishment; the Nirivian Island Expeditions Ltd. Fishing was the mainstay. They had a healthy business supported by word of mouth and a great T-shirt. I'd give up a big Lake Superior trout for one of those T-shirts or a certificate of citizenship. Fishing and boating remain a big part of the Nirivian lifestyle. We felt right at home. Indeed, the day before we arrived Russ had caught a twenty-three-inch speckled trout in the Nirivian homeland.

The declaration also has some teeth. The focus of Nirivia's state of mind is a proclamation focussed on preservation of the island's integrity. There are three objectives: multi-use recreation, no heavy resource extraction, and preservation for future generations. When one thinks of the uncompromising 1970s resource extraction polluters in nearby Red

Rock and Terrace Bay, it is easy to see the degree of serious attention needed. Nirivia in the late 1970s received treatments in the *Toronto Star*, the *Globe and Mail*, *National Geographic*, *Reader's Digest*, the *Minneapolis Star*, and others.[7] I asked Russ, now sixty-five years young, what he thinks of it all over thirty years later. His response? "Well, look what it created!"

So what is Nirivia now? Beth Foster, Robin James, Liz Calvin, David Taylor, Margot Peck, and I experienced warm Nirivian hospitality. Russ and Sharon were generous with their time, and we enjoyed a very hot sauna and cold Superior swim. "Look what it created!" Glorious boating travel with well-forested islands, just enough safe harbours and pebble beaches, grand views out to sea, and an inland view peppered with islands and high forested hills.[8] It is a sea kayaker's paradise … if the winds are calm and you have lots of time. The Nirivian state of mind would serve one well when travelling the many open water island hops out there: wait for the right weather, relax, take it all in, have a purpose, and don't take it all too seriously. Russ was an exemplary Nirivian, and we felt blessed to be a small part of this inspiring Lake Superior story.

What does the future hold for Nirivia? Russ mentioned many times that the idea was spawned from the carefree 1970s lifestyle. Today, the Nirivian elders who remain are Jim Stevens and Russ. Both live in Thunder Bay. Both see in their time out on the Nirivian islands a "true life." Jim, when asked about the true life of the islands, spoke of the spiritual impact of the place. As for the Nirivians' playbook, Jim said, "Out there, time goes with the sun." There are about a thousand certified citizens who have been touched by the "true life." Here we have another of Leopold's assertions of liberty — a hobby well played. Nirivia, a time for a clear "demarcation between hobbies and ordinary normal pursuits."

The comfortable, well-hidden geodesic domes (built from the 1970s Whole Earth Catalogue) at the Nirivia home base are in good repair. The sauna is a gem. The land use permit is secure, and younger family members will carry on the torch.

When the Nirivian founders claimed the islands, they did so as an "enchanted country" because it was there to be claimed. They did so for the environmental protection, with St. Ignace Island as the centrepiece. Now much of Nirivia is officially designated as conservation lands. The

Nature Conservancy of Canada in 2013 acquired part of an island cluster just offshore from Rossport. The resource extraction industries along the northern Lake Superior coast have cleaned up their act from the 1970s. Volunteer groups are maintaining campsites and remote saunas.[9] And Superior country is generally still revered for its spiritual impact, as Jim put it. Well done Nirivian elders, and thanks to Russ (the King) and Jim (the Earl) of Nirivia for the kind hospitality and joy of sharing some of the "true life" with us sea kayaking seekers.

A fitting way to close the Nirivian story would be to quote from the closing lines of the Nirivian national anthem, written by Nirivian citizen Norman Sponchia:

> And the flag of Nirivia flies over all souls.
> In the winds of Superior.
> When the waters start to roll
> The Nirivia spirit started to blow
> Oh Nirivia, the island nation of Nirivia.[10]

If a fitting anthem for Wendell Beckwith's Best Island were to have been written, it might go something like this:

> And the cabins of Wendell's Best Islands fills our souls
> with imaginative stories.
> In the winds of Wabakimi when the waters start to roll
> One can take comfort in the Beckwith spirit.
> Oh Wendell, a radical hobbyist seeker of liberty.

Thanks, Joss, for my important early introduction to seeking out remote people in remote places. It is a valuable life enterprise.

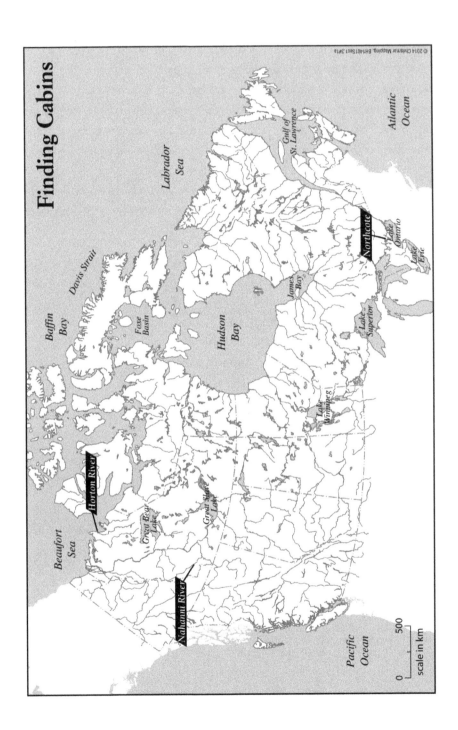

Finding Cabins

Baffin Bay

Davis Strait

Labrador Sea

Gulf of St. Lawrence

Atlantic Ocean

Foxe Basin

Hudson Bay

James Bay

Lake Superior

Lake Ontario

Lake Erie

Lake Winnipeg

Northcote

Beaufort Sea

Horton River

Great Bear Lake

Great Slave Lake

Nahanni River

Pacific Ocean

500

0

scale in km

© 2014 Chrismar Mapping, BH1401Sect.341a

3

Finding Cabins:
Stories from the Horton and Nahanni Rivers and
George Douglas's Northcote Farm

"I did not realize that the old grave that stood among the brambles at the foot of our farm was history."
— Stephen Leacock

Claude Lévi-Strauss dismissed travel books as "grocery lists and lost dog stories." I'm not so big on that one, but I can understand it. He also said, "If lions could speak, we wouldn't understand them anyway."[1] I love that one. In many ways, this is a travel book, but more to do with historical places to visit. I do not dwell on the travel but rather on the places. Cabins are central to this. And if some of the inhabitants could talk to us now of their time, we might struggle to understand. That is the challenge and fun in reading Vilhjalmur Stefansson, Raymond Patterson, and George Douglas. There are life lessons in their successful travels and in the places where they waited out a winter or that they called home for a time. The tales from these cabins in the bush showcase learning and comfort, misery and despair.

The Horton River flows north from Horton Lake, northwest of Great Bear Lake, to the Arctic coast six hundred kilometres north. It has a short canyon section midway along, but otherwise gently winds its way deep in an ever-changing charmed valley. Most notable are the crystal clear waters, the abundant wildlife (muskox, grizzles, and caribou in small groupings), and the hiking options at seemingly every bend in the river.

The Nahanni River flows southeast from the Moose Ponds to the Liard River and then to the Mackenzie River. It has four main canyon sections below Virginia Falls and rocks 'n rolls most of its length in a dramatic river valley. Most notably, this scenery is punctuated by Virginia Falls. For us, there was a general lack of wildlife encounters and select hiking from inflowing rivers and streams. Its waters are generally murky.

Northcote farm was the property of George Douglas (1875–1963). It was later owned by the Gastle family of Lakefield, Ontario, and now is in the hands of Lakefield College. Likely Samuel de Champlain portaged on the property to "Back Bay" en route from Huronia to Lake Ontario. It is on the Trent-Severn waterway just south of Young's Point and Stoney Lake, a waterway that has seen canoe travel for centuries. Today students at Lakefield College School regularly paddle up to the farm for overnight canoe trips. As a boy at Lakefield, I likely cross-country skied on the property more than a few times.

So, why link these places together here? Well, stories! Travel stories, but not the stuff of grocery lists. And if the characters taking us back into our northern Euro-Canadian history could speak today, one is left to wonder, would we understand them anyway? That is one of the intriguing qualities of travel books about which Lévi-Strauss might be misguided. Stefansson on the Horton, Patterson and Faille on the Nahanni, and Douglas of Coppermine fame at Northcote all move as far beyond "grocery lists and lost dog stories" into the realm of inquiring minds and the zest for exploration.[2] It is a noble challenge to capture some of their passion in one's present travels.

On the Horton in 2012, our group sought out Vilhjalmur Stefansson's cabin and other related stories from the land, both geological and historical. On the Nahanni, family and friends hunted out Raymond Patterson's and Alberta Faille's cabins and other related stories. In both cases, the stories were tangible in the recorded history, but the evidence on the land was scant. This combines to make the physical exploration most rewarding. Another reason to link these two rivers, in my mind, from the experiences had on each is the outward lack of adventure. Both these two canoe trips were event-free. That is, if an "event" is an adventure story of a scary grizzly attack, a canoe dumping in big water,

Joss Haiblen and David Taylor examining Stefansson's Horton River cabin remains.

or a dynamic weather event influencing the overall mood and flow of the travel. I'm okay with that. I don't need an adventure. On the Horton River, we had some grizzly encounters and the need for bear bangers, but with no consequence other than a feeling of great privilege to have had the experience. We had some river rapid running decisions and some rainstorm soakings and extreme heat to contend with, but no mishaps. Same for the Nahanni without the grizzlies. Not much to tell folks back home, you might be thinking. Herein lies the rub; when nothing goes wrong and nothing dramatic unfolds, then, for some, the trip might feel "adventureless." For some, mediocrity might even be the vibe of the trip, shrouding the experience both during and after. When friends back home ask for adventure stories, you feel you are letting them down.

Enter Stefansson to the rescue:

> My favourite thesis is that an adventure is a sign of
> incompetence. Few have disputed the Greek, or whoever
> it was, that said, "blessed the country whose history is

uninteresting," and no one … will dispute the statement that "blessed is the exploring expedition the story of which is monotonous." If everything is well managed, if there are no miscalculations or mistakes, then the things that happen are only the things you expected to happen, and in which you are ready and with which you can therefore deal … By keeping steadily in view the two maxims, "Better be safe than sorry" and "Do in Rome as the Romans do," Dr. Anderson and I managed to conduct for nearly five years a satisfactorily monotonous expedition.[3]

I had read Stefansson for insight about the Horton River. But what I got were gems of philosophy. Here's to monotonous expeditions. Sorry, few adventure stories on the Horton for me in 2012, just peace and contentment and the joys of travel with good friends.

Usually folks read travel literature for insights into the route to be travelled. Perhaps the traveller is the focus; perhaps the story is the focus. But often the lasting gem is a philosophical insight that catches readers off guard and stays with them through the rest of their own travels. So, to the Horton, to Stefansson's Horton.

John Lentz describes finding Vilhjalmur Stefansson and Rudolph Anderson's cabin on Coal Creek about one kilometre off the Horton River — though the more important route for them was the land link to their Langton Bay base on the Arctic Coast. Lentz describes a wooded area just north of Coal Creek. Should be easy to find, we thought. There was even a picture in the *Che-Mun* issue showing a bit of a slope behind the cabin. A clue.[4]

The Stefansson-Anderson expedition of 1908–1912 had the following intention: to live with the Inuit and with animal life. Stefansson was the ethnologist, Anderson the biologist. When at the Coal Creek cabin, Stefansson was living the dream. He was content to record his Inuit companions' stories and further develop his language skills. Anderson had no facility with the Inuit language and therefore travelled widely from the Coal Creek cabin.

Our thesis was this: that we were not looking for any waste places, but for land occupied by human beings; if those human beings were there at all, they must be Eskimo supporting themselves by the most primitive implements of the chase; and it seemed clear that if Eskimo could live there, armed as they must be with bows and arrows, and not only live there but bring up their children and take care of their aged, then surely we, armed with modern rifles, would be able to live in that sort of country as long as we pleased and to go about in it as we liked. Of course the thesis was bound to prove out.[5]

This passage certainly highlights the different times of 1911 for Arctic travellers.

Stefansson, in *My Life with the Eskimos* (1913), describes the cabin, which was "thirty or so miles to Langton Bay":

… we all put in two days in building a house frame and sodding it over roughly. The sodding was so poorly done that we later on had to do it all over again. The building was a simple affair. There were a pair of vertical posts about twenty feet apart and nine feet high, across the tops of which a ridgepole was laid. An essential feature of the walls was that they were not vertical, but sloped in, so that earth, no matter how carelessly it was thrown against the house, would fit in and not cave away as commonly happens when you try to build vertical walled houses in white men's fashion.[6]

From the Horton, we discussed the logic of this particular geography and a winter cabin location. André-François Bourbeau was our leader in this discussion. André is an outdoor survival educator. It's safe to say he sees the land differently than I do at times, and here his insight was invaluable. We discussed a distant hill edge spur that would offer easy access onto the plateau to the north. This would facilitate entry to the hunting grounds on a more "long vista" terrain. The cabin must be close to Coal Creek, must be in a well-wooded area, and must be sheltered from the exposed Horton River corridor yet close to the same for easy travel. Finally, the cabin site should be flat and perhaps close to a wooden downhill lie to drop trees easily.

In the hot sun, it seemed like a long hunt at the end of a full day of canoe tripping. Energy was waning, and the group had divided into two when André and others, staying true to the original assertion, found the cabin remains close to that same dominant spur we had seen from the Horton. The search was made harder by the fact that the Coal Creek watercourse was completely dry and quite braided with troughs in mid-August.

As expected, we first saw marks and axe cuts in what proved to be close proximity to roof remains (five to seven logs lashed together). These markings were covered in lichen, showing their age. There were no walls evident. The sod dominant indented wood walls were not evident. No door, no windows. This was a one-season winter throw-up tilt.

Such a quest is an exciting bonus to any canoe trip. The Horton is not a significant historical travel route given its proximity to the Mackenzie to the west. Stefansson sledded on the Horton River from Dease Bay on Great Bear Lake in December 1910, returning to Coal Creek. He travelled in an interesting circle via boat and sled from Coal Creek: from Langton Bay east to Coronation Gulf onto the Coppermine and then to Great Bear Lake via the Dease River, returning to the coast again on the Horton. And we thought our six hundred kilometres of river tripping was a long route. Visiting Stefansson's cabin on Coal Creek opened the door to his travels. We had something tangible to connect to. We had some passages from Stefansson on our trip, but I, for one, began reading his book in earnest following our trip. And a piece of the Arctic and another time lingers in one's mind and remains a little closer to one's consciousness.

Camped across from Whaleman Lake on an open plateau on the river, one might wonder why this curious name was chosen. Whalemen (men who hunted whales) walked south from Langton Bay on the Arctic coast, just as Stefansson and Anderson had done, to corral caribou for wintering-over food supplies. I had marked the site on my maps where the decayed remains of the corral and the funnelling wooden walls can still be seen. Problem was, I was about two to four kilometres downstream of the correct location. I figured all this out once the trip was over. Sometimes, that's the way it goes. I even remember, in hindsight, noticing the flattening of the river shore and thinking it was odd for this river. I had noticed the caribou corral site but hadn't realized it. Earlier we had seen a herd of muskox at a similarly unusual flattish shoreline. Oh well, something exciting for a return trip, perhaps. That imaginative spark of yearly groups of whalemen remains vague in my mind without the tangible evidence on the land that we were to have at Coal Creek in about ten days' time.

I paddled the Nahanni River in the summer of 2005 with family members and friends Sean Collins and Diane Gribbin. The trip was from Rabbitkettle Lake to Nahanni Butte. We were twenty-four days on the water, offering ample time for hiking.

Heritage on this river is synonymous with Raymond M. Patterson's 1954 book, *The Dangerous River*.[7] Patterson tells of his 1929–30 travels. But he also fuels the many stories that have made the Nahanni the dark river of fear. Added to this were sad Klondike Gold Rush stories. Few made it this way to the Yukon gold fields near Dawson in the late 1890s. Prospecting stories in the 1920s, too, seem to end badly, creating place names such as Deadman's Valley and Headless Creek. I wondered what I could possibly add to Patterson's rich treatment and descriptive prose of the river.

Then there was the surge of modern travellers gainfully serviced by regular bush flights and commercial operators (mainly Nahanni River Adventures and Black Feather). Books, articles, conservation, and park (and now park extension) initiatives all add to the coverage of this noble and, frankly, not so dark and fearful river. Again, what could I add? But once on the trail, Patterson's *The Dangerous River* seemed to sing out to us. Quotes from my spring read in preparation punctuated the geography of Virginia Falls and the Hot Springs. Song verses rang out as the stories told came alive on the trail, and the chorus was the fast flowing downstream in the mountainous, canyon-filled river. This is a well-travelled river, Headless Creek be damned. More than once I caught myself borrowing the chorus from other river songs as I sang my way down the river: "and we go on and on, watching the river run."

First off, I'm one of the rats to whom Raymond Patterson's partner referred. In agreeing to join Patterson, Gordon Matthews is quoted as saying, "Any country, where the Indians were still hostile and you can shoot moose from your bed and mountain sheep with a pistol is well worth seeing before the rats get at it."[8] I hope Matthews and Patterson might come to accept us modern rats, who fly into the country generally, not to mention flying into the river proper. Toronto to Yellowknife in one day isn't bad. It took John Franklin and company, in 1818, over a year to cover this distance by canoe. As rats go, I think we canoeists can be okay for the river, particularly if we get involved in current park extension efforts bent on preserving the river's watershed, not just its cosmetic corridor. When conveying his plan, at the stage when all was maps and geography and dreams, Patterson wrote, "Sometime soon I would do that [explore the South Nahanni, travelling upriver from the Liard River]. Strangely enough, I never doubted that I could, though exactly what I proposed to use in place of experience has since often puzzled me."[9] Here is a noble learner's enterprise in keeping with a favourite aphorism for explaining experiential education: "If a thing is worth doing, it is worth doing badly."[10] Patterson is a learner. He describes tracking upriver beaches, tackling a major upstream ferry below Virginia Falls, learning to live and travel through a Nahanni winter, and interpreting the crazy Nahanni chinook-ridden weather. We, as a family, were learners too in this grand country, far removed from our Canadian Shield base. Big water, like the Figure 8 Rapids, conjured up butterflies flying in formation.[11] We only hoped the formation matched the right river run. We too did an upstream ferry below Virginia Falls to enter Fourth Canyon. It was entered with a degree of uncertainty, shared with Patterson. The weather was black clouds and blue sky. The uncertainty was invigorating. Patterson had Albert Faille, a well-established trapper and gold seeker, to literally show him the ropes — the upstream tracking ropes to be exact. We had Patterson.

We planned a full-day hike at Scow Creek. From our camp on the river it looked ambitious. It was. Four thousand steady feet up and down with an on-your-knees finale caused the odd family member to experience a meltdown. Later we read Patterson's tale of Gilroy and Hay carrying heavy loads and the third partner, Angus Hall, travelling light. All had their own meltdowns with upriver paddling work: "they had had enough rivering to do them for quite a while." The prospecting partners hiked up Scow Creek with plans to ridge walk over to the north and west and descend into the legendary Flat River gold strike (an unproven claim). The lighter-ladened Hall had his second meltdown in frustration with the slow pace of his packhorse partners. He stripped down his gear and headed off with a rifle and a mosquito net. He was never seen again — a stern lesson for the meltdown type. I can almost see him now storming off in a huff along that well-defined ridge as the others, wiser and alive another day, struggle on below with supplies. We returned to our spaghetti dinner, thankful we didn't have to travel upstream and devote copious amounts of time to hunting. Dessert was a chocolate cake, as I remember. Not that Scow Creek needed more than its own rocky personality to be memorable, but the story does help etch the place in my mind.[12]

Quinn Henderson starting up Scow Creek/Nahanni River.

An aerial view of the Nahanni River from atop the Scow Creek ridge.
Photo courtesy of Sean Collins.

Patterson shares accounts of building a wintering-over cabin across the river from Prairie Creek. The Wheatsheaf Creek cabin was mostly built by Matthews while Patterson was hunting. It was named by Patterson for a friendly house that lay beyond the seas. He described an area well supplied with game and fine trees for building. The cabin was fourteen feet by thirteen feet, a bit small for two chaps. In his Nahanni Journals, Patterson writes passages such as, "Levelled off the shack floor, set up the stove and cut out the pipe hole … I put in the windows, lit the stove to air and dry the shack, made the door and did various odd jobs. The shack is going to be very warm and light — an excellent refuge." I can only wonder at the satisfaction experienced in such tasks when one is so removed from the next external heat source. We visited the site with expectations of connecting further with Patterson's story. Cabin foundation outlines provided difficult to discern, but to our glee we did discover an old wood stove, surely one that warmed the souls of these two northern travellers and dreamers. Such tangible discoveries added a crescendo to our river song. As I remember it, Diane found the stove half buried in the forest floor. The stove was surprisingly set back from the creek and river, I remember thinking, but this was a winter cabin. Shelter was the goal. Diane had

Diane Gribbin examining what just might be
R.M. Patterson's stove at Wheatsheaf Creek.

paddled down the Nahanni more than twenty times working as a river guide. It was fitting that she or Sean would find the stove. Later we frantically fought the current above the Splits to visit one of Albert Faille's cabins. I most enjoyed the bench near the edge of the river, perfectly located for viewing the sunset. While Albert never did find gold over decades of travels on the Liard and Nahanni rivers up from Fort Simpson, few would argue that his experience hadn't been golden. The riverside bench helped me secure this view. No lost dog stories here. Faille had largely been a teacher to Patterson. But Faille didn't have the writer's craft.

Patterson wrote: "Never in my wildest dreams had I hoped to see anything like this."[13] First Canyon, he noted, was two days' travel upstream, days he must have experienced as overwhelming for work and for visual pleasure, not to mention relief from the mosquitoes in the lower river flats. We floated First Canyon, stalling our progress to delight in our passing as much as possible. I imagined Patterson, Faille, and others tracking on the beaches, jumping from one side of the river to the other and then to the next beach. Hmm, what would they do here? No beach, sheer walls, fast current. Imagine the delight of their downriver run at season's end.

Patterson wrote of his first meeting with the awe-inspiring First Canyon:

> That passage through the Lower Canyon was the sort of thing that comes to a man perhaps once in a lifetime if he's lucky. The scenery is the finest of the Nahanni and the weather was perfect — clear, with cold nights and blazing hot days. And it was all strange and new: rounding a bend was like turning a page in a book of pictures; what would one see, this time and would this next reach hold, perhaps, some insuperable obstacles? But it never did, and always one found some way around by means of some new trick with the line or the pole. We were lucky too, with weather and good company and no obstacles.[14]

I would have changed places with Patterson to spend more time in this canyon and to sing his song of exploration; I think I understand his joy. Critical for this joy is lots of time to move upstream at a pace the river dictates.

So the Nahanni song, and certainly my song here, are both well connected to Patterson's *The Dangerous River*. The book provides a lasting testimony to earlier times when Nahanni travels were an up and down full-season affair. Indeed, my favourite part of *The Dangerous River* is the winter travel section not addressed here.

In reviewing the overall river song now, months later, I am reminded of a lyric by Ian Tamblyn concerning the Yukon River. It fits well. "Gold is gone, gold remains."[15] Patterson and Matthews, Faille, and perhaps even the lost Angus Hall in the hills above the river, all found little to no gold, but gold remains. Patterson wrote of this gold in flowing pages and Faille's river-edge bench at his cabin before The Splits sang the gold of countless sunsets and a dream for a good quest and zest for life. We all should be so lucky.

The Horton and the Nahanni were adventureless "monotonous" trips, one might say to link to Stefansson's thesis. But he and I were looking for different experiences in the remote north. He wanted study and recognition, discovery and enough fame to satisfy sponsors for future trips. I wanted to enjoy the grandeur of the Arctic river, to thrive in the techniques and joys of canoe camping with good friends, and to find enough historical stories to link my "now" with an intriguing "then." We both had our adventure fulfilled, call it monotonous or not. I think I can understand this guy, and that is a good feeling. As for Patterson and Faille, no problem understanding these guys. The excitement for exploration and for discovery, in the form of new canyons or gold, feels as universal as Stefansson's excitement for knowledge. It feels comforting to think, "I can know these guys" … sort of. Cabins and stoves and benches by the river edge that remain on the land really help this understanding feel tangible.

The Northcote property near Lakefield, Ontario, on the Trent-Severn waterway may appear incongruous beside the Horton and Nahanni river finds, but not so. It was with the same spirit of inquiry and intrigue that I drove (not paddled) up the grass-rutted lane to the Douglas homestead. Whereas I had expected more at Stefansson's Coal Creek and Patterson's Wheatsheaf Creek, this place was in better shape than I had imaged. The large riverbank white house with green roof stood tall and majestic, as did the barn — once full of canoes, now full of winter sleighs. The wraparound veranda of the main house gave a well lived in impression, as did the overall grounds where winter play on the open slopes and lake paddling and sailing used to abound. The two square, timber-log summer cabins are settling into the ground surrounded by brambles and foot-catching dog-strangling vine. They are very rustic and charming in that simple living, sparse needs, and few possessions way. I instantly fell in love with the place. The insides proved that all buildings need work. Indeed, that's why I was there. Here is history alive and well. The Douglas brothers' story of Arctic travel told in the 1914 classic *Lands Forlorn*[16] is a must read, and the characters who visited Northcote read like an early 1900s who's who of the north: John Hornby, Guy Blanchet, and P.G. Downes are highlights among them. Northcote was a conduit of northern affairs. But it was also a recreational playground for the related Greer and Mackenzie families.

George Douglas's homestead in Northcote.

Finding cabins, or what's left of them, doesn't have to be just an Arctic pursuit. Here, to my mind, is a house/cabin/barn all linked to arctic travel. Those same imaginative feelings grabbed hold as I wondered about George Douglas and all those who loved this grand property. My northern interest led to an invite by Bill Gastle and Kathy Hooke (George is her uncle by marriage). Bill and I, along with Richard Johnson from Lakefield College and Bert Ireland, all sized up the work needed to restore the main house into a liveable space again. The stone foundation needed to be reinforced and the house levelled on the foundation. The insides needed more than a Molly Maid cleaning. The veranda needed to come off to access the foundations, then get rebuilt. The roof must be covered anew. It is doable but expensive. The school envisioned summer programming. I envisioned northern literature and canoeing symposia. It all felt like a dream to me, but not to Bill and Bert, who started talking specifics of refurbishing and actual dollars.

Later that day (my second trip to Northcote), Kathy Hooke, the main Northcote/Douglas researcher, treated Bill and me to a fine lunch and kitchen sit about with her many photo albums of life at Northcote. Kathy and Bill swapped stories of Mrs. Douglas (twenty-three years George's junior) and George. George must have had fifty canoes. Seems he'd paddle down into Lakefield with one and paddle back with two. Kathy said George was on the water every day somewhere or nowhere in particular. Winter was a special time for family visits. Photo albums reinforce this, as ski and snowshoe outings (along with picnics and family portraits on the veranda) dominate the images of daily life.

I returned home from the Northcote day and went straight to my 1914 copy of *Lands Forlorn* and read with new vigour. The man behind the study had come to life. It is the same feeling one can get when finding an old stove and logs remaining at a cabin site almost lost to the ground and river flooding. It needn't be in the north to be about the north. But the Northcote site also sings a song of outdoor living. The photos are not of singing around the piano or dining in the formal dining room. Rather, folks at Northcote picnicked, paddled, hiked, and loved the winter. Later, the Gastle family started an annual sleigh ride, which one year attracted three thousand arrivals down the country lane. Today, the sleigh ride is still a Northcote event, as are school camping outings. History is brought to life in other ways than just northern travel; the school conducts an American Civil War re-enactment on the grounds.[17] I can't help but think George and Lionel Douglas would have been amused and might have gone canoeing. Yet, this speaks to a new life for Northcote, once a conduit to northern travel, now possibly to be restored to offer new energy and life to the place. This energy will involve lots of canoeing, camping, and winter recreation. It will involve experiential re-enactments, symposia, and a place to ponder Douglas's time here on the Trent-Severn waterway and on Great Bear Lake to and from the Coppermine. Douglas didn't write a grocery list travel account (nor did Stefansson nor Patterson), but he was a meticulous list taker who was well organized and, simply put, "got it right" in the North. I was to learn he got it right as a dweller at Northcote too. As for Patterson and Stefansson, it is good to have something tangible along with their travel accounts to help imagine the traveller. With Douglas, there is the added local and family histories alive on the Northcote farm. As Stephen Leacock learned, I hope people come to realize the cabins and houses among the brambles are part of history with these three early 1900s northern travellers. Herein lie histories with much to teach us that will help us reclaim the simple pleasures of outdoor life.

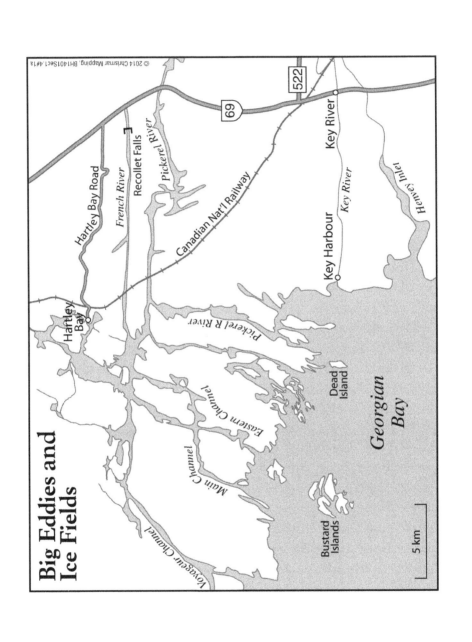

Big Eddies and Ice Fields

Hartley Bay Road

French River

Recollet Falls

Pickerel River

69

522

Canadian Nat'l Railway

Key River

Key River

Key Harbour

Hewey Inlet

Hartley Bay

Pickerel R River

Eastern Channel

Main Channel

Voyageur Channel

Dead Island

Bustard Islands

Georgian Bay

5 km

4

The French River and Georgian Bay: Big Eddies and Ice Fields in Spring Waters

"Historians worth their salt are storytellers."[1]
— John Boyko

I have been writing about my travels for forty years now. This little outing on the French River has always stood out because of the intense similarity of two moments: one at a rapid, the other a common experience dealing with lake ice canoe travel. Like many trips, it was also memorable for friendship, glorious weather, and the joy of time away experienced as time found. Now, over twenty years since the trip, there is an added quality of … well … concern. Am I honouring the Indigenous people who first travelled here in their homeland? Am I a player in a decolonizing movement that should connect all canoeists, as the canoe is part of our national story? When we tell a grand narrative, such as the Canadian national story with the canoe as a centrepiece, we will always leave out aspects of the overall story. Young Canadian scholars (younger than I, certainly) are asking canoeists to be aware of what is so often left out when folks like me speak or write about the joys and trials of our canoe trips.[2] The question decolonizing literature would ask is, are canoe trip travel writing and the white Anglo canoe tripper complicit in the oppression of Indigenous peoples? I hope to answer this here. I do think it is good that we are thinking about such things more now than we did twenty years ago. But first, some canoe trip writing — more trails and more tales that explore Canada's past.

On rare occasions, the canoe trip is more than any "re-explorer" would bargain for. Two such occasions were to grace one early spring trip on the French River between Ontario's Lake Nipissing and the north shore of Georgian Bay. In eagerness for the canoeing season ahead, my friend Joss Haiblen and I retrieved our canoe from icebound Lake Temagami. We portaged from an island to the mainland on the solid ice to head out for a week-long trip on the historic French River. The strong current on the river assured open passage, and we were confident Georgian Bay's icy shores would offer many open routes during spring ice breakup. We started April 28. It occurred to me that our Lake Temagami ice portage might just be a bit of foreshadowing.

The river was a joy, with no other boat traffic. Miniature icebergs were breaking off from the cliff shores and, best of all, there was a hint of budding spring greenery. Hey, no bugs! We enjoyed being out in early May, noting that the fur trade traffic between Montreal and Grand Portage (at Lake Superior) would have taken this route annually only a week or two later in the season.[3] All this added a spark of intrigue to our trip, but also a chilly reminder of the precarious situation of one wood-canvas canoe in frigid, rapid waters. I remember wondering how birch-bark canoes handled icy morning shorelines and mini river icebergs.

At Recollet Falls, this reminder was driven home. John Bigsby in 1824 described the falls with sharp contrasts: "It is very beautiful in its white waters and dark walls, bristling with dead and living pine, almost naked heights being close at hand."[4] It is always fun to read such poetic passages. We tend not to write like that now. I'd be more inclined to write of Recollect Falls: the canyon effect here is pleasing, but the falls are on a quirky angle, throwing off the symmetry. It is an unusual look. See, not very poetic.

A southern shore portage skirts the falls but leaves the canoes to embark into a powerful back eddy of whirlpools and waves. As a result of the much less than ninety-degree angle of the falls to the shore, a distinct eddy line drives a powerful current against the southern cliff face. In the summer, with lower water levels, it is an easy portage put-in. Not so in late April. This cliff face extends four hundred metres downstream, discouraging additional portaging. Once the beauty of the falls had been surveyed we were left with our own contrasts: flowing, patterned whiteness to the menacing, choppy black waters of the spring runoff below the falls. Forget the pines; there was a potential "dead and living" thought as we envisioned our canoe bobbing like a rodeo-bucking steer in the disturbed eddy waters.

We did not relish a four-hundred-metre bushwhack and steep drop back to the river, so we scouted the water and opted for a narrow channel by the cliff face. This demanded a direct and forceful lunge through the frightening eddy line. If all this sounds overly ambitious or foolhardy, indeed we likewise came to this conclusion, but not until we had been thrown about in the eddy long enough to confirm we were not in control. This was big water, big spring runoff water. Convinced, we ascended the ridge to portage.

Later that day we pulled out our collection of historic reading, selected to spice up our travels, and read the journal entry of eighteen-year-old Frances Simpson, the bride of Governor George Simpson, the domineering Hudson's Bay Company chief. It was the bride's maiden voyage into the Canadian interior — the *Pays d'en Haut*. She wrote:

> At the Recollet Portage breakfasted, and the weather cleared up, changed our wet for dry clothes, but on going from the foot of the Recollet Falls, were very nearly drowned under it, by a strong Eddy: indeed so near, that the spray from the fall showered over, and gave us another drenching; but by the exertions of the men at the paddle, regained the stream, and got into Lake Huron at 2 o'clock.[5]

Just over a week earlier in the year than this 1830s canoe party, we shared similar water and a similar anxiety. But there was one major difference that confirmed the soundness of our judgment for safety over risk-taking. The voyageur canoe of this portion of the first Trans-Canada Highway was the *canot de maître*, a thirty-six-foot-long, six-foot-wide fur trading workhorse powered by eight or more canoe men. Our sixteen-foot wood-canvas canoe was no match for this eddy line, considering Simpson's tale. History revisited has its joys and thrills, but in this case we were happy not to have tested our recreation. We portaged, but first we "nearly drowned under it, by a strong Eddy." Our "exertion ... at the paddle" taught us, in our tiny sixteen-foot canoe, to retreat.

Now I think of a passage from American poet Walt Whitman: "History is the swindle of the Schoolmasters."[6] You've got to get out and exert yourself at the paddle to fully understand the Frances Simpson passage and countless others. It was special indeed to connect to a passage so directly. My Schoolmaster's history classes were a preparatory grounding. We covered the curriculum in school; as I remember, the fur trade is grade six. Now I cover the terrain. To deeply understand an idea, you have to do that on your own.

I also think of the disconnect between physical experience and book or lecture work at university. While I was a young Physical Education professor in a Social Science department, I initiated a proposal for a new interdisciplinary course to be called Heritage and Issues of the Canadian Shield. The politics of the Temagami region were brewing major divisive issues at the time. We would spend a week in the region meeting the politics head-on from all sides and then spend the second week on a canoe trip with the history and literature of the area experienced with paddle in hand. The first was well enough received. Of the canoe trip week I was flatly told, and I quote, "That's Phys-Ed, that's fun!" The embedded assumptions here are that a Physical Education experience doing what you study is simply devalued. The other assumption is that fun has no place in education. Needless to say, the course didn't run (although there were multiple factors beyond the above), but I did learn a valuable lesson about the experiential approach in schooling. My interest in rendering the past as a felt experience had to be placed outside of a physical education language and framed more centrally in history and anthropology. The canoe trip became a "primal mode of travel" and camping became the "primitive arts." Winter camping became a means to study story, place, and technology. With time, I learned how to get proposals approved (or my superiors and colleagues grew tired of me). One thing remained constant: do not talk about fun.

Later that trip, while enjoying unusually warm weather on Georgian Bay, the reality of early May was again driven home through another experience recreating history. Our plan had been to paddle to the mouth of the French River, then east on Georgian Bay to Key Harbour Inlet, finishing at Highway 69. The northwest shore of the bay is broken up with many inlets and a maze of islands that provides shelter and safe passage but also (we were to learn) easily becomes clogged with the last of winter's ice floes. Basking in the heat as we paddled, we were surprised to quickly find ourselves nearly entrenched in ice. Again, the idea of contrasts best describes the scene. The ice was brittle yet firm, delicate yet compact; our feelings were excitement and concern, novelty and familiarity. I have been at the mouth of the French River many times, but never like this.

Our fascination with our historical precursors led us to many nights of digesting Arctic exploration literature, where folly in icebound water is common reading. Again, the link with Canada's travel heritage provides us with both a plan of action and serves to cloak the present experience in imagination and romance without diluting the challenge. We'd read enough to know what this ice might mean. Joss and I had both acquired background context to enjoy the intrigue of a potential icebound day.

Our plan of action had been laid down in a long tradition of writing devoted to such a situation:

> Such a condition of things was not the most enlivening, and it was a point of discussion with us whether the season of this land was spring or autumn. Upon reaching a hilltop we were well repaid for our labour. Away to the south and the east, as far as we could see, the ice-field extended, but to the north there lay much open water, and near the base of the hill there was a comparatively narrow neck of land across which we might portage our outfit and get to the open water. This we decided to do.

J.W. Tyrrell, a barren lands explorer, recalling this decision in 1898 at Dubwant Lake (translation: icebound lake) provided one option: we could climb the nearest height of land and, upon surveying the scene, perhaps mix portaging with sneaking our way along.

A journal entry from Franklin's first barren grounds travel en route to the Coppermine River in 1819 suggested travel on the ice, or plowing through, would be a questionable tactic: "The surface of the ice, being honeycombed by the recent rains, presented innumerable sharp points which tore our shoes and lacerated the feet at every step." Our ice as well appeared honeycombed and uninviting to both our feet and our canvas canoe. So uninviting that we didn't try it: this ice was too advanced in decay, or so we told ourselves. Perhaps we had read too many harsh accounts like Franklin's and the following one by George Back, from June 10, 1934. Back was leaving Timber Bay, where he and his men had built wooden boats on the edge of the treeline to descend the Great Fish River, later called the Back River. (An intriguing sidebar: I have looked at stumps from that 1834 boat building project on Artillery Lake.) Back's journal entry also bespeaks the hazards of walking on certain ice conditions: "on account on the badness of the ice, which was literally a bed of angular spikes, of many shapes and sizes, but all too sharp as to make mere walking a painful and laborious operation."

In 2010, just downstream of Nose Lake on the Mara River (see Chapter 1), our group paddled off for our first day on the water only because of friendly shifting ice. The ice was best described on this occasion as "candle" ice. It was again too rigid to plow through and too weak to land on. It provided a hauntingly beautiful sound and texture we were pleased to experience. We considered ourselves lucky on two counts. One, spring ice is something special to experience, and two, our day one progress was not thwarted. It was also special that we could look out of our float plane window and a decision could be made as to a specific landing spot based on that day's ice. Now there is a modern traveller's luxury.

George Douglas in *Lands Forlorn: The Story of an Expedition to Hearne's Coppermine River* experienced most of the above in the month he spent crossing Great Bear Lake in 1912 en route home from the Coppermine River. He describes an unusual phenomenon:

Ice at the start of the Mara River.

Crossing one bay in particular we were much impeded
by slush forming along the sides of the canoe just below
the water line … the conditions, whatever they were,
that made slush form lasted only about half an hour …
an accumulation near the bow made so much noise that
Lionel shoved his paddle along the waterline to see what
was the matter, and to our surprise scraped off the slush
in masses like water-soaked snow.

Douglas wondered if this was the same phenomenon Fridtjof
Nansen described as "Dead Water" while travelling in his ship, the *Fram*,
off the coast of northern Asia.

Douglas and party paddled any chance they had. They experienced
and described a wide variety of ice conditions. They were anxious to get
back to the Mackenzie River to catch the last steamer home. One can
read their account and easily put oneself into the action. Like Douglas,
who writes about many other travellers' experiences with ice canoeing

on Great Bear Lake and elsewhere, we too can fill our icebound time with friends' stories and travel literature episodes. It's like being part of the team. I know I am a bit player here, only twice having had ice influence my canoe travels, but I can still be more than a bench player.

Finally, Thierry Mallet, on a 1930 trip down the Kazan River, presented two options: either sit it out and wait for a windstorm to shift the ice as he luckily experienced on Ennadi Lake, or give up altogether, as he ultimately was forced to do further downstream at Yathkyed Lake.

Twentieth-century lifestyles and commitments dictated that we simply enjoy the Georgian Bay day. Tyrrell's option to climb for a view must wait for another trip. There was no sign of threatening skies, so waiting to see what the wind might do wasn't an immediate strategy. So, like Mallet, we returned whence we'd come.[7]

Even the odd explorer has been forced to backtrack. Our trip finished at Hartly Bay, where road access takes one to Highway 69. How great was it that we were four hours by car to Toronto and we were having an Arctic-esque ice experience thinking of the likes of Franklin, Tyrrell, and Douglas. Wonderful!

Overall, the trip remains in my memory as one where we experienced more than we'd bargained for. This, I am sure, is a common explorer's lament, whatever century you are in. I remember the last night of that canoe trip. There was an air of lassitude. Both of us resting against tree trunks, Joss smoked a cigar and read Margaret Atwood aloud while I half listened and simply felt really good. All this happened more than twenty-five years ago. Now I dare say the good that I felt was the deep satisfaction of a game well played, in which our Recollet Falls eddy bobbing and ice field paddling attempt were key moments. This satisfaction, I think, is about belonging and relationships. I'm not sure which is more accurate so I will use them both. With paddle, maps, and books in hand, I'd learned to want to belong to Canada's canoe country. I'd learned to seek relationships with those who had gone before in times that always seem more interesting than mine. From Indigenous trade routes to exploration history, I feel … well … Canadian, pursuing a paddler's connectivity. I should pause to remind myself that "good" schoolmasters were a part of that game well played. If their work is done well, they provide the stuff of context. Likely, they were storytellers also. You have to have the context and then the good story. If they cannot provide that, it does feel like a swindle. I was a young man who knew what he liked. I liked self-propelled outdoor travel with a good heritage story in tow.

Now, too, I have other context in mind that I doubt I could have pondered those twenty-five-plus years ago. I have read some identity theory and decolonization literature.[8] Some of it feels progressive and enlightening. Some of it feels guilt-laden. I realize there is a postmodern backlash to my desire for nation-inspired canoe trippers' relationships to the land.[9] I suppose one can "use" the canoe to fulfill such settler/invader desires. But, as I see it, the land, the canoe, and being Canadian taught me to celebrate canoe travel and feeling connected to lands past in the process. There is a truth and beauty here, I think.

Identity theory would have me appreciate that a nation is largely a fantasy. The canoe and canoe tripping are national symbols. One can strive to produce a Canada with symbols shrouded in an imperial nostalgia, where people (often white elite male canoe trippers, perhaps) mourn the passing of what they themselves have transformed. Decolonization would have me acknowledge the rip-off of First Nations peoples in which I engage. The newcomer takes up the canoe with a delusion that Indigenous peoples and ways are being honoured, but in reality we are appeasing ourselves after the violence of our imperial, colonial relations.

One can feel enlightened by realizing that Canada is always in a state of "becoming," and our activities and passions, like canoeing, are part of that becoming. We influence the nation, and it influences us. Canoeing is a borrowed Indigenous activity to which I can't truly belong — or can I? I might feel humiliated by my little voyageurs and Natives re-enactments or guilty for embracing an Indigenous craft, be it canoes or snowshoes (such brilliant terrain-appropriate technology), as a colonial oppressor. Or I might seek to broaden the story or enlarge the conversation to advance a respectful intercultural relationship. You do this by first coming to understand the Indigenous story of the canoe and of travelling and dwelling here pre- and post-contact. Emily Root writes of the decolonizing journey.[10] I have learned, largely from her, how to be on such a journey. This is messy stuff. At first, it might involve destabilizing some of the romance of canoe travel and paying attention to cultural oppressions. I, for example, am a white, Euro-Canadian canoe tripper: I do not feel responsible as a cultural invader, but I do feel accountable, and I have ample ways to act on that accountability. Here are a few quick examples from within my field of outdoor education. A friend wanted to use a Native symbol on a brand for his canoe company. I was asked my opinion on this. Simple: seek respectful relationships and ask the right folks. He visited certain Native elders to seek permission. In the end, permission was granted with some stipulations that all felt added to the initiatives with broader educational outcomes. One can and one must include Indigenous stories, be it by visiting rock art sites, attending events at ceremonial sites, or acknowledging Indigenous legends of the land or history. There is an Indigenous perspective too easily ignored. As mentioned elsewhere in these pages, if you are asked to speak on the history of the canoe and canoe travel in Canada, then Indigenous pre-contact trade routes and canoe activity should dominate.

In the 1960s, at the Serpent Lake Burial Mounds at Rice Lake, Ontario, as I understand, Parks Canada cut into one of the burial mounds and inserted Plexiglas so folks could see the graves and how people buried their dead centuries ago. Well, as a protest, members of the Hiawatha band of the area went to Peterborough (the closest urban centre) and dug up parts of a cemetery one night so folks could see the graves and how people buried their dead. The point is one *can* learn to break out of a Eurocentric view for that respectful intercultural relationship. This is a big part of that decolonizing journey Emily advocates.

When I read some of the decolonizing literature I want to shake the authors and critics and ask them, "What do you celebrate?" Criticism isn't a good enough answer for me. Truth is better, but there are many truths. I want to hear something like gardening, jazz, or … canoe tripping. To address the national stories of oppression, tied to the canoe or not, we need to be open to exploring the larger story. There will remain much to celebrate. We don't romanticize; we are imaginatively receptive to richer treatments. Were those voyageurs paddling Frances Simpson's canoe happy-go-lucky hired canoe men singing happy voyageur songs and wearing colourful sashes, or were they more like galley slaves, singing hymns or prayers and using sashes to avoid a common cause of death, a strangulated hernia? As the expression goes, "I'm just saying." I believe seeing both sides of this leads to richer knowledge, by opening the discussion rather than shutting it down.

I asked my colleague Emily Root to guide me in discussing the decolonizing journey. She, in an email, has responded to this question: "What do you celebrate or, perhaps better, support?"

> To me the obvious is, I celebrate a more honest version of Canadian history. I support respect — more respectful relationships. I support learning from Indigenous wisdom. I support overcoming ignorance. I support greater self-awareness. I support canoeing — in a way that helps to learn in and from Indigenous lands and with Indigenous peoples. But to be capable to be celebrating these things requires me to engage with difficult and (times painful) self reflection and critique.

I suppose what she is saying here is that ignorance is *not* bliss, or, as the full expression goes, "thought would destroy their paradise. No more; where ignorance is bliss, tis folly to be wise."[11] Rather, on the decolonizing journey, information is relational.

So can one "belong" to canoe trippers of Canada, or does acknowledging the invader, settler, oppressor story kill that relationship? I guess that is a personal question.

But I tend to remember the warm satisfaction of belonging and relationship felt that last night of a memorable canoe trip and accept enlightenment over guilt and humiliation. If I accept the burden of being a settler and invader I must accept the accountability to always learn and honour the "first" settlers, and to ever improve the production of the national story, including treatments of Indigenous peoples through time. Shared canoe encounters in a frothing eddy and ice fields on Georgian Bay and the Arctic, with a healthy respect for and curiosity about the past (all pasts), help build that Canada and strengthen at least one of its symbols — the canoe.

Deep Time and Deep Reflection

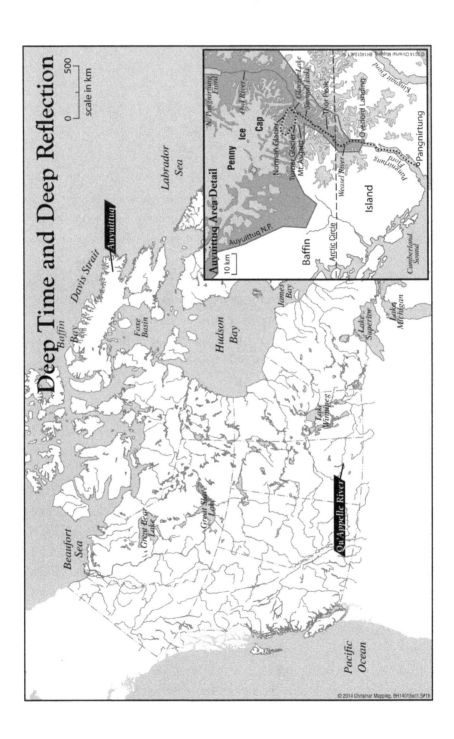

scale in km
0   500

Auyuittuq

Qu'Appelle River

Beaufort
Sea

Great Bear
Lake

Great Slave
Lake

Davis Strait

Baffin
Bay

Labrador
Sea

Foxe
Basin

Hudson
Bay

James
Bay

Lake
Winnipeg

Lake
Superior

Lake
Michigan

Pacific
Ocean

Auyuittuq Area Detail

N. Pangnirtung
Fiord

Owl River

Glacier Lake
Summit Lake

Thor Peak

Kingnait Fiord

Penny

Ice

Cap

Norman Glacier

Turner Glacier
Mt. Asgard

Weasel River

Pangnirtung Fiord

Overlord Landing

Pangnirtung

Baffin

Arctic Circle

Island

Cumberland
Sound

Auyuittuq N.P.

10 km

© 2014 Chrismar Mapping, BH14015#1 lb

© 2014 Chrismar Mapping, BH14015sec1.5#1b

5

Deep Time and Deep Reflection:
Baffin Island Ski Touring

"The physical landscape is baffling in its ability to transcend whatever we would make of it. It is as subtle in its expression as turns of the mind and larger than our grasp; and yet it is still knowable."[1]
— Barry Lopez

Certain landscapes lend themselves to questions about our place in the universe. But the first and foremost inquiry one must consider is the universe itself. I tend to associate such big questions with "deep time": that time you consider when you realize your hiking steps up the river valley might be dinosaur bones or the glacier snow you are gliding over is the ice foundation believed to have spawned the last ice age. Prairie rivers, particularly the Red Deer River in Alberta and the Saskatchewan and Qu'Appelle rivers in Saskatchewan, can do this. It's not just because of dinosaur remains or buffalo jumps or teepee rings; the landscape "feels" old — old and open with that big horizon view.[2] The same feel I get in open winter terrain. In 1985, I travelled by ski in Auyuittuq National Park on Baffin Island. Here I was completely absorbed by deep time and by its corollary, deep reflection. Later, in the Red Deer, Bow, Saskatchewan, and Qu'Appelle rivers in the Prairies, I got the spell again. Now I live on a high point on the Oak Ridges Moraine in southern Ontario, where the volume of glacial sand under my house means that the gardening sucks but I can always return to thoughts of deep time/deep reflection. I sit atop 180 feet of pure sand, a former beach, or so the fellow who dug our well (to 380 feet) told me. I thank that Baffin Island trip, though, for allowing geological time to be part of my repertoire of ponderous ideas. These ideas lead somewhere. "They expand the soul," as I heard actor Dustin Hoffman say once in an interview, and this expansion promotes utter contentment. Landscapes do this. Evening campfires and long, solo, meditative, rhythmic travel help. Literature helps too. Sometimes we need a little help to bring our thoughts out. The thoughts are there, but not able to be articulated. Baffin Island was, for me, a landscape ripe in deep time thoughts.

Our reluctance to say goodbye to winter brought three of us together for a ski mountaineering trip in Auyuittuq National Park. Its name is an Inuktitut word meaning "the land that never melts," so writes one guide book from the 1980s.[3]

After months of sorting equipment and reviewing maps, Mike Beedell, Gilles Couet, and I arrived on May 5 in the hamlet of Pangnirtung, sixteen hundred kilometres and five hours north by plane from rainy Montreal. Pangnirtung, an Inuit community of approximately sixteen hundred people, nestles in the valley shore of a majestic ocean fjord and serves as park headquarters. We arranged to travel by snowmobile into the park's glacial heartland via Pangnirtung Pass, which bisects Cumberland Peninsula from Cumberland Sound to Davis Strait.

For $125 each, Billy Etooangat agreed to take us the one hundred kilometres to the head of the pass by snowmobile. He described the route as *agoloon*, "rough trail," and we were to learn that this was something of an understatement. Our ascent of the frozen Weasel River to Summit Lake was a twelve-hour struggle. We often had to resort to ice crampons for gripping power as we wrestled snowmobiles and komatiks (sleds) up steep icefalls. We battled all night long against freezing headwinds that funnelled in an ever-present icy blast down the narrow pass. Coupled with the eerie twilight of the midnight sun, the furious winds were a harsh reminder of our distance from springtime Ontario.

The trip was a gruelling introduction to Auyuittuq, but the work, expense, and headaches were worth it to maximize our time skiing on the glaciers. We travelled by snowmobile past some of Auyuittuq's most awesome peaks, including Mount Overload and Mount Thor, at top speed in twilight and had little opportunity to savour their magnificence. At first I felt distracted and overwhelmed, psychologically disoriented you might say. But once on skis we had time to stand and stare, to watch the sun's light work on the mountains, to absorb their individual characters, and to slowly adjust to this mammoth landscape. At first, the physical landscape was baffling, as Barry Lopez says, but my psychological mindscape was also baffled. It was day one, and I secretly found myself yearning for the more southerly north that is treed and undulating, not open and towering. It was an embarrassing thought that I couldn't shake at first, but finally did with time and the slower pace of skis.

What is deep time? For me, it is the layperson's inability to contemplate the geological history of the earth. I can consider the last ice age, for example, and all that followed, and I can go back 4 million years into the creation of the Niagara Escarpment as a former seabed. But really, I'm struggling to get my mind there. I sympathize with Scottish mathematician John Playfair, who, in 1788 at the dawn of such thinking, said, "The mind seemed to grow giddy by looking so far into the abyss of time." I hear the scientist saying, "It blows my mind, man." He is also saying, I think, that the abyss of time takes one into the universe, the meaning of it all. Deep time is heady stuff. John McPhee put it this way: "Consider the Earth's history as the old measure of the English yard, the distance from the king's nose to the tip of his outstretched hand. One stroke of a nail file on his middle finger erases human history."[4]

Deep time demands that we consider the elbow, the shoulder, the tip of the nose. Not impossible, as scientists continue to study the earth, but I feel incredulous. I admit it. Consider this: in 2013 a four-year study called ice2sea discovered a previously unmapped 800-metre-deep, 750-kilometre-long gorge under up to two kilometres of glacial ice in north-central Greenland. It would have been cut by an ancient river more than 3 to 5 million years ago. Another study found a "ghost range" of mountains, similar to the European Alps, buried under Antarctica's glacial ice. These studies rely on data provided by radio waves penetrating transparent ice and bouncing off the buried bedrock.[5] One must pause to ponder the geological processes involved in forming such features and the processes that followed. For me, a human heritage type, it is truly overwhelming. Baffin Island's Penny Ice Cap was the same. I was skiing on an ancient glacier. What was I skiing over? What will be revealed if and when this landscape melts?

From Summit Lake we ascended Turner Glacier, one of many finger-like projections, or outlet glaciers, from the dominant Penny Ice Cap, which is believed to have spawned the last great ice age. Glaciers that originated here slid for eons across the continent, gouging out the Great Lakes and exposing the scoured rock of the Canadian Shield. Some scientists also believe that the next ice age will originate here. We decided our trip was giving us a glimpse of the world to come as well as a view of the ancient past. Such geological speculation worked our imaginations overtime, and we laid plans to reach the ice cap proper, so we could view the fields of this polar desert from its apex. Ice cap anyone? We explored in an orderly way: we would establish a base camp, then play nearby, climbing snow rises and rock ridges to find viewpoints and seeking out suitable pitches for Telemark (free heel) ski runs. Then we'd move on to a new base camp. Slowly we ascended from 500 metres at the valley floor to 1,950 metres on the ice cap.

We hauled our gear with plastic children's toboggans, then carried only day packs for trips from base camps. We also cached food at various central camps to lighten our overall load. The rigours of heavily laden skiing were often set aside for day-trip explorations in a skier's heaven.

Our Auyuittuq experience (reduced to its simplest terms) involved lengthy, laborious climbs up a long glacier's finger, with the objective of rapidly descending it again. To the detached outsider, this may appear absurd. But for us, the slow, steady climbing meant there was time to really see the ice walls, rock formations, and hanging glaciers. We had little sense of urgency. Our sleds, lovingly labelled buggies, were a joy to haul compared with backpacks.

Coming down was a test of our skiing skills. Snowplowing with a speedy sled on mixed powder and packed snow took total concentration. On less steep pitches, or on free skis without our loads, we would play with turns or cruise along, surveying the landscape around us. The terrain changed as snow texture, light, and shadows created new images as we moved through the day. By evening light, we gazed up at the rocky landscape on high, learning the intricacies and complexities of an environment that challenged our senses. Ours was a slow-paced, personal journey to know the land.

On the glacier network and the ice cap itself, we enjoyed a balmy 20° C inside our sun-drenched tents. Daily highs outdoors occasionally hit 10° C, allowing bare-skinned skiing and even a snow shower of sorts, with much picture-taking and the kind of merriment that comes only with rolling naked in the snow, then lunging for the comfort and security of your Ensolite sleeping pad for cold feet. (Glacier giggles are only for the healthy with a large respiratory capacity.)

Evenings, on the other hand, meant the return of typical winter conditions — averaging -15° C, with a low of -30° C. When evening shadows lengthened, we sped up our preparations for sleep.

We hit the valley floor after a rapid final descent off Norman Glacier, and there we encountered an abrupt change in the weather. Wind-driven snow pinned us down in our tents one day while on a forlorn ascent back up Turner Glacier to find one of our food caches. In such extreme conditions, proper equipment and clothing, knowledge, and caution are essential. However, there is more to safe travelling than proper equipment and techniques. In Baffin Island's mixed beauty and harshness, common sense and humility must govern your actions. Your attitude is always more important than your equipment.

We travelled out to Pangnirtung by retracing the snowmobile trip we had made two weeks before. We had five days at a pace that allowed us time to see the valley we had initially sped through. We also enjoyed more snow this time, and this meant good skiing. The ample time we had meant we could stop and stare on skis where we had rushed past before. How often we rush past exceptional places. Akshayuk Pass was nominated on virtualtourist.com in the Eight Wonders of the World contest. Mount Thor is the world's greatest sheer vertical drop at 1,250 metres. It is impressive from a valley floor standing on skis with a few days of food left. Truthfully, that baffling disoriented feeling returned in Akshayuk Pass with its towering rises, funnelling winds, and deteriorating winter conditions. Not to mention I blew out my three-pin toe binding on my ski boots. I felt I was a long way from home — the Canadian Shield — and that was a good thing. I have learned how to "be" in this Arctic landscape.

Heading up onto the Penny Ice Cap.

There was much evidence of spring. The icefalls were treacherous, as thin ice, gravel, and mud stretches replaced snow and slowed our progress. From an emergency park shelter, we radioed headquarters to arrange a final snowmobile trip from the park boundary at Overload to the terminus of Pangnirtung Fjord.

Once back in Pangnirtung, we realized how remarkable the environment was that we had skied. Big inquiries, such as how this landscape was made, bring one to deep time/deep reflection. To understand this land, it is best skied in April or May. It is a place to stand and stare, a treat to the senses, and an opportunity to hear the eerie, silent language of the ice fields. You learn, too, about your complete insignificance against the backdrop of time and space in such a titanic landscape. This certainly is a writer's cliché, but it is also certainly true. The Baffin landscape is certainly a land to ponder.

While this idea of a ponderous place was certainly an Auyuittuq phenomenon for me in 1985, it has also been a continually perplexing quality in certain landscapes I have travelled. In 2013, on the fast flowing Keele River, travelling three hundred kilometres to the Mackenzie River, I paddled in awe of the glacial river cutting a deep time and recent time (geologically thinking) swath through the Mackenzie Mountains southwest of Norman Wells. Here, for hundreds of years, the Dene people have been walking inland from the Mackenzie River in the spring to hunt upriver on the Keele. Later in the early fall season, they would return to the Mackenzie River. This I can understand.

A replica moosehide boat housed at the Prince of Wales Museum in Yellowknife goes a long way towards helping the easy comprehension. While flying into this river, one can easily pick out choice walking routes in the mountainous terrain. Smooth historical comprehension and fine hiking terrain with no hikers: such is the northern interior here. What I cannot understand are the pre-glacial qualities and the overlying glacial features. The valley has been carved, but its rocks might predate glaciations in the millions of years. This is a ripe place to ponder, a good place to be paddling downstream. As Jamie Bastedo says in his fine book *Shield Country*: "In Shield Country, rock is the ecological bottom line. It determines the lay of the land, the pattern of vegetation, the flow of water."[6] Putting the rock, the river, and the glaciations all together — this I cannot fully comprehend.

I remember our perplexity when looking for teepee rings with Parks Saskatchewan employee Joe Milligan while overlooking the Qu'Appelle River. What a stunning river valley on the often misunderstood Prairies. We had the opposite view at the Akshayuk Pass with Mount Thor or when I started a canoe trip under the Stelfox Range looking over to the jagged Delthore Range of the Keele River. Instead of the vertical gaze in the valley floor, overlooking the Qu'Appelle River one has a horizontal view and the sense of a great, depressed land corridor more than a river. Qu'Appelle River traveller Norman Henderson put this best:

> The Qu'Appelle Valley is a great burrowing from the end of the last ice age. Here, about fourteen thousand years ago, the continental ice sheet stalled for a few centuries during its northern retreat from the warming climate. Vast volumes of melt water flowed west to east across the ice sheet face, cutting deep into the belly of the Plains. I stared out at the great empty valley, a mile or

Qu'Appelle River Valley.

more across at nearly three hundred feet deep, and tried
to imagine it overflowing with ice water and the blue-
tinged berg-bits of super compressed glacial ice. Only
the thin shimmering line of the river bore testimony to
the mighty floodwaters of the past. From this distance
the remnant river, only thirty yards across, seemed
unworthy of the great valley inheritance bequeathed it
by its glacial forebear.[7]

The Qu'Appelle, like the Keele River and the valleys of Auyuittuq, is
a glacial feature. Indeed, one can say that Canada is still largely a glacial
landscape. This makes the Penny Ice Cap, possibly whence it all spawned,
a very ponderous, perplexing, perfect place to stand and stare in search
of deep time and deep perspective.

Educator Steve Simpson wrote, "… using literature in outdoor education … illustrates perceptions the reader already realizes and presents
new perceptions that the reader has, to this point, never considered."[8] I
agreed on both counts, but I think there is more of the former happening

than the latter. I believe literature largely distills ideas and draws them out rather than instilling, creating, or producing them. It is the central tenet of ecopsychology. You do not produce an ecological consciousness in people as an educator; you draw it out. It is already present in you as a latent spiritual impulse.[9] To ponder deep time is in us. It is good for us. Yes, it expands the soul, which I believe is distilled, not instilled.

Let's consider utter contentment. For camp director and canoe trip guide Mary Northway, utter contentment was one of three main ways to answer an ever-present contemporary question: Why go camping? She put it this way: "… experiencing a sense of harmony between the world and oneself that resolves all conflict and releases new springs of action." Connected to this thought, she recalled a lazy, sunny moment paddling Redstone Lake in Haliburton, Ontario. The other two main reasons to go camping for Mary were "… achieving of a goal in spite of adversity, [and] participating in an enterprise that increases gaiety and enjoyment."[10] There you have it, three succinct reasons why we go camping. I've always liked this reasoning. I think pondering deep time and finding the utter contentment of that sunny moment paddling Redstone Lake that "resolves all conflict" often go together.

When I read passages in literature denoting utter contentment, I am drawn to them. The passages often shed light on a pre-conceived idea or pre-instinctual feeling I hadn't had yet: something on the tip of my tongue, so to speak, or rather the tip of my cerebral cortex, tip of my held pen, tip of my "this gives me the shivers" body. It is there, but waiting for articulation, waiting for help. Literature can be that help!

Halldór Laxness, a famous Icelandic author, wrote of an idyllic spring day by a flowing stream. From his novel *Independent People*:

> … after a day or two the brook had grown little again and all the snow had melted from the mountain. Had the brook lost its charm, then? No, far from it. Clear and joyful it flowed over the shining sand and pebbles, between its banks white and withered grass, its joy eternally new every spring for a thousand years; and it told

little stories, in its own little tongue, its own little inflections, while the boy sat on the bank and listened for a thousand years. The boy and eternity, two friends, the sky cloudless and unending. Yes.[11]

There really is something forever about the river and those who watch it flow. Yes. And the river often serves as a metaphor for strength and timelessness: the boy and river eternal, two friends. Who on a river trip, whether summer or winter, has not paused to ponder the river's eternal flow? Mike, Gilles, and I certainly did this on our Baffin Island spring river ice trip back out to the ocean.

It is a prominent deep time reflection that literature can expose and enhance, and it is good for us, really good for us. Elliott Merrick, in his 1942 treatment of Labrador winter river travels, like that Icelandic boy on the riverbank, captures that ecstasy of the flowing river and reflective time. Merrick captures the ideas of the highs and lows of outdoor travel. The lower the lows, the higher the highs. That post-rainstorm morning when all the gear is wet and the rain continues into midday can get pretty bleak. But my goodness, what an evening high when the sky clears and all is dry again by bedtime; you are in paradise. The fire is warming and reveals all its wisdom for those who stare and ponder. Yes, Elliott Merrick captures much of deep time and deep reflection with the following passages:

> Oh, the happiness that fills us in as strong and quiet as Grand River. Just as the river never stops flowing down under the ice, so this ecstasy will flow forever in our hearts, carrying us with it to the limitless sea of hope and understanding and sympathy. In this life where one can conceal nothing, not even from oneself, it seems we have found ourselves out for the first time, found what we really are and what living is. It is like getting to the bottom of things, as though from this as a starting point we could live true. All of it has not been pretty,

but the gem-hard beauty of these months has freed the soul like some sweeping tragedy that is too splendid and transcendent ever to be tragic. Last night I thought this life was a brutalizing ordeal, a long, long chain of pain that one numbed oneself to endure. Tonight I think that we have touched the earth's core and found meaning. Whatever it is we sought, we have found. We hold it in our hands, dreaming by the fire.[12]

There is a Norse expression for all this: *Terrenget Underviser*, meaning, "the terrain does the teaching." Canadian literature is rampant with such sentiments of the power of nature to draw out contemplative thought. Yves Thériault's central theme in his novels such as *Agaguk* is "he who fails to respond to nature-as-teacher is doomed to emotional and spiritual sterility."[13] In *The Shallows: What the Internet Is Doing to Our Brains*, author Nicholas Carr reports that we are losing our contemplative skills.[14] No, it is worse, we are losing our ability to even know we once had such skills. In our digital age, perhaps this study of deep time, utter contentment, and nature as teacher of contemplative attention seems nostalgic. After all, by way of an example, the Oxford dictionary review committee recently decided to delete certain nature words from continued inclusion in the junior dictionary. Words like *acorn*, *fern*, *heron*, and *dandelion* have been eliminated so that computer age words such as *blog*, *chat room*, and *database* can be added.[15] Personally, I find this troubling. Losing our contemplative and deep nature awareness is the central problem here. Carr writes, "We don't see the forest when we search the Web. We don't even see the trees. We see twigs and leaves ... whenever we turn on our computer; we are plunged into an ecosystem of interruption technologies."[16]

Enter the idea of neuroplasticity. Carr introduced me to this idea, though obviously from his research it is clear the idea has existed in brain research for decades. Here's the idea: the brain can change its way of thinking with new cultural practices. The written word changed our way of thinking from oral storytelling. Now is the computer changing the way we think from the book era? Put plainly by Nicolas Carr: "Our way of thinking, perceiving, and acting, we now know, are not entirely determined by our genes. Nor are they entirely determined by our childhood experiences. We change them through the way we live — and, as Nietzsche sensed, through the tools we use."[17]

I'm worried! If this research is right, then we lose a certain humility that feels "natural" in places like the Penny Ice Cap in Baffin Island. Will skiing about with friends for fun — but really of utter contentment — be replaced with another source? Will that source be from an interruption technology? Will our mind prefer to always be elsewhere? Will pondering deep time and a deep contentment follow us as we shift our language in the direction the Oxford dictionary has decided to advance? I only know I want to hold onto the feeling of utter contentment I can get when travelling on the land. Places where deep time feels omnipresent advance this. As singer-songwriter Todd Snider sings, "I may have been born yesterday [in terms of dwelling in the computer era], but I've been up all night." I'm not prepared or preparing to lose that contemplative spirit with nature.

Margaret Atwood has encouraged us "to let the wild in." What does this mean? Surely there is a need to ponder, to embrace "the other" so to speak.

PART TWO

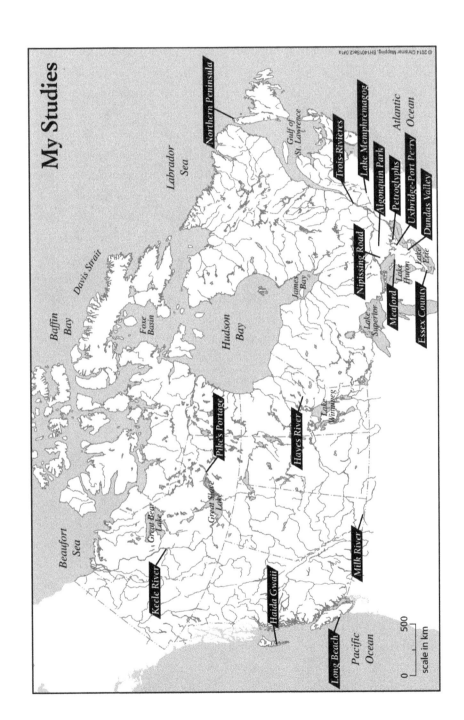

My Studies

Northern Peninsula

Trois-Rivières

Lake Memphrémagog

Algonquin Park

Petroglyphs

Uxbridge–Port Perry

Dundas Valley

Atlantic
Ocean

Nipissing Road

Meaford

Essex County

Lake
Huron

Lake
Erie

Lake Superior

James
Bay

Hudson
Bay

Labrador
Sea

Gulf of
St. Lawrence

Baffin
Bay

Davis Strait

Foxe
Basin

Pike's Portage

Hayes River

Lake
Winnipeg

Great Slave
Lake

Great Bear
Lake

Keele River

Milk River

Haida Gwaii

Long Beach

Pacific
Ocean

Beaufort
Sea

0   500

scale in km

INTRODUCTION

Perspectives

"A simple intuition, a single observation, can open vistas of unimagined potential. Once caught in the web of an idea, the researcher is happily doomed, for the outcome is always uncertain, and the resolution of the mystery may take years to unfold."[1]
— Wade Davis

With the completion of *Every Trail Has a Story: Heritage Travel in Canada* in 2005, I shifted gears a bit as a traveller. In the ensuing years, I have continued to travel widely in Canada, but have had fewer years of gathering stories through exploration than the thirty-plus years represented in *Every Trail*. That said, I have also become more and more engaged in local excursions and stories. Often these are the stories that are lying in wait. For example, I had known about John Muir living in the Meaford area, I had known about Native marker trees in southern Ontario, I had known the war canoes I paddled as a kid were special, but I'd never followed up on these close to home stories. My studies here represent time devoted to learning more about my vague or underdeveloped knowledge. My studies also represent surprises discovered serendipitously. For example, while under contract to write the Canadian section of the *Northern Forest Canoe Trail Guidebook*,[2] I discovered Gérard Leduc and his work on the Jones Mill sites among other Lake Memphremagog area historical anomalies. This has led to strengthening the time for casual exploration of those discoveries on the land and in the literature that tell the stories we are not hearing in Canadian history.

Some stories are assertively pursued to gain the insight of others. I travelled out of my way a bit to visit my Danish friend Svend Ulstrup to learn about his perspective on Bronze Age canoes. I joined Paul O'Hara one day to seek out a Native marker tree and followed up on many of his discoveries. My research here, whether discovered or planned, is almost always as a secondary researcher, following the leads and research of others who are fully devoted to a specific line of inquiry. I am happily all over the Canadian map. Paul O'Hara, Robert Burcher, Svend Ulstrup, Dave Standfield, and others presented within are grounded in a story. I am a sideline reporter fascinated in their work. My studies represent perspectives gained largely where other folks are not looking. I have gained respect for those who work outside the dominant story. The perspectives within are mostly lesser-known viewpoints or ones outside the dominant story.

Historical Anomalies

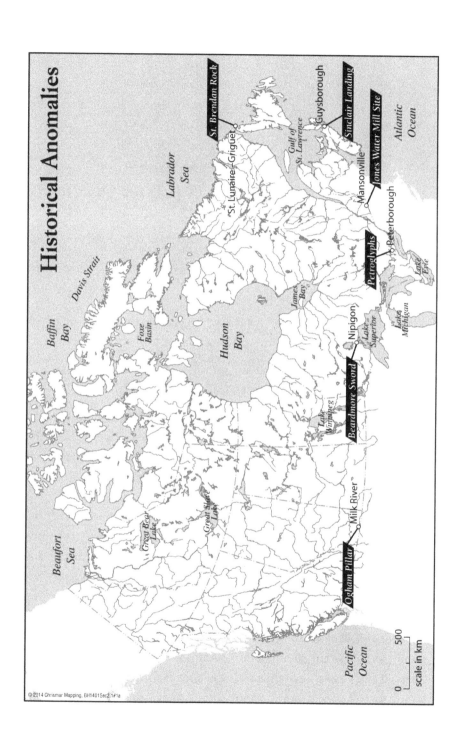

6
Historical Anomalies:
To Deny It or Rely On It, That Is the Question

"What I have seen is a fascinating struggle between 'hard' scientists trained to dissect data and draw conclusions of probability, and historians hesitant to embrace a non-conforming interpretation."[1]
— Alice Beck Kehoe

I told a friend about the Beardmore Sword, a Viking relic found on a Native travel route between Hudson Bay and Lake Superior. He said, "Oh yeah, I've heard of that. It's a fraud." He knew next to nothing about any of the sword's details as an archaeological anomaly, but still he had an opinion. Tell other friends, like Robert Burcher or Gérard Leduc or Daniel Kolos, and you get a flurry of inquiries and hypotheses. Within a few days, Robert for one, thanks to much research and lately the internet, will have contacted authorities and connected several of the dots needed to have a substantial theory brewing. I prefer Robert's approach. I am a self-proclaimed "rely on it" rather than "deny it" person. That doesn't mean I grab onto a wild idea. Rather, I think we have an accepted, unchallenged version of our history and many have a vested interest in and psychological attachment to that particular version. Some odd historical finds have been proven to be hoaxes, but some remain unexplained and challenge convention. Some appear to be denied outright without good cause. I like to believe one can be truly objective. I do question this, though, because both "deny it" and "rely on it" sentiments seem to swing opinion in one direction or the other from the get-go. The Beardmore Sword, for example, has been proven not to be a hoax, but the next find might be. The Kensington Runestone found in Minnesota, possibly Viking in origin, is a mess of controversy (see Kehoe's book). It is best to try for that middle ground, but hard to hold an objective position. Dissect all the data available, weigh probabilities, and generate a hypothesis for the scrutiny of others: that is the task that befalls historians and archaeologists in the face of the wealth of incongruous finds on Canadian soil and in the waters. I will lean toward my preferred "rely on it" stance. Easy for me, as I have no vested interests that I am aware of other than the love of a good, engaging story and friends who share that same quality as historical anomaly snoopers.

Anomalies are, in the words of receptive anthropologist Alice Beck Kehoe, "at once the bane and the fun of science."[2] She advocates that "anomalies play a critical role in science, pushing researchers to refine or reject theories."[3] I agree! "If the evidence makes you uncomfortable given your theory or opinion on a topic, pay attention, you are about to learn something." My friend Garrett Conover shared this with me in conversation amidst many an anomalous subject.

I have a few here. The 1560 water mill and the undated winter solstice site in Potton Township near Lake Memphremagog, Quebec, stand out for me. Basalt stones found in Newfoundland likely served as ballast stones that weighed a ship down and were easily discarded when a load was taken on at a Viking landing site. There are many such anomalies out there, often in clusters that collectively inspire the possibility of many a historical rewrite. Others include the Peterborough petroglyphs in Ontario, inscriptions on Atlantic shoreline rocks, and woven cloth at a Baffin Island archaeology site. I can only scratch the surface here but will share sources for my studies.

First, my story with historical anomalies. I started in the early 1990s with Barry Fells' research into the Ogham Pillar on the Milk River shoreline in southern Alberta.[4] Ogham is an ancient Celtic alphabet made up of grooved writing that can look like elaborate tally marks. The Ogham Tract suggests there are seventy varieties of this ancient script. I went to the Milk River for a good paddle and to see the Ogham Pillar for myself. Local historian Alva Beir met us on the river and showed us the sites. Later I compared the etchings at the Milk River with examples of Ogham. It is compelling stuff, to which Alva said, "It's there, you can't deny it." I've always remembered that simple advice. These etchings in the soft stone certainly do not look like anything connected to Native peoples. The story is a curious one. Could early travellers have advanced upriver on the Mississippi and Missouri to this Milk River headwater tributary in pre-Columbian times? The Ogham Pillar is not easily explained.

Only a year or two later in 1998, while sea kayaking on the eastern shore of Nova Scotia, I had a chance meeting with Henry Sinclair's modern clansmen. Seems the Sinclairs of the world (there were about five hundred of them gathered), were having a six-hundred-year celebration of Henry's landing at Guysborogh Harbour, Nova Scotia. Henry Sinclair, Earl of Orkney (1345–1404), allegedly travelled with Venetian merchants the Zeno brothers, who recorded his travels into the interior of Nova Scotia in 1398.[5] I got the bare-bones story from descendents.

Paddling on Milk River.

Wait, slow down — who the heck is Henry Sinclair, and what of the Zeno Narratives that allegedly record his travels? This led me to Fredrick Pohl's work on Sinclair and the Zenos.[6] Then I was hooked. I knew Columbus travelled with maps in 1492. Yes, maps of the New World. Jacques Cartier arrived in 1534 with Native populations waving to his ships and drawing him in to trade. Clearly not a new practice, this New World landing stuff. Still, the Ogham in southern Alberta and Sinclair in Nova Scotia (or his Knights Templar buddies, anyway) were different. There are full-blown explanation stories to anomalies like the Ogham Pillar and the Zeno Narratives. I soon realized that once you enter this world of brewing forbidden history and archaeology, there is no escape. As Paul Eluard has said, and I am fond of saying, "there is another world, but it is in this one." I enjoy the destabilizing of history. I like what British poet John Keats called "negative capability": "that is, when a man is capable of being in uncertainty, mystery, doubts, without any irritable reaching after fact and reason."[7] Keats rejected the idea of rigid, perhaps biased, theories and categorical knowledge. This quality is needed when exploring historical anomalies.

So I kept going into the present. I read Farley Mowat's Alban theory. I visited Gérard Leduc in Mansonville, Quebec, and read his works, which led me to Michael Bradley and the Knights Templar, religious refugees in North America theory. I diligently read Gavin Menzies' treatment of possible Chinese landings on both the Atlantic and Pacific coasts and later his treatment of the Minoans' travels, circa 2500 BC, revolving around extracting copper from Lake Superior.[8] Some group had to have extracted the currently estimated two thousand tons (approximately 2 million kilograms) of copper from the ancient mines (although this may be a low-ball figure). Deb Diebel, a friend of Robert Burcher, knowing of our mutual interests, set us up for a meeting. I still remember her saying, "You just have to meet this guy!" My brother, Gordon Henderson, made a film (90th Parallel Productions, titled, *The Norse: An Arctic Mystery*) on the archaeological finds and work of Pat Sutherland in Baffin Island. Why was she allegedly fired (my words) from the then-Museum of Civilization for finding and sharing her discoveries of a Viking settlement's (my words again) activity on Baffin Island? Woven cloth dated to around 1000 AD is an anomaly indeed. Perhaps it is true, as author of *Forbidden Archaeology* Michael Cremo states: "Scientists who find things that should not be found sometimes suffer for it professionally.[9]

Time to focus on specific examples. Trips to the Jones water mill site have my imagination spinning. Both Gérard Leduc and Michael Bradley have written about the site in Potton Township of the Eastern Townships in Quebec. Gérard quotes the 1850s Jones pioneer family: "The impressive cut stone foundations had always been there."[10] The first settlers here arrived in the 1790s. The mill was there then. Indeed, settler families have an oral tradition that maintains that stones from the water mill, where the water flows down toward Lake Memphremagog, were used to build foundations for their first houses. Gérard helped coordinate a 1992 archaeological dig at the site sponsored by the Quebec government. The foundations have two clearly defined walls with a right-angled corner. There is a square opening sluiceway for water to run and a larger slab cut stone over the opening. This is not the work of Indigenous people. Pioneers who must have lost track of their history is a fair surmise. Two datable artifacts were discovered at the site. Easy, do a carbon dating analysis and you likely have your time period, at least. Saving government money was the reason given for the process not to proceed officially. Yet fifteen years later the same carbon dating was employed at the Cap Rouge site near Quebec City, revealing a settlement ruin from Cartier and Roberval dating from 1540–1543. Hmmm, what happened to saving government money? Gérard spent his own funds to receive an objective date for the mill site through the standard carbon dating channels. Voila, the year 1560 (plus or minus sixty years) came up for the hemlock wood stake and charcoal samples. Still, the official government word on the site was 1850s pioneer. I'm going with 1500.

Now, a water mill doesn't exist in isolation. There would likely have been a small community taking shape around such a mill. Fascinating, a great discovery of an early interior (not on the St. Lawrence River) and pre-Cartier/Roberval settlement. Important? I think so. Premier Jean Charest at the time of the Cap Rouge archaeological discovery said: "This is one of the greatest discoveries in the history of Quebec." Why the pass

The Jones water mill site.

on the Potton site? It likely isn't French. It might even lead to a better understanding of pre-Columbian landings and interior travel. It doesn't stop there. A stone's throw (for an Olympic athlete) away from the mill site is the former Indian Rock, now called the Potton Celtic Rock. The rock ledge has a series of engraved glyphs that certainly look like Irish Ogham alphabet writings from the fourteenth century. Coincidence? Certainly anomalies abound at this Lake Memphremagog area site.

I should add that I only came upon this story in 2003 when writing the Canadian section of *The North Forest Canoe Trail Guide* — the Lake Memphremagog–Missisquoi River section.[11] Members of those same pioneer families, in this case the Jewetts, suggested I contact Gérard. I had already visited the mill site and the Celtic stone on local leads. Expecting to only be reporting on portages, canoe put-ins, and restaurants, you can imagine my pleasure in learning the above story. But why is this a local, not nationally known story? Well pre-Columbian settlements or non-French settlements in Quebec, despite some solid evidence for one or both, are not the stuff of favoured theory. Deny it? That's how it reads to me.

So, who then, and why there? This is a problem. The Jones water mill site is but one anomalous item of evidence. The evidence of pre-Columbian landings and travels in North America exists and stories are woven connecting the evidence. For example, the Potton Celtic Rock with Ogham script dating to 1100–1300 AD linked to the mill site suggests Celtic origins. Michael Bradley, working with the Memphremagog evidence, suggests a Knights Templar settlement perhaps connected to Henry Sinclair's travels inland from Nova Scotia on one or all of the New England "river roads": the Connecticut River; the interconnected waterway of the Hudson River, Lakes George and Champlain, and the Missisquoi River; and the St. Lawrence and St. Francis rivers. Three possibilities. Gérard Leduc differs with Bradley on the possibility of the Sinclair story extending from Nova Scotia to Lake Memphremagog, but he is now a committed Knights Templar researcher given his Potton discoveries.

In November 2013, Gérard Leduc took my friend Paul Laurier and I into a location west of Lake Memphremagog, that Gérard believes is a winter solstice site. This would certainly be a pre-Columbian and pre-Colonial site (Loyalists arrived here in the 1790s). The day was glorious, with clear views from the raised bench above the North Branch of the Missisquoi River in the shadow of the Sutton Mountains, showing Jay Peak in Vermont to the south and the dominant Owl's Head Mountain to the east. A fine panoramic lookout. A grand place for a grand observance, certainly.

Gérard Leduc showing a rock etching alignment for the winter solstice sunrise.

Walking up a long established trail, we first saw a rock-lined depression with dry wall masonry (built without mortar). Gérard pointed out this construction practice, suggesting possible centuries, not decades, of age. Then we saw three small vertical boulders deeply buried in the ground in a straight line from the lined depression. On the furthest stone are two very clear grooved line markings. *Easily missed*, I thought. Gérard pulled out his compass, as he had done before for keeners and skeptics alike on winter solstice group visits. One line shows a definite north-south direction corrected for the magnetic declination; the other line points towards the winter solstice sunrise azimuth. Exciting! Only then do we notice we are on a level tennis court sized raised terrace from the gradual slope. A well-built stone wall with steps in ruins is a surprising and out-of-place dominant feature. Gérard reminds us that 1940s aerial photographs reveal the slope was once an open pasture. I wondered what the slope might have looked like pre-1500s. Certainly it's possible to imagine a well-built staging area on this platform. Perhaps the depression once was full of water for purification from a creek that is very close by. A house was later built here, perhaps using the ready-made depression. New foundations over older foundations are common in the region: activity built on former activity. Walking directly westward off the key grooved mark on the key solstice stone took us to a man-made boulder cairn. Here, with the brilliant open forest and November light, Gérard noticed a strange human marking. It was a new discovery for Gérard and just a part of Paul's and my overwhelming sense of the special place we were seeing. This petroglyph was studied by epigrapher Michel Boutet, who interpreted the markings as referring to solar-lunar intervals.

Gérard thinks it might be a letter of an ancient alphabet. We lingered. There was a calming pleasure in taking it all in. But taking what in? Clearly the alignments carved in well-placed stone speak to a winter solstice site. Okay, who would establish such a site and such a practice? I could delight in the mystery, connecting it to the Jones mill site about ten kilometres away. Early settlers and Native peoples showed no tendencies toward such activity. We marvelled at the stone wall, standing for hundreds of years. Gérard thinks the site is connected to a short-lived pre-Columbian settlement in the Lake Memphremagog area. Celtic people? Knights Templar? Vikings? The carbon-dated Jones mill site from 1560; the lion's head gargoyle found in 1985 in the creek of the mill that is, according to a Montreal archaeology professor, the remains of a medieval sculpture; Ogham writing on a dominant stone — there is too much here for coincidence, and pre-1500s is no longer a speculative call. I, for one, am receptive to Gérard's opinion and curious as to why he is shunned by the academic community, who, in many cases, do not even explore possibilities or visit the sites. There is much more to this story.

Discoveries are happening fast. Pat Sutherland's woven cloth (among other artifacts) from the Viking era at an archaeology site in Baffin Island appears to have gotten her fired from her Museum of Civilization job. Sutherland is part of a "rewriting history" movement, if that is the right name for it. She says, "The Arctic was not this isolated, marginal place as is often assumed. In the centuries around 1000 CE, it was really a nexus for the people from the old world meeting with people from the new."[12] She has found whetstones for sharpening metal tools, woven cordage, notched wooden sticks used by the Norse people to record trading activity, and evidence of smelted metal. Seems like a Viking site to me.

Then there is the recent Faroe Islands story. From the Faroes to Iceland to Greenland to Canada — island hopping makes the idea of early trade from Atlantic crossings seem very doable. Not to mention Arctic currents to propel them along. Indigenous hunters wanted exotic trade goods. Early Celts needed copper, and the Norse needed timbers to build Arctic settlements. Remember, temperatures were much warmer circa 1400 and earlier. With the Viking L'Anse aux Meadows site confirmed as a boat repair station in northern Newfoundland, it makes sense more sites will be discovered. Still, I wonder why there is resistance.

Scottish researchers have found evidence of very early habitation (350–550 AD) on the Faroe Islands (the first link on the island-hopping northern transatlantic crossing to North America) that makes pre-Viking ocean crossings more acceptable. Found recently on the Faroes' island of Sandoy are traces of charred peat, barley seeds, and evidence of human efforts to control erosion that date five hundred years before the established Viking colonization of the Faroes in the ninth century.[13] All this fuels the fire of seemingly mythical accounts of Atlantic crossings. The medieval Irish text *Navigato Sancti Brendani* (*The Voyage of St. Brendan*) is a centrepiece here. Did Brendan in 570 AD island hop to the promised land of the New World (Newfoundland)? Tim Severin, a British adventurer in the 1970s, went to great efforts to replicate Brendan's voyage in a replica medieval leather sailboat.

Inscriptions on a harbour rock face in Newfoundland continue to keep the story of Saint Brendan the navigator alive. Time will tell. New evidence continues to be decoded both in Canada and Ireland. Mike Church of Durham University says of the archaeological discovery: "There are no truths, per se. You have to put together the evidence and then argue from the evidence for a specific interpretation."[14] Sometimes the evidence is the bane and fun of it all. Historical anomalies abound.

This is all wild thinking if you are entrenched in the conventional version of history, but the anomalies beg attention to my mind. Many a historian and archaeologist will tell you that "history is the lie that we agree on." This should at least open the doors to inquiry when new interpretations come forward. As educator Henry Bugbee has said, "Risk yourself in the possibility of meaning."[15] In the case of anomalies, this means weaving a story, connecting the anomalous dots, and putting it out there to be scrutinized. I respect this approach particularly when the conventional story sometimes seems blind to new information. Susan Sontag, in an introduction to Icelandic author Halldór Laxness's classic novel *Under the Glacier*, put it this way: "Imagining the exceptional, often understood as the miraculous, the magical, or the supernatural, is a perennial job of story-telling."[16]

Enter Robert Burcher, who follows anomalies with the best of them.

Robert Burcher found his avocation as a historian through his family's sensitivities to Canada's Native peoples. On a family trip in the 1960s to Petroglyphs Provincial Park near Peterborough, Robert was more than casually intrigued. Years later, this childhood intrigue would see him write *The Leather Boat*, in which he offers a different interpretation of the Native rock art.[17] Put briefly, the rock art image believed to be a spirit boat that exists in the dream world to take the shaman between upper and under worlds also looks a lot like a sailboat with two masts, not unlike the leather boats used in Ireland circa 500 AD. You can see such a boat in action in the replica used by Tim Severin in his 1976–77 transatlantic voyage to recreate

St. Brendan's journey. For a culture that, as far as we know, were not using sailboats, why call them into play in art? One might expect a spirit canoe.

Then there is the issue of the unusual arrowhead-like images that an early interpretation describes as depictions of manitous. Well, Robert presents a very compelling idea that they are amphorae — big clay jars hung cleverly in ships so stored water would be easily retrieved with no spillage. Also, could the "rabbitman" image on various sites be a man wearing a horned helmet? Could the great creator (or Gitchi Manitou), sometimes shown with legs and body supporting a radiating sun, be a man supporting a *Trumpa Creda* — a two-thousand-year-old Gaelic Bronze Age horn?

These Burcher interpretations make sense pictorially. The rock art looks like representations of physical items or actions. Also, the Peterborough petroglyphs stand out among Ontario sites for the different images compared to more conventional Native rock art. Also, the nearby Trent-Severn waterway and related foot paths between Lake Simcoe and Lake Ontario were a well-known Native trade route. We know Champlain travelled the Trent-Severn waterway from Huronia to Lake Ontario in the early 1600s, and we know Native populations travelled and traded extensively by canoe-friendly waterways. We also know that European boats from the Viking period (850 to 1100 AD) were travelling extensively into the European interior, using the Volga River, in the main, to access the Black Sea and the Byzantine Empire to trade.[18] The European boats of various periods would have been capable of travelling river and lake country. One can argue that the spirit world images of the petroglyphs could be depicting encounters with pre-Columbian interior travellers. This site doesn't stand alone. There is a similar petroglyph site in Michigan.[19]

You will hear none of these stories at Petroglyphs Provincial Park. The *ke-no-mab-gay-wab-kon* (the "rocks that teach") site offers no rock art interpretation literature, of which there exists a wealth. This is, in a word, frustrating. The "teaching rocks" offer a single conventional interpretation that makes sense in Native spiritual understandings, but not in context with other Canadian Shield sites. It has been suggested that some petroglyph images at the Peterborough site have not been highlighted for display (melted black crayon is used) or that these same images were consciously allowed to erode. Even worse, one theory suggests that they were ground out once area Native groups took control of the site. And what image is allegedly lessened? A Viking ship similar to images such as the Boslund ship at sites in Sweden.[20]

It doesn't hurt my pre-Columbian traveller position that as I gather up material from various site visits, meeting maverick scholars and, of course, reading books, I am reading the hot-off-the-presses *Who Discovered America: The Untold History of the Peopling of the Americas.* You guessed it, it isn't suggested to be Columbus, Cabot, Cartier, or Erikson.[21] So who? That turns out to be a very big question with lots of ideas.

Let's catch up with Robert Burcher and his most immediate investigation.

When you are researching ancient Celts it is best to avoid the pull to follow threads of Viking anomalies, but once you are in, so to speak, there isn't a "one culture" story that unfolds smartly. It's a mess. Gérard found the same thing in the Lake Mempremagog area. Here's a highlight or two from Robert's anomaly hunting: several inscriptions on Newfoundland coastal rocks. The "rely on it" camp are looking and seeking expert analysis; the "deny it" camp are losing sight of the mounting evidence.

In 2004, I followed a road sign titled "St. Brendan's Rock" just outside St. Lunaire–Griguet on the Great Northern Peninsula. I had a plane to catch at Deer Lake, so it was a rushed early morning affair. Following the boardwalk (common to Newfoundland trails) led me to the end of the boardwalk construction. There was the road sign to the site, but the trail was not yet complete. I floundered about looking at rocks in the area but ran out of time. I later learned that Gary Bussy was the local historian I should have consulted. There is always an important local fellow. But I didn't revisit it once back home. Enter Robert. He had pursued the inscription with Bussy at the St. Lunaire–Griguet coast. Turns out that the boulder the locals (and the highway road sign) call St. Brendan's (presumably from circa 500 AD) is more likely connected to the Tartessian culture from today's Iberian peninsula, Spain and Portugal. The Tartessians predate the Celts of St. Brendan's time by a thousand years. Man, I wish the boardwalk had been complete and guided me to that site. I'll be back ASAP. There's more! Two other sites in Newfoundland are currently under analysis. One from the Placentia

Bay area might just prove to be Phoenician, a culture dating back three thousand years. Phoenicia today encompasses the countries of Lebanon and Syria. Another inscription found near St. John's has been recognized as medieval Latin.[22] These three examples are all under investigation at various labs in Europe and Canada as of November 2013. The quick disregard for such anomalies worries me. I can only imagine how Robert Burcher and Gérard Leduc handle this? How did Alva Beir put it to me in the early 1990s on the Milk River at that Ogham Pillar: "It's there, you can't deny it." A calm and confident Robert and Gérard would say people need to learn about the big picture and then comment.

Background work involves, among other things, following the work of other maverick scholars. Gavin Menzies is one. He suggests the quest for copper and tin in the Bronze Age (3200–500 BC) had certain cultures travelling far afield. Surface copper and copper mines at Lake Superior sites possibly played a big role in transatlantic journeys. Menzies has the Minoan culture (3200–1450 BC) obtaining Lake Superior copper for hundreds of years.[23] We do know that the copper was extracted in large amounts long before Columbus sailed the ocean blue in 1492. How much copper was extracted, you ask? Estimates range from 1.4 million kilograms to as much as 230 million kilograms.[24]

Back to Robert Burcher. He had heard a story in Newfoundland of a woman cleaning out some tuckamore bush to extend her backyard. She turned up some unusual inscriptions and made a few calls. The woman had found what appeared to be Viking runic inscriptions. She confirmed this by internet research. Robert could see by the lichen on the boulder that partially covered the inscriptions that they were of great age. The woman also mentioned that she had found a report of a Viking ballast stone of rare basalt found on the beach in her village. The squared boulder of basalt rock, unusual for Newfoundland, just might prove to be a ballast stone. Ballast stones weigh down a ship to keep it upright, in this case perhaps a Viking ship coming from Iceland or Greenland. The ship arrives empty, discards the ballast stones, and takes on a load of timber needed at home in Greenland. Now where is basalt found? Disko Bay in Greenland for one, as well as Breidafordjur Bay in Iceland, within sight of Erik the Red's farm. Alas, this beach in Newfoundland is the same location where Farley

Mowat claimed the Vikings landed in 995 AD at Tickle Cove. Mowat's book *Westviking*, which made this controversial claim in the 1960s, was largely discarded like a heavy ballast stone in the New World.[25] All coincidence, perhaps, but I find myself marvelling at the ease with which this story unfolds from evidence on the ground. The Newfoundland ballast stone is now under investigation comparing it with Icelandic basalt.

How to sum all this up? (First, our history is a mess, a glorious mess. It isn't just about Cabot, Cartier, Columbus, and Erikson. It is much more and much earlier. Alice Beck Kehoe is right: "Authorities can be dogmatic." She suggests that all too often we, the curious reading public, hear the news of anomalies as the bane of science, not the fun of science. And hence, "we get selective memory such that only belief-sustaining information is recalled" and "expectation of certain results with failure to recognize contrary data." Worse, we tend to ask for the same. We tend to jump on the idea of the hoax quicker than the possibility. She continues, "The Columbian myth is so entangled with notions of European superiority and American [Canadian] uniqueness the challenges are distressing."[26] Second, our history is fun. The excitement in rethinking the Peterborough petroglyphs rock art using the possibilities posed by Robert Burcher is compelling. The walk to a winter solstice site in Quebec's Eastern Township is an adventure in possibility. Even my premature walk to Newfoundland's St. Brendan's Rock, while frustrating, was still a fun time laden with enthusiasm which later bore fruit. My visits to the Jones mill site in the Lake Memphremagog area and the carbon dated evidence found there is hard for even the confirmed skeptic to refute. The evidence of something pre-Columbian or just post Columbian is there.

The stories that are woven from the evidence are evolving and continue to take shape while they are ignored or avoided (or so it seems to me). I will continue to follow the evidence and evolving new history. As for the Beardmore Sword found in May 1931, close to the Blackwater River south of Lake Nipigon, I encourage you to travel to the Royal Ontario Museum in Toronto and ask museum staff to see the iron sword from the Viking era. It is on display but not marked as found in Ontario. Ask why a possible explanation for this historical anomaly is not provided. You may discover this attracts some attention![27]

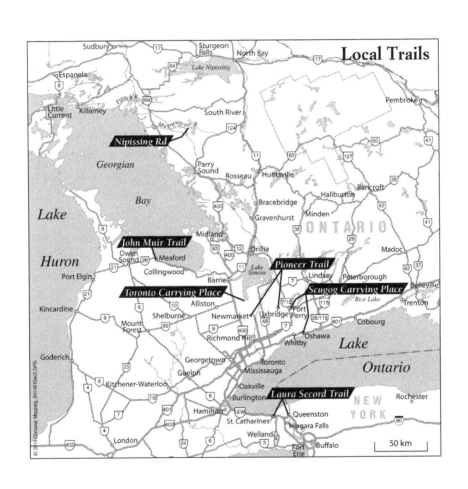

7

The Delights of Local Trails

"Mankind, in its eternal quest for food, treasure, and living space, has left a crisscross of trails over the continents. Many of these trails are centuries old, and some go back thousands of years, further than my written historical record."[1]

— Sigurd Olson

Local trails: I'm for 'em! I've always had an aversion to the idea that history is "somewhere else." Worse is the idea that the outdoors/nature/ the bush, whatever you like to call it, is out there — somewhere else. Local trails are often linked to history and are a good way to showcase that the outdoors can be right here. I'm referring to the so-called weekend warrior who travels three hours each weekend for outdoor recreation, or the Arctic canoe tripper, or the teacher/outdoor educator — all of whom might pass over the local for the exotic destination. Home terrain should not be overlooked or devalued. I suppose my mantra here is to explore it all, away and at home. And know that trails criss-cross the continents everywhere.

That said, when backyard trails tell something of the story of home then you have a real winner. I have a few examples of personal favourites here, where the stories compelled a local or a regional outing for me depending on where I was living or holidaying at the time. All these tales are local for someone. What are your local trails with a good tale to tell?

Old Man's Lake. The name has a pleasing ring to it. I bet there is a good story here. Well, it turns out there is.

I had long been intrigued by the colonization roads in Ontario. The Opeongo, Parry Sound (Great North Road), and Nipissing roads were all opened up in the late 1800s supporting early logging activity and initiating settlement and farming. Each road has its own intriguing collection of stories, but they share one central point of colonization history: the huge lie of farming potential.

Theologian Thomas Berry in his book *The Great Work* said, "our world of human meaning is no longer co-ordinated with the meaning of surroundings."[2] The great work is to reconcile this separation. Exploring the early colonization roads between Rosseau and Commanda (just south of Lake Nipissing) is an excellent way for Ontario folks to reconnect with their surroundings. In the process, I daresay one adds richer meaning to the land and to one's associations with its people. Talking with old-timers, reading local histories, and getting out on the land can serve as an initiation toward a membership with people who wisely know their roots and, above all else, are connected with their surroundings.

I had the chance to leave my summer cottage for a fall weekend bike ride exploring places and people on the Nipissing Road.

Nipissing Road opened for year-round traffic in 1874. Exploration, white-man style, had occurred in 1837 when a canoe route from the mouth of the Magnetawan to the Tim to the Petawawa rivers, over the Algonquin watershed dome to the Ottawa River, proved that a canal route wasn't feasible. The hope had been to secure travel ways north beyond the American border. Loggers also preceded the colonizing road in the 1850s. White pine, seven feet at their base, were noted. The first recorded river log drive was in the spring of 1857, on the lower Seguin River. The 110-kilometre Nipissing Road was for settlement; settlement meant farming, and farming meant prayer, hard work, and more prayer in these parts. Many turned to logging.

From Harry and Elenor Bell of Magnetawan, I learned about Old Man Bell of Old Man Lake. Isaac and Jane Bell travelled from Rosseau to the Magnetawan area in 1876. They were originally from Scotland but had settled in Ireland. They were married in 1845 and left for Canada on their wedding day. That's putting a marriage to the test! Not to mention that Jane was thought to be twenty years Isaac's junior. The Bells settled north of Toronto, where they farmed the land.

By the time that Isaac was sixty-five, he and Jane had six sons and three unmarried daughters. They needed space for their growing family. Hey, Toronto was growing north even then. So, as family lore has it, Isaac Senior carried a bag of flour and a bag of sugar up the road with one cow. Every time he tried to load the bags onto the cow, the cow would lie down. He couldn't get much to grow, though the success of rhubarb at least staved off scurvy. A small comfort! Spence and Croft townships were opening up, and Isaac, among the first settlers, had room to spread out his family. In 2006, this same extended family shared stories that captured my imagination on a bike-riding foray into the trail's lore.

There was much to learn. Why the unusual roof style? Answer: so you could get more hay in the barn. Eventually folks knew that construction style, so it became common for houses, too. Harry remembers his father using coal oil as a remedy for the common problem of head lice when loggers returned from the winter harvest. What killed the six Morden children, aged between ten and one, in 1902, as evident in the Methodist cemetery? Answer: diphtheria. I did not ask for more details about this one. Muriel Peck (nee Bell) remembers school days at the Spence School. She tells tales of walking to Midlothian to play field sports on one winter's day, and being overwhelmed by the volume of snow while walking to school in snowshoes.

The evening of stories and my own reading of local history proved uplifting. Even though Ron Brown, the great ghost town snooper, named the road "the Road of Broken Dreams,"[3] people certainly seem to remember the good times first. Perhaps the broken dreams are reserved for a second evening of storytelling. Either way, the Nipissing Road and side bike trip into Rock Hill are fine local trails for exploring.

Hard times were certainly connected to the once-hamlet of Rock Hill, six kilometres off the Nipissing Road to the east. Rock Hill was described as a deserted village in 1932. Why is Rock Hill so far off the road? Why the sparse evidence of the community now? What of the lives now marked by ten to twenty grave stones on the hilltop cemetery,

Chris Blythe examining grave stones at Rock Hill Cemetery.

surrounded by forest? I was certain Rock Hill has a story connected to broken dreams. On the following weekend, with curiosity, my friends Chris Blythe, Peter Carruthers, and I bicycled into Rock Hill, a mere dot on topographic maps. Evidence of buildings, fields, and wells, but mostly the lovely cemetery filled us with questions and rewarded our efforts. Still, much of Rock Hill remained a mystery. One could surmise it was not named Rock Hill with the promise of good farming to come. Certainly this must be a name formed from broken dreams and worn-out backs.

One grave caught my eye. The Brown family grave at Rock Hill connects to Elenor and Muriel (my main Nipissing Road contacts) via their mother, a Brown. Families may have struggled at Rock Hill and elsewhere, but many stayed in the area.

In the early 1900s, Rock Hill was a village serving logging camps close by. At first the logic of Rock Hill being so far off the Nipissing Road was a curiosity, but given the early twentieth century logic of logging, it all comes together. Rock Hill was very close to the streams that feed the headwater of the north Seguin River. The logs were hauled out of the bush to the first available downriver, high-water spring flow. The north Seguin would get the timber to the mills in Parry Sound. In the late 1800s the virgin white pines in Spence Township were among the highest priced stand in the world. Rock Hill now makes sense. When the trees were gone, the people moved on. But not without the odd story to tell. The following is a story recorded by Donalda Reid Brown (Muriel's aunt, who taught Muriel at the Spence School from 1933 to 1938):

> I remember Mel telling me about the Sunday afternoon when some of the lads at Reid's camp walked to Rock Hill to see the haunted house. They'd heard the story about Hooper shooting Cooper in an argument over ownership of a horse, then shoving his body into a well. When the lads went there the deserted, dilapidated house still stood though it leaned eastward.
>
> They entered through a creaking door, Jimmie in the lead. He bounded up the old stairs way ahead of the others who followed more cautiously. Just as they discovered the lethal bullet hole half-way up the stairway, a heavy thump sounded from the kitchen, followed by another, and another. This was too much for them fellows! They scrambled down the stairs and ran for Reid's camp like scared rabbits. When Jimmie returned later, he told them that he had dropped rocks through the stove-pipe hole just to scare them. First they didn't believe him but then they had a good laugh.[4]

No buildings were standing in 2006 when I explored the open terrain of Rock Hill, but this story still helps bring the place alive.

There remain special locations all along the old Nipissing Road, Rock Hill most curious among them. Town sites sprang up (ten hamlets in total) roughly corresponding to a day's journey for a team of horses. Presumably it was enough per day for the people as well. Rye, named for Rye, England, was once a thriving community with a general store, a church, a post office, and up to four hotels. That was in the 1880s before the railway to the east forever changed the transportation patterns in 1886. All that remains of

Rye is a cemetery and some building foundations. A similar fate befell Bummer's Roost, Seguin Falls, and Ashdown. Only Magnetawan, fifty kilometres up the road from Rosseau, remains thriving today.

With pleasant towns such as Rosseau and Magnetawan as destinations, and with many cemeteries and buildings such as the Spence School along the way, there is much to see en route, complemented by thirty-two historical plaques.

Some of the trail has succumbed to the bush, waiting to be discovered; other sections remain accessible only by mountain bike or on foot. A bike is the best way to get a feel for the trail with its varied surface options today. Upon some of the more remote trail settings, you can still see and feel early corduroy road work (the laying down of logs to aid the passage over wet ground). It is best to be self-propelled and moving slowly to properly experience this. This is not a driving trip, but it is a rewarding trip into a past worth remembering. Old Man Isaac Bell makes for a powerful presence as one contemplates the shift from canoe routes to land trails through near-northern Ontario. From this we moved to railways and straighter roads still.

There are people who can follow their roots back to families who were the first settlers in this region. This is exciting. Colonization roads open the heart and mind to this past. Seek out the old-timers along these routes today and be prepared for a story or two to broaden your perspective. In the end, discovering just who *was* the Old Man of Old Man's Lake proved an exercise of ongoing learning of the best kind, the kind that connects people back to the land and their surroundings. It is great work indeed.

More great work on local trails was done by me in 2013. Following my friend Robert Burcher around is always a good idea. I joined him for one of his local walks, one connected to John Muir.

The Trout Hollow Trail starts by a quiet, well-shaded park close to downtown Meaford, Ontario. It follows the Big Head River upstream about three kilometres. Then you cross the river by fording the stream and return along the opposite bank. Great views of the river along the banks help make this a lovely trail. But wait! John Muir, the John Muir of American conservation history, once lived along the river. Now here's a curious story itching to be told.

John Muir was born in Scotland in 1838. He and his family moved to Wisconsin in 1849. By 1864, Muir was on his wandering way to Trout Hollow to join the Trout family as a hired hand, along with his younger brother, at the family mill site. Likely he arrived by the Hamilton/Guelph/Durham road to Owen Sound. First he visited Niagara Falls. It is known that he discovered the much prized calypso orchid in bloom at Holland Marsh near Bradford, Simcoe County. This is important because apart from the glorious botanical find, the date places Muir in late May 1864 in Simcoe County en route to Meaford. The botanist and inventor was, like the Trout family, a member of the Disciples of Christ congregation; Muir had probably arranged the mill job with like-minded folks. As a pacifist, he escaped the turmoil of the American Civil War. Muir settled into a mill worker's life until the mill burned down on February 21, 1866. In this time Muir improved the mill machinery's production with a semi-automatic design to create rakes and broom handles. In his free time, he explored local terrain.

The Trout Hollow mill has long been well known as a square rock and brick foundation up on the riverbank. The "fair log house with cobbled gables and an elm bark roof" that was the workers' home near the mill site had not been identified. In June 1998, in advance of the gathering of the Canadian Friends of John Muir, local historical sleuth Robert Burcher (see Chapter 6) poked around the mill site looking for the cabin. It is thought that the mill burned because of sparks from the workers' cabin chimney. This offered some directional and distance clues. But it was a gopher hole that won the day. Archaeologists love gopher holes. These critters, after all, dig up layers of ground strata. In short, they can bring up stuff for easy exposure. As Robert remembers it, the gopher hole exposed some ceramic pottery shards. Nearby were flakes of mortar from the cabin chimney. This site looked promising. The landowner at the time committed to pay for a proper archaeological dig. Voila, cabin found.

With Robert Burcher and Marty Bruce, I walked the Trout Hollow Trail, forded the Big Head River after examining the remains of the mill dam, and visited the west riverbank's flat site, which still shows mortar pieces and that thoughtful gopher's archaeological dig.

The view up Big Head River toward John Muir's cabin on the Trout Hollow Trail.

A pottery shard found at the John Muir cabin site.

There is no historical plaque. There is no roped-off area. The mill's foundations and the workers' cabin are integrated well back into the Big Head River's forest banks. A lovely trail, lovely river, lovely story of the early days of John Muir, and tangible physical remains of Muir here in Meaford, Ontario. Muir would go on to become the first president of the Sierra Club, a leading voice for the establishment of western frontier wilderness preservation in America, and an influential author supporting spirituality for nature contact and enlightened well-being. For the more than two hundred people who, on June 13, 1998, walked the trail to the Trout family's mill site, it was a pilgrimage to pay homage to the influential man and his humble but inspired time on the Big Head River. To me, in May 2013, it was the same, and a pleasant walk on a now well-travelled local trail.[5]

Closer to home. Two years into my new home terrain on the Oak Ridges Moraine, I'd settled in and had a strong urge to learn about my local trails. Amidst the Moraine's rolling hills, rivers, wetlands, and mixed forests are a number of small settlements dating back to the first settlers walking into the region on trails.

In 1806, twelve Quaker families from Pennsylvania travelled in horse-drawn wagons over the new cart track from the new market of Newmarket to the Uxbridge valley. They followed a trail that is now Vivian Road. Local historian Allan McGillivray told me about a section of this route which is no longer a roadway just north of Regional Road 8, north of Siloam and Roseville. It was exciting to knock on an area farmer's door to seek permission to walk their farm lane into their woodlot, where a slightly raised earth bed is likely evidence of an early corridor road through a wetland area. I was on the early settlers' road heading east from Yonge Street in 1806. It is worth noting that this easterly trail from Yonge Street connects with the east branch of the Holland River, which heads north to Lake Simcoe and south via the Humber River trail travelling into Lake Ontario at Toronto. So this west-east settler trail meets not only Yonge Street but also the Toronto Carrying Place, travelled by Native peoples for centuries and later by explorers de La Salle, Thompson, and Franklin and troops heading west in the War of 1812. So often in Canada the portage trail gives way to the road. Discovering local trails often starts with waterways and portages. There are few as famous in Ontario as the forty-six-kilometre Toronto Carrying Place, crossing what de La Salle called in 1680 "the peaks of very high mountains"[6] of the Oak Ridges Moraine.

It was Governor Simcoe who commissioned the building of Yonge Street after struggling up the Toronto Carrying Place in September–October 1793. He didn't have an easy go. Elizabeth Simcoe mentions a "terrible bog of liquid mud." That bog is now the Holland Marsh, long since drained and prime agricultural lands today.

At an upper branch of the West Holland a Native named Old Sail advised the Simcoe canoe party to return from Lac de Taranto (Lake Simcoe) via the eastern branch of the Holland River. Historian Heather Robertson hints that Old Sail might have been helping by advising an easier route that avoided the Holland Marsh, or hoping to keep the expanding European presence away from a First Nations burial ground.[7]

I cross the east branch of the Holland River regularly by car at Green Line, the top of the 404 highway. Here; Old Sail's possible subterfuge, de La Salle's "very high mountains," and even Dr. Chris Beswick and his Quaker friends (soon to follow Yonge Street to the new market at the opening of the Uxbridge valley) can all come forward to a wandering mind. There is a fine local walking trail along the Holland River just north of Newmarket.

Evidence of the 1806 Uxbridge Trail.

But the Toronto Carrying Place wasn't the only route north from Lake Ontario. Further east is another waterway-turned-trail-turned-road that is largely lost to modern drivers while waiting for a traffic light at Simcoe Street and Rossland in Oshawa. Again the Oak Ridges Moraine would need to be ascended.

The Scugog Carrying Place followed Oshawa or Farewell creeks and the roughly northern streets of Simcoe and then later Ritson Road, dropping down to present-day Port Perry. Another route arrived at a location further east on Lake Scugog south of Washburn Island. Confusing! Historian Grant Karcich calls the Scugog Trail "a dynamic structure that evolved over time."[8] Karcich also suggests the trail has been in use for seven hundred years between Lake Ontario and Lake Scugog, continuing west on the Nonquon River to a portage joining with the Beaver River (near the hamlet of Wick) and north to Lake Simcoe. From here, the Kawartha Lakes and the headwater that is now Algonquin Park was a destination, as harvesting the land preceded the contact and exploration period that saw so much travel to Lake Huron and further west.[9]

The present-day towns of Oshawa, Port Perry (where a Mississauga campground existed alongside the first settlers of the 1820s), Cannington (where there was a portage around a rapid), and Beaverton (at the Lake Simcoe terminus to the trail) all owe much of their existence to the Native carrying place.

My friend David Taylor and I, with two cars, one canoe, two bikes, and hiking boots, set out to see those parts of the trail that can still be explored in a self-propelled manner. The Beaver River Wetland Trail certainly can get one in touch with the landscape. This local route runs sixteen kilometres following the river, which in a time of higher water levels a hundred years ago and today in seasonal high waters can be paddled into Lake Simcoe. We also explored how the Nonquon River to the Wick (Beaver River) portage might have looked as we viewed possible put-ins and takeouts for canoes. It is fun to think that one rough translation for *Oshawa* from the Ojibwa language is "leave the canoe to travel on foot."[10]

It is also fun to imagine the passage of settler Philip Sproule, who quotes his grandfather John Sproule in the 1820s, saying: "I could look from my window and see an Indian in the lead, carrying a rifle. Behind him came the Indian women carrying the canoes on their heads while other Indian men brought up the rear."[11]

Closer still to my home on the Oak Ridges Moraine, south of the town of Uxbridge on Concession #7, is the Glen Major Fishing Club in the former hamlet of Glen Major. Evidence of past glory days is the Glen Major church.[12]

Back off the road are now excellent walking and ski trails. Thanks to a heads-up from Allan McGillivray, David Taylor and I walked a familiar trail with the new insight that the route was once likely part of a street plan for Glen Major. As advised, watching for mounds from the trail, we found the well-preserved rock foundation of a Glen Major house. We learned that the house burned, likely in the early 1900s. As the story goes, William Beverly and friends were playing cards when a fire broke out. William died in 1910. The moss-covered stone walls evident today were a part of the hamlet's mills and farms; the fishing club and the church are not all that remain.[13]

Over two hundred years ago, Laura Secord made her famous walk to warn the British troops at DeCew House in Thorold, Ontario, about the imminent threat of attack by the Americans who had stationed themselves at her home along the Niagara River at Queenston Heights. She had overhead the American battle plan and was compelled to act at great threat to her own life.

Today one can follow her route within roughly one hundred metres of the original trail. Special footbridges have recently been built over major roadways, and the black swamp is now Glendale Campus of Niagara College. Yes, there are changes. Laura is reported to have departed in the early morning using her need to milk the cows as her excuse to leave the house. She also used the cows as a shield to set off for her sixteen-hour walk.

The thirty-three-kilometre walk, now called the Laura Secord Legacy Trail, is roughly an eight-hour trip. The trail is part of both the Trans Canada Trail and the Bruce Trail. Laura's walk was on June 21, 1813. On June 22, 2013, over a thousand people opened the new trail. Changes, yes, but the Secord homestead where Laura raised seven children is still standing, and the British headquarters at DeCew House is an interesting stone ruin. Best of all, parts of her Niagara Escarpment trail are trails still.

A Friends of Laura Secord group oversees the trail and the memory of the Secord family. The current president of the group is Caroline McCormick, Laura's great-great-great-granddaughter. It must have taken great courage to make that 1813 walk in a war-torn landscape. Laura had earlier rescued her husband from the battlefield of Queenston Heights with musket ball wounds. She would climb the escarpment just nine months later with notions of saving her homestead and family of five children from an American takeover. Thanks to her warning, the British lieutenant organized strategies which led to the surrender of over four hundred American troops largely at the threat of attack by mostly Mohawk and Kahnawake troops. It was a decisive moment in the War of 1812.

In 1860, Laura heard of plans for a document that was to be signed by surviving Niagara soldiers. Now she stepped out into prominence. Laura Secord insisted on her name being placed on that important list of war veterans. Not an easy task for a woman who had not claimed any notoriety in the years following her walk. When the Prince of Wales heard of her story he arranged for her to receive £100 in gold ($5,000 Canadian today). Today we can enjoy not only Laura Secord chocolates but also a fine local trail that will certainly help preserve her story.[14]

Other local trails in places I have lived have also been explored. In my first home, Ottawa, I think first of voyageur and fur trade history heading up and down the Ottawa River, followed by barges of lumber in the log drive eras. However, every year I take great delight in cross-country skiing the local trail that is the Gatineau's Ridge Road. Beyond serving as the main artery into the Gatineau Park's extensive trail system, the Ridge Road was indeed once, wait for it, a road leading Irish immigrants to farms atop the Gatineau escarpment. Now, this isn't farm country. John Welsh, who in 1899 had purchased the property just below the escarpment — near Booth Hill, for the regular Gatineau Park cross-country skiers — from Thomas Wright is believed to have benefited from abandoned farms atop the escarpment along the Ridge Road. He was there to cut lumber for his property. It is a dramatic turn of mind for the recreational skier to consider the toil of clearing the land, which was later abandoned in despair, along this main ski artery.

The Ottawa Ski Club was formed in 1910. Now *this* is ski country! A train had existed since 1892 and continued well into the 1950s, taking skiers north to Chelsea, Quebec. These folks would then ski into the trails with the Ridge Road as a centrepiece. By the by, another faction of the club were ski jumpers who before 1910 had erected a 115-foot ski jump in Rockcliffe Park, Ottawa. The club built day ski lodges, and the Welsh farm, which grew potatoes, onions, and cabbages, eventually became The Old Mountain Lodge at Kingsmere, which, along with the Wattsford's Kingsmere Lodge, lasted through the 1950s until their eventual demise to Camp Fortune and the downhill ski craze. A rope tow was first built in 1940. It is easy to remember in Ottawa that downhill heel secure skiing started from cross-country free heel skiing.

Today there is a petition to return to the old heritage names for the trails. The Ridge Road, for example, is number one, as it should be if numbers are necessary. In 1977, the National Capital Commission adopted a number system for the trails to the outrage of most of the regular skiers. In 2010, as part of the Centennial events of 1910–2010 for the Ottawa Ski club, the initiative to re-establish Pipe Dream, Chicken Run, Burma Road (Trail #3), and of course the Ridge Road was launched. The plan to revive the heritage trail names is still in question. As Gatineau historian Charles Hodgson simply and correctly states, "What is the heritage of a trail without the name[?]"[15] I agree and am grateful for the heritage plaque that exists along the Ridge Road ski trail today, reminding folks about those nineteenth-century Irish farmers who ... well ... cut a fine ski trail in the bush north of Ottawa. And who, in so doing, helped inspire a fine bit of country road poetry:

> Slender and white from the tree tops
> Points Chelsea's gleaming spire;
> See, round the road's next bending
> A Maple tree or fire![16]

Then again, I could have selected lyrics from "Chelsey Morning" by Joni Mitchell, who woke in the mid-1960s to a lovely Chelsea morning and wrote sound advice for all those boarding that ski train in Ottawa for the Gatineau trails most accessible from the Ridge Road.

In Lakefield, Ontario, just north of Peterborough, where I lived for two years, is the infamous Northcote property. Infamous, that is, if one knows one's early twentieth century Canadian exploration history. At Northcote, the Douglas family entertained and corresponded with many a northern explorer of the time. Central among them were John Hornby and P.G. Downes. To visit this property, now in the control of Lakefield College School thanks to a recent bequeath from the Gastle family, was a stirring moment. The house with its grand porch by the lake and massive shady willows easily paints a scene from another era. Here George Douglas and his brother Lionel planned their Arctic exploration to the mouth of the Coppermine River via Great Bear Lake and the Dease River. It was a very successful prospecting trip. Nothing stands out other than good planning and efficient travel. Hence, we tend to know little about fine Arctic travels. At Northcote, George researched the travels of Samuel de Champlain with the Huron on the Trent-Severn waterway. He determined that Champlain portaged along the Northcote farm, finishing the portage from near Young's Point in the back bay behind the house. Bill Gastle has promised me a trail walk along the old portage (when water levels here are significantly lower). I skied up the farm property often and enjoyed its rolling terrain and long-used recreation trails. Kathy Hooke, George Douglas's niece, shared with me family photo albums. I was struck by my own experiences on the same trails. A 1913 photo of Stella Greer at age fifteen taken by George at Northcote skiing with long wooden boards and a single long pole now hangs in my house — a reminder of local trails with rich memories through generations.

Here also, decades earlier, Susanna Moodie was known to travel for visits. A particularly good berry patch still evident on the property was in part a drawing card. It is easy to imagine Highway 28 heading north of Peterborough as a horse-and-buggy cart track to Northcote and beyond into the then wilds of the Ontario bush.[17]

Finally, very close to home — out my back window — is "Little Switzerland." That is what the Toronto Ski Club in 1938 called the hilly region north of the Dagmar train station. For $1.80 return fare, keen "ski runners" would arrive in one hour from Union Station, Toronto. Teams of horses and sleighs would transport the skiers the short distance to the hills. Many locals provided weekend bed and breakfast lodging. There are still ski areas and a wealth of bush trails here. Skyloft Hill was then called Big Ben. Lakeridge Ski Resort, a short distance to the east, was then called the Devil's Punch Bowl. Skiers could easily move between the hills on their cable bindings. Originally the lift was a horse-drawn sleigh ride. Eventually, a rope tow was installed. Now there are chair lifts, of course. But it is not hard to think of skiers on these local trails and slopes. The recently logged terrain meant that there were more open slopes then than now. It is easy for me to be jealous of the winter fun of a ski day in those pre-war years. Cable bindings and raised heels meant skiing was a healthy mix of terrain — up/down and along/across skiing and then over to a neighbourhood farm house. I have an old Dagmar ski map from the 1940s: no house yet, but my property is on the ski trail map.[18]

Everybody has a local trail. That trail has tales. Those tales are housed in local history books and on the trails themselves with people like Elenor Bell, Robert Burcher, Allan McGillivray, William Gastle, and more. With time on these trails you too can become one of the folks keeping the stories alive and helping "the great work" continue. For the most part I have addressed here local trails that I have some affiliation with. I love the Grey Owl phrase to be "Keepers of the Trail."[19] I hope to not only be such a person but also inspire others to do the same. This, in part, comes with one eye on the historical context and the other on the future care of the place. If Thomas Berry is right, and "our world of human meaning is no longer co-coordinated with the meaning of our surroundings," then the delights of local trails are a good start on the great work of reconciliation with nature and history.

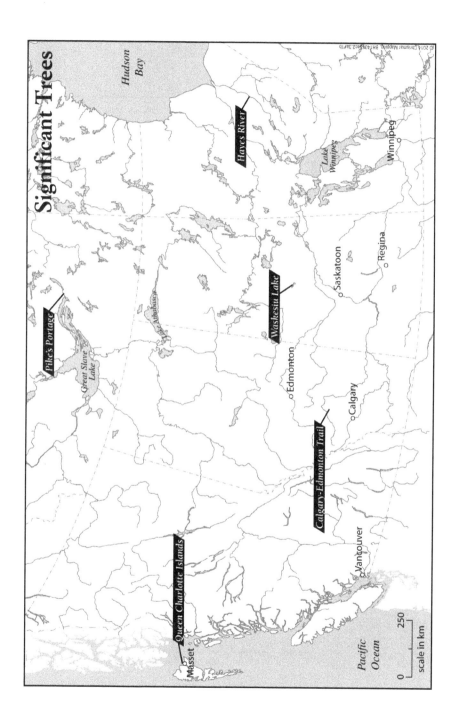

Significant Trees

Hudson Bay

Hayes River

Lake Winnipeg

Winnipeg

Saskatoon

Regina

Pike's Portage

Great Slave Lake

Lake Athabasca

Waskesiu Lake

Edmonton

Calgary

Calgary-Edmonton Trail

Queen Charlotte Islands

Masset

Vancouver

Pacific Ocean

0   250
scale in km

© 2014 Chrismar Mapping BH140SSec2.5a#16

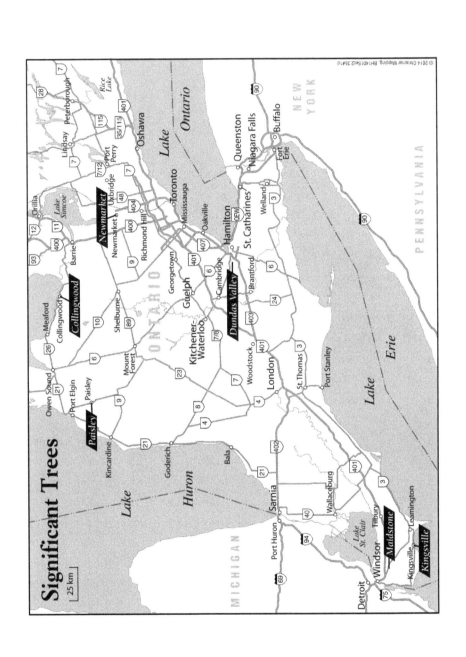

Significant Trees

25 km

8

Significant Trees:
Touchstones to Other Times of Living and Travel

"Trees are your best antiques."
— Alexander Smith

I've never met a Native marker tree I haven't liked! What are you talking about here, you ask? Trees! Significant trees! Specifically, marker trees that have been manipulated and reshaped by humans hundreds of years ago such that they take on a distinctive deformed shape today. We will also discuss significant heritage trees recorded in historical literature or local histories that tell a fine story of practices of a time before road signs. Trail marker trees, lobsticks, meeting trees, church trees: I will just scratch the surface here. And what should happen is that you will never repeat Ronald Reagan's famed response; as Governor of California, facing environmental groups and logging issues, he blasted out, "When you've seen one redwood, you've seem 'em all."

Dotting the landscapes of forested Canada are special trees, brought into service as early trail signs. In Canada, mostly in the deciduous forests of the lower Great Lakes, the Native marker tree, also called Indian marker tree, is gaining attention, and further north the lobstick conifer (pine and spruce) is still a famed presence talked about as a ghost from the days of footpaths, cart trails, and canoe portage routes. All these trees are the road signs of their time. Travellers have always needed signposts.

People also need to revere the land as visitors and dwellers. Significant trees distinguished by age and location can help remind us of our humble place and short time on this earth.

The rebound of attention for Native marker trees stems from three main sources, as I understand it. In the early 1900s there were scholarly treatments of folks reporting on and recording these trees that often coexisted as trail markers with early road construction and road markers. Certainly many marker trees were lost back then to road construction and simple aging. Folks didn't know what they were. Today in America, Dennis Downes and Don and Diane Wells, in two new books, have brought the trees back into our consciousness. In Ontario, Hamilton botanist Paul O'Hara has begun the process of sending out a call for marker tree sightings to fellow botanists throughout the southern part of Ontario.[1] Simply put, he started looking and followed up on all the leads that have been pouring in. Paul has recorded over thirty marker trees in Ontario to date. Brilliant! Let's get into some details.

Oaks, maples, Shagbark hickory, and beech trees have all been recorded as Ontario marker trees. How are these trees deformed to the point that they are recognizable as marker trees? First you bend a hardwood sapling of about eight to ten feet. Rope or rawhide attaching the tree to the ground will be enough. A year later, new shoots reaching straight up towards the sky appear. All but one or two of these are cut, and a new trunk growing parallel to the ground is started. Once it has started maturing, the horizontal trunk is cut, and voila, a bent right angle tree pointing in whatever direction you selected. The curious shape has the look of a bent elbow with a characteristic flat knob at the elbowend. After two hundred years you have the deformed, distinctive tree you can see today. But in no time you have an identifiable marker tree. In fact, as noted, if you leave two vertical leading shoots well spread apart, you might get two trunks growing vertically. The deformity creates an issue of size. These old growth trees needn't be the largest trees in a mixed forest today. The deformity can stunt the trees' growth.

Why marker trees? Remember, they are the first road signs. Why road signs? Well, first, a directional marker in a landscape without significant linear features to follow, such as a creek or ridgeline, is gold to a traveller. But as an exit sign, a marker tree might indicate a choice gathering site (this could be medicinal plants, a berry patch, or flint), a cool water spring coming out of the ground, a good place to ford a stream, or a portage sign. Paul O'Hara, much like me, saw a reference to Native marker trees and that was it. I saw one of Paul's references. He has found on his own and has been referred to marker tree locations in Burlington (two marker trees a hundred metres apart), in Oakville (four in a wooden area south of Queen Elizabeth Highway likely to mark a stream crossing),[2] on Fairchild Creek in Hamilton Region, in Wainfleet Township in Niagara, in Norfolk and Elgin counties, and many more: Owen Sound, Kincardine, Kingsville, and Gananoque areas. Paul visits each location, meets the people who have local history insight, and collects fine stories connected to each tree. In a minor copycat way, I have done the same.

What would you do if you received an email like the following?

I am doing American Chestnut surveys for the MNR in the Golden Horseshoe and I am currently in the Dundas Valley. There are several trees in the woods adjacent to Gravel Pit Road which is right off Mineral Springs. In pre-settlement times the Dundas Valley was loaded with Chestnuts, which were a staple of First Nations.

While I was there I noticed this tree. It is right on the edge of the 'gravel pit', so the grade is completely disturbed to the right of this photo. The nose is quite distinct and I am thinking this could be a marker that has been partially buried by the activities of the gravel pit. Below this area where the tree is pointing looks like the remains of a cart path. I think it would be curious to dig at the sides and see if there is the arch of a true marker tree.

Cheers, Paul

I was there in a flash.

With fellow curious local history friends Daniel Coleman and John Terpstra, Paul guided me to a remote (for Dundas Valley at the head of

Lake Ontario) location that seemed to make no sense today but, if Paul was right, surely made sense in its day of prominence. We found a vertical trunk and nose exposed in an earth bank. "Modestly promising," I remember thinking. It was like digging for buried treasure. We worked hard and fast between four friends and three shovels. Soon we had a significant tree elbow exposed. Yup. This not particularly impressive red oak might be a marker tree for something, perhaps a gathering site. In the end, Paul decided the tree was probably pushed over by the activities of the gravel pit and discounted it as a marker tree. Even though this find was not a clear-cut example, I had the bug. I would need to visit more marker trees, and thanks to Paul, I had options close enough to home.

On a glorious September day in 2013, I headed to Essex County, a land of tomatoes, cucumbers, and the odd Native marker tree. Paul had identified two trees in the area. A lovely woodlot off of Highway 401 bordered by the Puce River in the Maidstone Conservation Area has a distinctive Shagbark hickory tree. You can't miss it along the family-friendly 1.5-kilometre trail. I met a family out for a morning walk. Grandparents with their grandchildren. Wonderful. I told them about the marker tree, which they knew as the tree their kids climbed for pictures. I sensed they have had kids climb that tree for over thirty years. It is pleasing to think that the tree has remained significant for centuries. I wondered if that hickory's meaning for them intensified with this new knowledge.

The second tree I visited that day was along the Wigle River flowing into Lake Erie. Paul has described this one, a giant white oak, as "the Mother of all Markers." Easy to see why. It is massive and extremely bent. A local from the Kingsville Golf and Country Club called it the "bent oak" and added, "Eh, everyone around here knows about that tree." Sure enough, Kyle Booker, one of the golf pros, and a long-time course member, Paul Lemieux, and I had a great chat about the tree and its role in the life of the magnificent golf course, which first started on this site ninety years ago. The tree predates golf in the area by at least another hundred years.

Trails drawn on a 1791 map by Crown surveyor Patrick McNiff are almost certainly connected to these trees. It appears that early Native trails-turned-settler trails crossed the Wigle and Puce rivers. One can surmise that the trees served to mark choice river crossing sites. Rivers

At the Kingsville marker tree site.

generally had more volume in those days. The Kingsville oak is on a trail following the Lake Erie shoreline, continuing around the Detroit River and then along Lake St. Clair, joining up with a Thames River trail. The Thames is connected to the Grand River and then to Lake Ontario. The Shagbark hickory at Maidstone is likely on a trail loosely following Route 3 between present-day Leamington and Windsor. McNiff's survey shows a sandy ridge with swamp country on either side. The Puce River appears to flow across the trail just after the sandy ridge. It's a guess, but a good guess, and adds meaning to the distinctive trees.[3]

Only a month earlier, I was paddling by Red Dog Mountain on the Keele River in the Northwest Territories, a noted site for the local Dene to leave ritual offerings on their travels walking and rowing (in moose-hide boats) to and from the inland mountains to the Mackenzie River. I am familiar with northern travel, but rarely think of the walking trails of the north. Clearly, given the Dene peoples' seasonal patterns on the Keele River, there were established walking trails with their own marks. Perhaps stone cairns. Now here I am in the most southerly town in all of Canada again experiencing a significant site for Indigenous peoples. North or south, people travel and need road signs and landmarks.

To close this discussion, I have been reluctant to use the term "Indian" marker trees. "First Nations" is too general a term for the variety of tribes who were likely involved in this practice of deforming trees for trail markers. Second, it is likely that early settlers adopted this same practice in some cases. That said, the moniker Indian or Native marker trees will likely endure, and that isn't a bad thing. Paul said it best: "The weight of history is not with colonial history, it is with aboriginal history." I remember being asked to give a keynote talk to canoe paddlers on the history of canoe travel in Canada. Appreciating this weighting, I spoke of the pre-contact travel routes of Indigenous peoples before touching on the Mackenzies, Thompsons, and Franklins. I wish I knew about Native marker trees then.

More generally, there are records of significant trees that logically follow the re-shaped trail marker trees theme. One general category of significant trees is meeting trees. The majestic trading tree on Timothy Street in Newmarket, Ontario, is one. While not reshaped, it is certainly a marker tree on a busy Native trail system that unquestionably predates early settlers arriving in the 1790s. There was the trail running north–south paralleling Yonge Street, which replaced the Toronto Carrying Place along the Humber and Holland Rivers, but there were also trails heading north from the Rouge River and Oshawa Creek headwaters. Artifacts have been found along these routes. My guess is there were once marker trees too. Perhaps one may still be identified.

There were many trails heading north and south from Lake Ontario. The Oak Ridges Moraine must have been a prime hunting and fishing ground. Salmon running rivers abound from the Moraine headwaters of the Don, Duffin, and Rouge rivers. Caribou once happily mingled with moose on the well forested uplands. Only after it was logged out did the deer arrive from the south.

While the original elm trading tree was cut down in 1947 because of Dutch elm disease, the town council wisely replaced the elm with an Emerald Queen maple tree and added a middle traffic island dividing the road. Today the traffic island is gone. In 1980, the 1947 replacement tree was replaced yet again. A healthy maple graces the spot with a historical plaque. The road is no longer divided at the tree, and the current tree no longer towers above the neighbourhood houses and other trees such that it could be seen looking west while paddling or walking along the Holland River. But the memory remains. Today one can drive by and remember what gave Newmarket its name: it was a new market on a fur trader's foot-path well signposted with a trading tree. And a tree remains there today.

Tracee Chambers, who for twenty-six years has owned a house that is in the early 1930s photos of the trading tree, showed me early images of the tree and filled me in on more recent developments. A house that was around when the original elm stood tall burnt to the ground in December 2012. The loss of the road twinning happened in the late 1990s. Tracee remains proud of living beside the current maple tree that is meant to remind everyone that here resides the new market that has become Newmarket. That is how she put it to me.

I reckon Tracee's perspective is a rich one. She can sit back on her front porch imagining the original trading business of William Roe and Andre Borland. Starting after the War of 1812, they were known to drape trade goods such as cloth rolls and blankets on the branches of that majestic elm clearly visible from the Holland River valley. They merely had to display the trade goods and spread the word they were

Tracee Chambers outside her home beside the Newmarket trading tree site.

open for business. Trade goods came from York (Toronto) and furs came from the Algonquin and Haliburton highlands. It is a practice well played throughout much of Canada for hundreds and thousands of years. It is charming that a third-generation tree stands today just off a busy urban street in a quiet neighbourhood to help us engage with such a rich past.[4]

The trading tree was just north of an eighteenth-century Mississauga encampment along what became Yonge Street. The Mississaugas would trade moccasins, maple sugar, baskets, glass beadwork, and miniature birchbark canoes to local settlers. Seems that the tourist industry started up early in these parts. Pre-contact times would have seen items such as birchbark rolls, furs, shells, agricultural products, and minerals for tools all changing hands. Buffalo robes and copper have been found in northern Quebec, and birchbark canoes were made on James Bay trips by trading furs for birchbark rolls. It is interesting to imagine the trading tree on a busy day.

The trading tree, generally a meeting tree, might also be referred to as a tidings tree, a place to receive news. I think of this because Paisley, Ontario, did have a tidings tree. East of the Teeswater Bridge, near the junction of the Saugeen and Teeswater rivers, once stood a giant elm. This tree eventually succumbed to Dutch elm disease in 1968. At this time, the tree was believed to be over three hundred years old. That would mean that when the earliest settlers to the area tied their rafts to the shore along the river in the early 1850s they certainly used this dominant elm. As the town of Paisley grew around the tree, in the same way that the trading tree was once the centre of a growing Newmarket town site, the tree evoked a certain reverence from the town's folk. The tree became known as the tidings tree and served as a town meeting place. Here folks would post town activities such as a barn raising or items for sale. When a town newspaper was introduced in 1865, the practical importance of the tidings tree diminished, but not the symbolic quality. Paisley artist Cindy McKenna has created a tidings tree painting depicting hanging jars on the trees branches provided by Paisley residents. In this and other ways, the tidings tree lives on as a significant part of the heritage of Paisley's townsfolk.[5]

Miranda MacKeen, an outdoor educator with the Upper Thames Conservation Authority, told me of a meeting tree in her area. Seems you just need to mention your interests in this regard and the examples come to you — a fun way to do research, as Paul O'Hara and I have discovered. Miranda put me in touch with Bob and Nancy Ross. Bob and Nancy live on a two-hundred-acre property north of Kirkton, Ontario. Close to the middle of one of their managed woodlots is an area meeting tree. That is how the tree is known in these parts. It is a tower beech tree. You can't miss it. Bob remembers his grandfather (born in 1891) taking a young Bob out to the tree. In Bob's words: "I was told if I ever owned this property, I should never cut the tree down." I visited Bob and the tall beech meeting tree in November 2013. I learned lots about rural Ontario farm country that day. Between the grid concession roads the farms tend to run five farms east to west and five farms north to south. Bob's farm is in the middle, and the woodlot with that dominant beech tree with the odd-shaped, extensive, and gnarly crown is in the middle of Bob's farm. Bob's kin have been six generations on the farm, and the tree was already significant in Bob's grandfather's time. When the first Ross to the area arrived in the late 1840s, the beech tree, which would become a community meeting tree, was already well established.

Author John Valliant writes, "trees were the continent's first churches, government buildings and fortresses ..."[6] Treaty oaks are another meeting tree idea: less church, more government building. America seems to have a better record of such trees. Valliant tells an interesting story of the sole survivor of the once-prominent Council Oaks in Texas. In this noted sacred grove of local Comanche peoples, the first border agreement was declared and signed. The five-hundred-year-old Treaty Oak, however, was poisoned in 1989 in an occult ritual over unrequited love. The perpetrator, Paul Cullen, was sentenced to nine years in prison for the act. The tree received significant rehab, which has saved a third of the original grandeur of the Lone Star State's symbolic tree. Former presidential candidate Ross Perot wrote a blank cheque for the restoration work.[7] Perhaps research will turn up treaty trees (government meeting trees) in Canada.

The lone pine marker is another example of a once significant meeting place tree. W.H. Williams in 1881, travelling on the Calgary/Edmonton Trail in Alberta, which maintains that name to the present as Highway 2, recorded the following:

A little before noon we reached a clump of grey willows and found ourselves fairly in the timber. In this immediate vicinity there is a large spruce tree known to freighters and *voyageurs* as "lone pine." It is here that they begin to "pack" wood on their way south, usually taking enough to last them to Calgary, unless they are travelling very light, in which case they depend partially on the sparse growth of stunted willows to be found along the banks of Sarvisberry Creek for a supplementary supply.[8]

Williams was travelling north into better treed country. That night Williams noted they were "fifteen miles from the ford where we have to cross." I can't help but wonder if there wasn't a significant marker tree there as well, just not recorded.[9]

Also on the prairie terrain of Alberta, explorer and fur trader David Thompson tells a story of the "One Pine." In October 1786, Thompson, with six men on horseback, headed into Piegan country to winter over with them and "induce them to hunt for furs, and make dried Provisions." Thompson recalls the following story:

Our road lay through a fine country with slight undulations of ground, too low to be called hills, everywhere clothed with fine short grass and hummocks, or islands of wood, almost wholly of Aspin and small, but straight growth. About the tenth day we came to the "One Pine." this had been a fine stately tree of two fathoms girth, growing among a patch of Aspins, and being all alone, without any other Pines for more than an hundred miles, had been regarded with superstitious reverence. When the small pox came, a few tents of Pee a gans were camping near it, in the distress of this sickness, the master of one of the tents applied his prayers to it, to save the lives of himself and family, burned sweet grass and offered upon its roots, three horses to be at its service, all he had. The next day the furniture of his horses with his Bow and Quiver of Arrows, and the third morning, having nothing more, a Bowl of Water. The disease was now on himself, and he had to lie down. Of his large family, only himself, one of his wives, and a Boy survived.

As soon as he acquired streng[t]h, he took his horses, and all his other offerings from the "Pine Tree," then putting his little Axe in his belt, he ascended the Pine Tree to about two thirds of its height, and thee cut it off. Out of revenge for not having saved his family; when we passed, the branches were withered and the tree going to decay. For three and twenty days we marched over fine grounds looking for the Indians without seeing any other animals than a chance Bull Bison, from the killing of a few we procured our provisions.[10]

Again one wonders how many significant trees existed as markers for superstition, navigation, and comfort in the open plains, heavy forests, and lake country.

Back to my home terrain in Ontario. There is an interesting category of trees one might call commemorative or graffiti trees. I suppose this category name depends on what the graffiti represents. East of Owen Sound, just off Highway #26, the Bruce Trail crosses into a rich mixed forest woodlot north of the road. Here, with a ten-minute walk, you will arrive at the Polish soldier tree.[11] In 1942, a soldier from the Tadeusz Kosciuszko Polish Army training camp operating in Owen Sound in the early years of the Second World War carved a memento in the soft bark of a beech tree. I visited the tree on a wet first snowfall day in late October 2013. I love the now common feeling of a pending discovery. The Bruce Trail Heritage Tree Scavenger Hunt link on the trail's website meant I was confident the soakers I was experiencing would be worth it. I knew where I was going. The tree is truly a grand mature beech. Written is the soldier's name, Zolnierz, the year, 1942, and the opening words of the Polish national anthem, "Poland has not yet perished." I would have noted the letters in Polish, but as the tree has aged the lettering has spread and scar tissue has expanded. I took a moment to consider what might have been the circumstances of the time spent here in the woods in 1942 by a likely homesick soldier thinking of the turbulent times of a Poland perishing under the weight of Nazi Germany's occupation.

Another curious tree still standing is the Halfway Tree, a meeting tree of sorts. It is not a Canadian tree, but it is too good and eccentric a story not share. The burr oak is just south of Brodhead, Wisconsin. It marks the halfway point between Lake Michigan and the Mississippi River at the shortest distance between the two. The walking trail of the eighteenth and early nineteenth centuries became a stage coach route turn, Highway 81 today. Dennis Downes, marker tree snooper extraordinaire, believes there would once have been many accompanying marker trees along this route. As early as 1832 the distances were paced off by Native runners and confirmed by the U.S. survey crew. Reading Dennis's book *Native American Trail Marker Trees* is a calling to jump in the car and head to Illinois, Wisconsin, and Michigan.[12]

That said, Paul O'Hara's work provides more than enough incentive to keep my explorations closer to home in Ontario. I have started the simple process of looking for marker trees in my home terrain on the Oak Ridges Moraine and have begun to "ask around," as Paul puts it, to area historians and botanical experts on the ridge. I've had one false call to Paul where I'd been seeking the Dundas Portage between the head of the lake at the Dundas Valley and the Grand River. Patrick Bermingham and I in 2009 knew of the concept of trail marker trees, but details were hard to find. Our tree had right angle limbs but not, as we have since learned, the distinctive shape. Still, it was enough to start me on the trail. I'd like nothing more than to be able to be among the folks who have responded to Paul's request in the Field Botanists' of Ontario newsletters for living trail marker trees and related significant landmark trees. Thanks to the work of Paul here in Ontario and of Dennis Downes and the Wells, the hunting is made easier, but time is not on our side. This was an old practice, and the remaining trees likely do not have much time left standing.

Another style of marker trees to discuss here is the lobstick. More distinctive to the northern boreal forest of spruce and pine trees, the lobstick has garnered much attention in parts of Canada as an iconic symbol of a bygone era of trail markers. I will let a historical voice describe a lobstick tree. In 1845, R.M. Ballantyne, clerk with the Hudson's Bay Company, paddled from York Factory on Hudson Bay to Norway House, Manitoba. He writes from the Hayes River:

> At sunset we put ashore for the night on a point covered with a great number [of] lopsticks. These are tall pine-trees denuded of their lower branches, a small tuft being left at the top. They are generally made to serve as landmarks; and sometimes the voyageurs make them in honour of gentlemen who happen to be travelling for the first time along the route — and those trees are chosen which, from their being on elevated ground, are conspicuous objects. The traveller for whom they are made is always expected to acknowledge this sense of honour conferred upon him by presenting the boat's crew with a pint of grog, either on the spot or at the first establishment they meet with. This then considered as having paid for his footing, and may ever afterwards pass scot-free.[13]

For well over twenty years, I discussed the mystique of lobsticks at our first portage with university groups on camping trips. It just so happened that our first portage had a prominent pine jutting out into the forest skyline by the portage. This was a coincidence, but it gave me the idea to start infusing our trip with a discussion on engaging with the canoe travel heritage of which we were a part. I would also mention my former teacher from the University of Alberta, Stu Mackinnon, who, as I remember, travelled about Canada one summer hunting out remaining lobsticks. Stu isn't with us anymore. I wonder if I remember that story correctly, or have I romanticized Stu and his lobstick interest?

As for actual lobsticks still on the land from the fur trade era, I like to think that I'll still see one. I have likely found a famous lobstick stump on Great Slave Lake. At the start of the five-kilometre Pike's Portage there

Warburton Pike's sketch of the lobstick tree marking the beginning of
Pike's Portage, Great Slave Lake.

was an outstanding lobstick tree marking the beginning of the portage.[14]
It was cut by Warburton Pike and James MacKinlay in 1890. Many who
travelled this gateway to the barren lands mentioned it. J.W. Tyrell took
an excellent photograph of the lobstick in 1900. Still on this portage, my
friend Gordon Hommes wrote to me about his 1991 canoe trip from
Yellowknife to Baker Lake. In Gordon's words: "we did 'discover' what was
almost certainly another lobstick at the other end of that first long trail, at
the west end of Harry Lake. It was one of the very few tall trees in the area,
a dying white spruce, with the branches high in the tree long ago cut off."

In 2007, when I paddled up to that end of the portage, I either
missed it or the tree has since fallen down. I prefer to think the former.

Today, there is a Lobstick Inn in Jasper, Alberta, a replica lobstick
tree at the Waskesiu Golf Course dating back to 1935, an academic journal out of Grande Prairie titled *Lopstic: An Interdisciplinary Discussion
Forum of Creative Thought, Social Commentary and Scholarly Research and
Debate*, and a 1920s historical fiction titled *The Lobstick Trail*. Recently,
Merle Massie wrote in the *Globe and Mail* recommending that the lobstick become a national biopolitical symbol.[15] That lobstick replica at the
Waskesiu Golf course will be coming down due to old age on September 2,
2013, and a new lobstick replica will be planted on the distinctive first fair-
way. The golf course was built in 1935, and the superintendant of Waskesiu
National Park (formed in 1928), J.A. Wood, had the idea of a tree to

remember the lobstick trees on the shores of Lake Waskesiu.[16] Today, the symbol lives on, and the time of marker trees lives on in our imagination to wisely keep the days of walking trails and portages in mind.

Back to John Valliant's notion of church trees: it's an interesting idea. I think this can be a very subjective category. I have one. It is a tall old growth white pine on a portage trail between Dewdney and Chiniguchi lakes in Ontario's shield country. I have stopped here with summer campers and university students for over three decades. We would perform the girth test of spreading three bodies' arms stretched around the tree and often take a group picture. There was always a moment of quietly standing and staring and then a discussion of what constitutes "old growth." This pine is likely well over two hundred years old. It is a part of my life and likely has special qualities for some of those wide-eyed campers and students too. Many, of course, pass by, the tree going unnoticed. For me, as an educator and canoe tripper, the Dewdney white pine is a church tree. Many people will have their own special trees that they revere. This is good. For some the pines north of Lake Obabika in Temagami, Ontario, are their church trees. I have seen Anishnaabeg ceremonial flags on the trail to this grove of pines. Others return regularly to the tall pines on the hill on the north end of Old Crow Lake in Algonquin Park. These are wonderful destinations on canoe trips. I expect to visit each forest again in the years ahead.

Finally, Peter Kelly and Douglas Larson, in their book *The Last Stand: A Journey Through the Ancient Cliff-Face Forest of the Niagara Escarpment*, reveal many ancient cedar trees previously unexplored for special qualities. Once core samples of cliff-attached trees were taken, it was shocking to learn that some of these gnarly cedars are the oldest trees in Canada. Lion's Head, Ontario, on the Bruce Peninsula, is the place to go. There, three cliff trees, named by Kelly and Larson the Three Kings, the Snake, and the Ancient One, have birthdates of 971 AD, 795 AD, and 688 AD respectively. For the Ancient One, that's 1,326 years old.[17] My visit here will be a touchstone to another time indeed. The Ancient One predates the Viking era. Lots to ponder here. The church tree is not only a personal idea. It can exist in a personal, local, and national manner.

In the early 1990s, on a visit to the west coast with a young family and steady showers in the rainforests of Vancouver Island, I visited the Carmanah Giant. This is a Sitka spruce tree that became a big part of the anti-clear-cut logging protests. The Carmanah Valley in these years attracted national attention. I jumped on the bandwagon, intrigued to see the forest and its showcase giant spruce that rises ninety metres and is likely over eight hundred years old. I was painfully aware that I could only reach the tree, with two kids under six years of age on a family weekend outing from Victoria, thanks to the logging road giving access to the terrain. That said, the Carmanah watch trail guides were present to ensure sound environmental practices were met. The region was spared full cutting. The tree remains, and I have a vivid memory of its girth (you could lose calories walking around this tree) and towering presence. It remains symbolic to me of the good fight and changing attitudes. It is a church tree.

Another local environmental movement–focussed tree is the infamous Golden Spruce of the Yakoun River Valley in the Queen Charlotte Islands, also called Haida Gwaii. The tree has been felled by the disgruntled and talented Grant Hadwin. He was protesting the short-sightedness of "university trained professionals" and the related destructive practices of logging companies, practices in which he was highly skilled. John Vaillant, whose book *The Golden Spruce: A True Story of Myth, Madness and Greed* is a biography of the tree, the B.C. forests, and Hadwin, tells a compelling story of an outstanding church tree and of people (the Haida, the Port Clements townsfolk, and really all of us) done wrong.[18]

The crushing irony is that while Hadwin's act of protest (cutting down the tree — a remarkable feat even with today's chainsaws) stirred intense anger and sadness, his inspiration was largely shared by a majority of Haida Gwaii's population. The tree was known to the Haida as *K'iid K'iyaas*, meaning "Elder Spruce Tree." As the legend goes, the tree was once a young boy transformed into a tree. There are not many single trees for which there is an associated legend, but the spruce tree with golden needles, a biological anomaly, is one. It is a dense story. In brief, the tree has fallen. The culprit, Grant Hadwin, is missing. He didn't arrive at his court date and was last seen kayaking across Hecate Sound to the islands. New life is growing from the nurse log, which was thoughtfully left where it fell. And one is left to visit the stump site where a mythical, one-of-a-kind church tree, the Golden Spruce, once stood.

On the other side of the environmental-inspired protest from Grant Hadwin and the Golden Spruce is the story of the California redwood Luna. In the year 2000, the unidentified cutter left Luna badly damaged. The cutter, believed to be a local logger, was, in Valliant's words, enraged "by the interference of environmentalists in what most west coast loggers feel is a God-given right."[19] Luna, the redwood church tree, was made famous by an activist, more aptly put tree dweller — an ultimate tree hugger, Julia Butterfly Hill, who lived for two years in the tree as a protest to proposed logging of Luna's forest. This section of forest has not been logged.

Reshaped marker trees, lopped-branched lobsticks, meeting, or church trees — it is a special feeling to be travelling on trails today wondering if you will see a landmark tree or wonder where on your route such a tree might have existed. One can ask, What is my special relationship with a certain tree in my life? In conclusion, I delight in the thought of the voyageur travelling with Alexander Ross or the member of the Red River Settlement in Manitoba who shouted out one day from a canoe on Lake Winnipeg, "That's a lop-stick, I trimmed eighteen years ago."[20]

I might just go for a walk out on the trails on my scrubby forested ten acres and cut a lobstick. Hey, why not start a reshaped marker tree or designate a meeting tree? Perhaps one of the trees planted on the property in 2013 will someday become an area's church tree. Cultures and trees move on, but good traditions are worthy of our continued attentions.

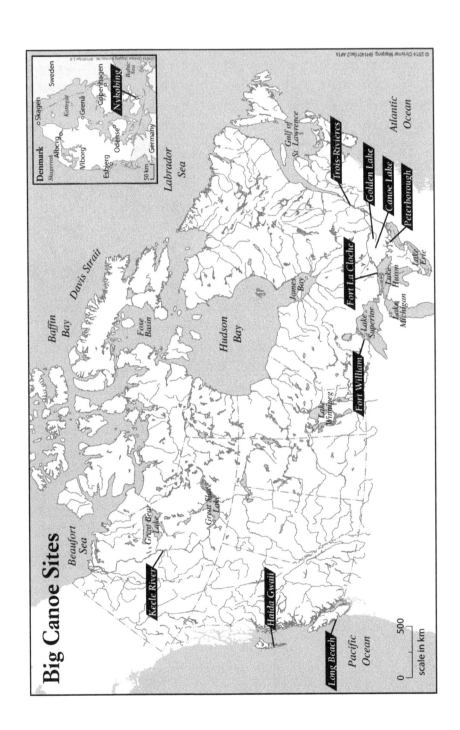

Big Canoe Sites

Long Beach

Pacific
Ocean

0   500
scale in km

Haida Gwaii

Keele River

Great Bear
Lake

Great Slave
Lake

Beaufort
Sea

Lake
Winnipeg

Fort William

Lake
Superior

Fort La Cloche

Lake
Michigan

Lake
Huron

Lake
Erie

Peterborough

Canoe Lake

Golden Lake

Trois-Rivières

Hudson
Bay

James
Bay

Foxe
Basin

Baffin
Bay

Davis Strait

Labrador
Sea

Gulf of
St. Lawrence

Atlantic
Ocean

© 2014 Chrismar Mapping BH140156c2.AI1A

Denmark

Skagen

Skagerrak

Alborg

Kattegat

Viborg

Esbjerg

Odense

Grenå

Copenhagen

Nykøbing

Baltic
Sea

Germany

Sweden

50 km

©2014 Chrismar Mapping Service Inc. 011401156c2.2.6

9

Big Canoes and Their Builders

"Does it linger in our consciousness merely as a nostalgic relic, and only because the moulders of contemporary sensibilities have not yet succeeded in transferring popular perceptual allegiances to some modern digital icon? Or is the canoe genuinely evocative of sentiments and experiences that remain widely entrenched and are constantly being adapted through renewal?"[1]

— Jamie Benidickson

Big canoes — I love them. Bronze Age replicas, dragon boats, voyageur *canots de maîtres*, you name it. To my mind, when you get eight or more canoe paddlers working together, you are in a big canoe. The teamwork, the rhythm, the glide: it is a wonderful feeling for the usual solo and tandem canoeist. Then there are the builders of big canoes. My eldest daughter, Ceilidh, and I, under the superior guidance of Roger Foster of the Carlisle Canoe Company, built a sixteen-foot tandem wood-canvas canoe in 2009. It was hardly a modest undertaking. We are proud of our efforts, grateful to Roger, and in awe of anyone taking on the creation of a good canoe more than twice that size. To be connected to big canoe traditions, even in modest ways, is a special feeling. I will share some of those feelings as I touch on a collection of big canoe traditions.

In a dragon boat race in 2013, I found myself with a few friends but mostly with folks I didn't know. Many had never been in a canoe, let alone a dragon boat. Many had never experienced the exhilaration of a canoe race start. I was new to the dragon boat race, but not to the canoe race or big canoe race. It was an excited group and an intense two plus–minutes with each heat of five hundred metres. It wouldn't have mattered much how we did; the joy of the event was the spirit of participation for most of the forty-eight teams. That said, we won our division. We were mixed doubles, a second tier of racers winning our first heat and the finals by a hair. We were all surprised and elated. Now I think back on it and realize the undertaking involved in staging such an event for forty-eight boats and the challenges involved in getting twenty people together to go for a paddle. It was truly a special day. I look forward to repeating the day on the shores of Lake Scugog. The event was called the Dragon Flies Dragon Boat Festival in support of breast cancer research. I was aware of being connected to a variety of histories that June day.

Dragon Boat racing on Lake Scugog in Port Perry.

The breast cancer connection started in 1996 with breast cancer survivors racing to promote awareness and research. This is just one significant history that has flourished. A quick review of websites today points out that over 2 million paddlers participate in dragon boat festivals each year. The growth rate of the sport is at 22 percent annually spread around fifty countries. That is a phenomenon in my books. The modern era of dragon boat racing began in 1976 in Hong Kong when post-communist forces revived the ancient tradition. The international scene started in 1986 when six boats were brought over from Hong Kong for races at Expo '86 in Vancouver. The rest is history.

The early history, of course, has an appeal that adds to the overall spirit of friendly competition I enjoyed that day. First off, competitions have been taking place annually for over two thousand years. There have been religious, military, and folk customs and traditions associated with the races. The boats themselves are dragons, symbolized by boat hulls painted as scales, a dragon head for a bow, and paddles representing claws. Dragons are thought to be wholesome and deserving of respect and honour. I'll say!

As expected, there has to be an origin story. One such states that in the classical age of China's history, at the time of Confucius (551–479 BC), Qu Yuan, a loyal scholar, poet, and advisor to the emperor, committed suicide as a protest to warring states. Throwing himself into the river with a heavy rock, he was gone. Local fishermen rushed out to save him, beating drums and flailing paddles to disrupt the fish from eating the body. His act of protest ultimately inspired the dragon boat race. Another origin story involves the medieval *Jingda*, or competitive crossing. Here a mock battle involving teams of about thirty men would compete for dominance in a river crossing. This half race, half mock combat event became a fine spectator sport with ornately decorated boats. Two related origins, perhaps? Dragon boat races are a way that many people connect to canoeing these days. I could never have imagined this in the 1960s when canoe racing was canoe regattas at children's camp and canoe clubs.[2]

How easy it was at children's camp, where I cut my teeth getting in the camp's forty-two-foot war canoes at every opportunity. I remember it like it was yesterday. The challenge was made. A group of about thirty-five ten-year-old kids challenged thirty-five older kids to a war canoe race. It was a classic summer camp activity with one difference: the wood-canvas canoes were big — really big. With thirty-plus kids in each canoe, wide enough for three across and built to be untippable, we raced our hearts out. The older kids always won, but it didn't matter. It was a fun, thrilling ride at top speed. The guy that built the canoes, Stan Murdock, was still at camp when I was ten years old. He was in his late sixties then. I knew who he was but wouldn't dare talk with the living legend. He worked on the canoe fleet in the canoe shop near the edge of the camp. It was an esteemed position at a camp where canoes were king! The shop itself, with its old photos, wood stove, and aura of the best of traditions, all added to this special place at camp.

Over forty years later, I appreciate those childhood races as truly special events: not to mention those special glimpses of Stan Murdock. A child's lack of attention to detail has matured into a strong desire to fully appreciate the master craftsmanship of Stan Murdock, those two war canoes, and the camps that have relied on them for over eighty-five years. The canoe shop, now under the direction of Dave Standfield, holds this aura of tradition still. Attending the Wooden Canoe Heritage Assembly at Paul Smith's College in 2012, at the invitation of Rob Stevens, has given me the impetus to gather historical details and share a fabulous wooden canoe heritage story with like-minded folks.

First the two canoes. As far as I know, they are the largest wood-canvas canoes in the world. They are forty-two feet long, fifty-nine inches wide at the midpoint, and twenty inches in depth. They were made at the Peterborough Canoe Company in 1925–1926. A standard thirty-six-foot mould was cut in half so six feet could be added. The wood used was cedar for planking and ribs, oak for gunwales and keels. This was a special work order from Taylor Statten (known as the Chief at Camp Ahmek for boys and Camp Wapomeo for girls). The Chief wanted extra-large canoes to serve as the main transportation system for the two widely spaced camp settings. The girls' camp involves two islands. There are seats for over thirty campers, but forty paddlers are not out of the question. Once the canoes were made, the thirty-six-foot mould was reassembled, and there have since been no requests for canoes larger than the thirty-six-foot voyageur canoe. One theory for the Chief's need for the extra space was as a means of evacuation in case of fire. The two canoes arrived at Algonquin Park by train in 1926 on a flatbed and were soon involved in controversy. That same summer, ten boys and one staff died on Balsam Lake, Ontario, when their thirty-six-foot war canoe from the Peterborough Canoe Company swamped two miles offshore. At first, editorials in the newspapers advocated that large canoes at children's camps should not be used as "utility boats." Later, the jury deliberating on the case recommended "legislation to banish war canoes from all boys' camps." So begins the history of war canoes at Camps Ahmek and Wapomeo. Some camps burned their war canoes. Other camps put the boats in storage, while others continued their use.[3] The Chief had a picture taken with fourteen boys sitting on one gunwale for a camp brochure promoting the forty-two-foot two-of-a-kind canoes as unswampable. Suffice it to say, the canoes and the two camps weathered the storm. These were genuinely unique war canoes.

Stan Murdock was born in 1900, and in the early 1920s he was an apprentice with the Peterborough Canoe Company. Together with his father, he helped build these war canoes and saw them head away to places unknown. Stan couldn't take the wood dust in the factory, so when the Chief called down to Peterborough for a canoe maintenance man and builder for his children's summer camps, Stan was an ideal choice. Imagine his excitement when he arrived at the Algonquin Park camps to discover the two-of-a-kind war canoes were the workhorses of the two camps. Stan built a fleet of canoes and fixed them for the next forty-six years. He retired in 1972. The canoe shop is still going strong today. Repairs and new canoes are being made; however, now campers are involved in wood-canvas canoe building projects. Man, I wish they'd had this operational in my day … I mean, Stan's day.

I had been at camp for eight years by 1972. Stan was a quiet, calm, larger-than-life figure. All of us kids kept our distance out of reverence for this master craftsman. I started on staff at camp in 1973 and only then would have had reason to interact with Stan. One opportunity missed, but paddling Stan's war canoes was certainly not a chance missed. I was in those boats every chance I had. I loved them. I loved paddling them in regattas, and I loved simply looking at them.

The Taylor Statten camps war canoes, Canoe Lake, Algonquin Park.
Photo courtesy of Marc Laurier.

Happily, I can love them still. That said, the canoes have only been re-canvassed once, in 1979–80, by Bill Statten and Don and Dave Standfield. Dave is now the "Stan Murdock" of camp, and I'm sure there are kids at camp who see Dave as that same calm master craftsman.

Dave tells me the war canoes need to be re-canvassed, and once the canvas is removed he is concerned there will be some rotting of wood under the three keels. He has to add significantly to the canoe shop to create a heated space for the winter work. One boat is to be repaired in each of two winters, but first an internal exam is needed. Dave speculates that if there is rotting he will have a major repair job in the next five years.[4]

Swapping canoe building and refurbishing stories among the wooden canoe heritage folks at Paul Smith's college in 2012 helped me realize that what can so easily be taken for granted as an older "beater" canoe, even a rather big canoe, might need to be rethought of as an on-the-water art form. The Taylor Statten war canoes are masterfully crafted heritage boats. Their daily use for eighty-six summers simply furthers this point. I also realized at the assembly that the war canoes and Stan Murdock are a story to be shared. I hope to be around to celebrate one hundred years of intensive daily summer use by these canoes, of which I have been a part. Heck, I'll organize a regatta race in them ... as long as they let my then-aging bones compete.

While camp days and those camp canoes are long past me, paddling big boats is not. That said, the easy nature of the boat always in the water, enough paddlers almost always present, and a necessary trip across the lake or a whimsical race always in the wings is not likely to be repeated. I hope the camp kids today appreciate those canoes. Beyond the next dragon boat race or perhaps a future rental of a *canot de maître* from Naturally Superior for a Lake Superior trip, big canoes remain a cherished but hard to have experience.[5]

My 2011 visit with Danish boat-builder Svend Ulstrup comes to mind as one of those hard to have moments. I didn't even get to paddle Svend's eighty-four-foot Bronze Age replica boat. It was enough to experience it in his canoe yard. I do hope to be involved in a future launching of another Bronze Age replica. I'm expecting a call from Svend someday with an invite. Here is a slice of the world of an eccentric big canoe builder in the modern era.[6]

"I think democracy must have started in a canoe." Okay, this statement is not the sort of thing you hear regularly. But from the mouth of Danish boat builder and educator Svend Ulstrup, such is the norm. He is a man full of aphorisms. He is a man who makes two countercultural thoughts prominent: from Bruce Cockburn, "the trouble with normal is it only gets worse," and from another singer, the late Pete Seeger, speaking about Woody Guthrie, "Any darn fool can make something complex; it takes a genius to make something simple." Svend Ulstrup is not normal, and he is genuinely simple. Let's go back to democracy in a canoe.

Svend builds kayaks and canoes. He figures so far he has built over two thousand, mostly in educational courses, for about six thousand people. He has been at this for over twenty years. He's built umiaks (skin boats from the Arctic), birchbark canoes, and, oh yeah, one eighty-four-foot Bronze Age water craft. A really big canoe complete with a mythic creature masthead!

In the canoe all eyes face the same way, making all paddlers equal according to Svend's thinking. Rowing facing backwards was the way of the Iron Age Viking boats that came later. In Viking boats, leaders faced the direction of travel, while the rowers faced the leaders. Democracy, or an earlier form of it, possibly had its beginnings in a canoe. Makes you think, doesn't it? Genius or goofing around, it was hard to tell. Zabe MacEachren and I spent two days with Svend and his wife, Annalie. We paddled in his Greenlandic skin-and-wood frame kayaks and admired his badarka design, both of which he builds in educational courses. It was hard to ignore the eighty-four-foot (that's twenty-five metres), forty-two-paddler Bronze Age ocean boat in the canoe yard, with its double bow stem and middle wide enough to serve as a stage for a jazz quartet. Building kayaks for a living in Denmark might be enough to make you eccentric, but build a Bronze Age boat (oops, canoe) and involve local curious folks in the building and paddling and you win a certain notoriety. Almost as if he hadn't thought of it, Svend came to realize that it is hard to get forty-two folks together for an afternoon paddle. Hence the canoe sits in the yard, and Svend has started (indeed, the day we left) to build a smaller version, not necessarily more sea-worthy, but more practical for an afternoon outing. It will require only eighteen paddlers and be thirty-two feet long.

These canoes must be flexible for the big waves of the ocean. "The feel of the canoe is like a worm in the water,"[7] Svend says. The flex can be almost frightening on the ocean fjord by Svend's workshop. In big waves, the bow may disappear from sight to the stern paddlers. Svend had documented the inaugural canoe launch. The pictures are almost shocking. That many people in one canoe. Happily, the oceans were warmer when these boats plied Danish waters, and warmer overall temperatures meant four seasons for trade far afield. Bronze Age folks were the precursors to the Vikings, and it was the Iron Age that made possible the shift in shape from the more flexible skin canoe to the Viking rigid wooden hull. Think iron rivets by the year 1000. Let's remember, Indigenous peoples in Canada started their Iron Age with materials brought over from Europe in the 1400–1500s. The canoe had served and continues to serve them well on lakes, rivers, and oceans.

We never felt far from the Bronze Age with Svend. We examined many Bronze Age rock art canoe images from Scandinavia in his library. We visited a burial mound site en route to catch our bus out of town. The rock art was very similar to Canadian Shield images, particularly those at Petroglyphs Provincial Park (minus the double bow to cut the ocean waves). Svend used rock art both as an inspiration and a design template. There were no blueprints from the Bronze Age. Svend's rawhide skin covering theory has validity given the seaworthy qualities of his canoe. It may seem speculative to us, but not to Svend Ulstrup. But we *look* at ancient rock art; Svend *studies* it.

Earlier in my trip, it had been casually pointed out to me that there were Bronze Age burial mounds, "here and one over there too." Without particularly looking for them, four were pointed out from a specific vantage point. Svend said that one hundred years ago there were over two thousand such mounds peppering the Danish landscape. Now, given advanced farming practices, this has been reduced to about two hundred. Svend's interest in the Bronze Age, given this wealth of artifacts and his intense awareness of Danish heritage, made my Danish landscape experience seem alive with a past that would make a Canadian history buff salivate. Bronze Age boat building is a natural extension for a kayak and canoe heritage builder. It seems normal as a mark of genius. That said, the kayaker who gave us a lift to Svend's place felt compelled to warn me that "he is a bit of a kook." I think she might be missing this heritage-to-waterways connection.

Thinking over our time with Svend Ulstrup, I realized, "We need this guy." He can help a hurried, harried people make valuable healthy connections in time and space with heritage and places and technology. Svend's approach to life and education help keep alive ways of living on the earth that now seem distant. I am reminded of the poster of 1881 found in Steven Heigthon's novel *Afterlands*. The poster is for an actual presentation Captain Tyson gave to the Arctic-hungry audiences of New England concerning the survival of many crew members and Inuit set adrift on an ice floe from the Howgate Expedition for 196 days before rescue — a true story, and a true poster. After all the promotional material, the poster finishes with, "told with the graphic power of actual experience."[8] In today's world of virtual realities and over-hyped events, I'm inclined to think cynically, "Imagine that, actual experience!"

Svend Ulstrup in his boat works yard beside a Bronze Age replica "canoe."
Photo courtesy of Svend Ulsrup.

Well, Svend has it — "actual experience" that is. His lifestyle and work have graphic power that stands out distinctly today. Finally, little about Svend is normal, and there is a simple genius in that. For all these reasons, I feel inspired to write about him.

You cannot write about big canoes in Canada without mentioning the birchbark voyageur *canot de maître*. There was a day when there were many canoe builders. John Tanner (1780–1847), who was taken captive as a boy in the late 1790s from the Kentucky River and travelled mostly in and beyond northwestern Ontario, mentions a desire of his adopted tribe to conduct a raid. This led to what appears to be the spontaneous building of a fleet of canoes. His entry makes it sound like they said, "Hey, let's stop here and build ten or so canoes so we can raid our neighbours to the south."[9] In those days, it appears canoe building wasn't a specialty trade.

With the advancement of the fur trade, the canoe factory became a fixture in the successful emerging trans-Canada fur trade canoe route. The voyageur *canot de maître*, at thirty-six feet long and five-and-a-half feet wide, became standardized in the early 1700s. By 1751, the memoirs of Colonel Franquet, Military Engineer-in-Chief for New France, make several references to the fur trade *canot de maître* factory at Trois-Rivières. He claims a production rate of twenty canoes per year made by Algonquin and French builders. Later, after the British takeover in 1763, more displaced Iroquois builders worked on the standardized craft for the heavy demands of the Montreal-based North West Company traders.[10] These businessmen pushed the trade to the Pacific, with such names as David Thompson, Simon Fraser, and Alexander Mackenzie serving as explorers and traders. The voyageurs, canoe men who didn't typically write, are usually understood through the cursory writings of the explorer, surveyor, or trader. Oh, how those canoe men must have been mesmerized by the rhythmic meditation of paddling in large teams.

Changing canoe route patterns with the Hudson's Bay Company take-over in 1821 increased the demand for the smaller twenty-six-foot canoe of the western interior; along with an increased scarcity of materials this led to the Trois-Rivières factory's closure. It is interesting that there are limited factory records of any canoes being built beyond thirty-six to thirty-seven feet. I suppose this highlights the specialness of the Taylor Statten Camps' forty-two-foot war canoes and Svend Ulstrup's eighty-four-foot canoe.

In the Montreal-based North West Company's heyday (1803–21), as many as seventy to eighty canoes were made each year to travel the route from the Montreal to Grand Portage, Fort William, and the Great Lakes on the way to the Athabasca and the Pacific. Each year, this same number of thirty-six-foot birchbark canoes were decommissioned or reserved for minor local runs. The St. Lawrence–Great Lakes run was clearly demanding.

Shawn Patterson, Fort William Historical Site Collections Curator, and I went over the math on the phone one day. Combing the fur trade records shows that, in their heyday, about forty to eighty *canots de maître* left Montreal in the spring for Fort William. Eighty is certainly the exceptional figure. If you average fifty boats over those years going to Fort William, the main canoe run west, and factor in the lesser runs, such as a route north to Abitibi, you might get seventy to eighty boats total. That is four-hundred-plus canoe men (if eight paddlers per canoe) for a modest estimate of fifty canoes heading west for the Fort William rendezvous.

Coming east from the western interior it is estimated, again in the 1803–21 heyday, that there were roughly 150 canoes working in the interior coming east for the Fort William rendezvous laden with furs. At four canoe men in these twenty-six-foot canoes, that's six hundred canoe men. In total, over one thousand canoe men would arrive in Fort William in the fur trade fleet of canoes. Amazing. That's a lot of birchbark and a lot of builders between Trois-Rivières, Fort William, and certain interior building locations.

Why the standardized sizes? In the fastidious fur trade business, standardized shapes and sizes were important. You would need to know from trip to trip how much you could put in the canoe. Also, for the *canot de maître*, one can surmise that thirty-six-feet was as big as a group could comfortably portage. The consequence of a fall must have weighed heavily on their minds. Repairs consumed time. There is also the question of a craft holding its shape out of the water. At some size, presumably beyond thirty-six feet, a canoe out of water is susceptible to not holding its shape. Practical stuff, this.[11]

Repairs are also interesting. About halfway along the route between Montreal and Grand Portage/Fort William, the North West Company established repair stations. One such station existed at the mouth of the Mississagi River by the present-day town of Little Current. The most permanent repair station (which also served as a fur trade post) was at Fort La Cloche.[12] Like most of the Great Lakes fur trade route, this is excellent canoe travel still. It is exciting to imagine a thirty-six-foot fur trade canoe pulling into what can now be choice campsites at the Mississagi or La Cloche for repairs and a good rest for tired canoe men travelling on fur trade routes.

As the demands of fur trade travel waned, the big canoe eventually shifted to become a racing canoe, the feature event at canoe regattas in the late 1880s. New materials, wood-canvas and cedar strippers, replaced birchbark. Eventually, replica canoes were built of fibreglass for retracing fur trade routes and summer camp use. The standard thirty-six-foot *canot de maître* refuses to sink away.

One story I particularly like involves the 1955 commission of a birchbark *canot de maître* by builder Matt Bernard. Bernard was a former Chief of the Algonquin of Pikwàkanagàn. He was seventy-nine years old in 1955. He responded to the request from David Gillies (president of Gillies Bros. and Co. Ltd., lumber manufacturers) and head staff of the National

Museum of Man (later the Canadian Museum of Civilization, now named the Canadian Museum of History in 2014). The fear was that a true replica birchbark canoe demanded a kind of craftsmanship and materials that were difficult to find then. Bernard, with his sons and grandsons, completed the replica (based on an 1810 model used for decades) in September 1957. They launched the canoe in Golden Lake in the Ottawa Valley to check on its seaworthiness, then trucked it off to Ottawa's museum that same afternoon. Seems a shame to me; it should have had a trip first, at least a paddle on the Ottawa River. In the summer of 2012, over fifty years later, the impressive largest birchbark canoe in the world has been returned to Pikwàkanagàn, specifically returned to Omamiwinini Pimadjwowin, the Algonquin Way Cultural Centre, and to its birthplace and the birthplace of its builders.[13]

In October 2013, Christina Ruddy, the Project Coordinator for the Pikwàkanagàn Cultural Centre, learned that a prefab steel structure could be purchased. In point of fact, I called her that same day. The fundraising has been ongoing to bring the canoe back officially. Acquiring an economically feasible structure had been a holdup. The building site is on traditional grounds and the band's powwow site. The tradition of birchbark canoe building is now continued by Stanley Sarazin and family. The Cultural Centre has a collection of smaller canoes. The *canot de maître* returning home is a gem of a big canoe story spanning … well … my lifetime.

Since, the 1960s there has been a growth in traditional canoe building craftsmanship. Wood-canvas, cedar strip, and even birchbark canoes are being made again by specialty builders. Recently, Dorset, Ontario, builder Rick Nash was commissioned to build a thirty-three-foot birchbark canoe. He started the project in 2012 and with some stops and restarts will be finished construction by the summer of 2014. But we are a long way from the days of John Tanner's journal entry describing a needed war canoe building event, a community-building event.

Similarly, the West Coast dugout big canoe tradition is in a revival mode. In 1873, James Swan travelled to Haida Gwaii (the Queen Charlotte Islands) on behalf of the American Smithsonian Institute. He reported canoes "very large and capable of carrying one hundred persons with all their equipment for a long voyage."[14] Dugout canoes on the west coast were recorded at lengths of ninety feet (thirty metres) and used on lengthy coastal trade routes as well as battles. There were many clashes involving the early contact trading relations between Europeans and the proud coastal tribes. John Vaillant, in his brilliant history of Haida Gwaii centered around the mystic Golden Spruce (see Chapter 8), captures the drama of big canoe paddling on the West Coast.

> Travelling in these giant cedar canoes, the Haida would regularly paddle their home into, and out of, existence. With each collective paddle stroke they would have seen their islands sinking steadily into the sea while distant snow-covered peaks scrolled up before them like a new planet. Few people alive today have any notion of how it might feel to pull worlds up from beyond the horizon by faith and muscle alone.[15]

The big dugout canoe of West Coast Indigenous peoples' traditions has seen a revival largely credited to the construction and paddling of *Loo Taas* ("Wave Eater"). This fifty-foot Haida design, built by celebrated artist Bill Reid and Haida carvers, was readied for the 1986 World's Fair in Vancouver. It later travelled, by Haida paddlers, from Vancouver to Skidegate. Frank Brown, of the Heiltsuk Nation, also built a big traditional canoe for the 1986 Expo. In 1989, Frank accepted an invitation to join the "Paddle to Seattle" gathering. Here Frank issued a challenge for other Indigenous groups to meet again in community-built canoes for a 1993 Bella Bella Qatuwas (People Gathering Together) festival. Twenty-three canoes made the journey. So was born Tribal Journeys. Today, one can visit yearly Tribal Journeys hosted by various communities. Here, the canoe and the journey are healing tools, a performance of sovereignty and a prime educator of Indigenous cultural values and community spirit.[16] I had the good fortune of seeing a stopover of a Tribal Journey in the mid-1990s at Long Beach on the west coast of Vancouver Island. I was taken by surprise by the energy and dedication to these summer journeys as I talked with paddlers pulling up to the shore for an arranged stopover celebration.

Here was yet another big canoe tradition: this tradition is about celebrating canoes, builders, and journeys. It is also a revived practice shaped by cultural resilience and resistance. In the words of Misao Dean, "Rather than seeing the canoe as a means to further integration into Canadian nationality … indigenous peoples see the canoe as a technology of resisting the Canadian state, and of resisting colonialism."[17]

I missed asking about the validity of this statement concerning resisting colonialism with a group of Sahtu Dene on the Keele River in 2013. About two weeks after I left the river (I had anticipated meeting the group) a camp of moosehide boat builders was on the riverbank site putting finishing touches on a boat. It would travel the final section of the Keele River to arrive at Tulita, formerly Fort Norman, on the Mackenzie River for a seasonal celebration. Yellowknife's Prince of Wales Museum houses a 1970s moosehide boat. I did see that in 2013. The best I saw that summer. I considered whether the Dene builders couple cultural resistance with cultural celebration. A missed opportunity for me. I asked Al Pace about this. He did see the moosehide boat newly on the water and the builders' site along the Keele River shore.

Certainly builders today are aware of preserving deep and rich traditions. They have their own local history of boat building. And we all have intriguing passages in the travel literature. George Douglas, when homeward bound in 1912 from the mouth of Coppermine River and Great Bear Lake, wrote in his journal:

> Fort Norman/Tulita: a party of Montagnois Indians turned up at the post one day from some far eastern tributary of the Mackenzie. They had killed a number of moose and with the skins for cover and saplings for a frame they had built a large boat and journey down the river bringing in the meat. The boat showed great ingenuity in design and construction, and was really a thoroughly serviceable craft. As soon as they had disposed of this meat, they crossed the river and struck by some overland trail back to their hunting grounds on the eastern

slope of the Rockies. They sold their boat to the factor of the northern Trading Co. who broke it up for the skins.[18]

From Tulita, they had likely headed toward the Keele River watershed and would return again to the post in the next summer to bring meat, furs, and the moose fur boat "cover" all for sale. Now that's practical. I was sad to have missed the moosehide boat building on the Keele riverbank that summer, but it was pleasing to know it is still active on the rivers Keele and Mackenzie.

The big canoe tradition has a way of linking large cultural questions and issues and drawing big meaning out of individuals and groups. It is only right to note that the big canoe resurgence as a cultural expression of celebration and resiliency is not alone. In August 2013, the first totem pole to be raised in Haida Gwaii in 130 years found a home on Lyell Island, on the site of the signing ceremony to create a national park reserve jointly managed by the Haida Nation and the federal government.[19] This puts an end to clear-cutting. It also showcases what can be accomplished with diplomacy: a commitment to relationship building rather than conflict management.

A moosehide boat at the Yellowknife Museum.

The thirteen-metre totem pole depicting images of animals, spirits, and human forms weighs in at three thousand kilograms. Head carver Jaalen Edenshaw and thirty-three Haida Eagle clan members worked on the celebratory totem at the Haida Heritage Centre at Skidegate with a healthy support staff. About four hundred people travelled out into Windy Bay for the raising, many in Haida dugout canoes.

The circle of onlookers involved a wide spectrum of West Coasters including local RCMP and government representatives. Peter Lantin, president of the Haida Nations, stated that day: "The legacy pole tells the story of how we work together for a common good, resulting in the successful care of land and waters for the benefit of all peoples." Not just euphemisms, people were seen to be in tears during the raising. For decades to come, powerful images will be seen of bear, raven, wolf, and the "five good people" representing the leadership who, in 1985, blocked the advancing logging road.

Tears of joy are rare in complex environmental cultural issues. This legacy celebration is really for all Canadians. Here, along with the resurgence of West Coast dugout canoes and the 1950s birchbark canoe returned to Pikwàkanagàn, is relationship building in action. There is a long way to go, mind you, but the legacy totem pole rose in August 2013 and annual canoe gatherings help show the way. In the same way, dragon boat events, Svend Ulstrup's experimental archaeology in Bronze Age replicas, and the restoration of Camp Ahmek and Wapomeo war canoes all foster a healthy spirit that traditions matter whatever your culture. To know the tradition and experience it wisely, you have to study the background contexts and the positives and negatives in the past.

Be it dragon boats, camp war canoes, Bronze Age replicas, Indigenous peoples' canoeing renaissance, and the war canoe race capstone to many a canoe club regatta — the essence of it all is the feel of teamwork on the water, the rhythm, the glide, the joys of group effort. The opportunity for all the above does not readily present itself too often. And herein lies the greatest appeal; it will always be special to join a group of twenty or so paddlers for an outing, be it for recreation, celebration or resistance. Fine traditions tend to remain and being part of the big canoe tradition is one to probe and celebrate.

PART THREE

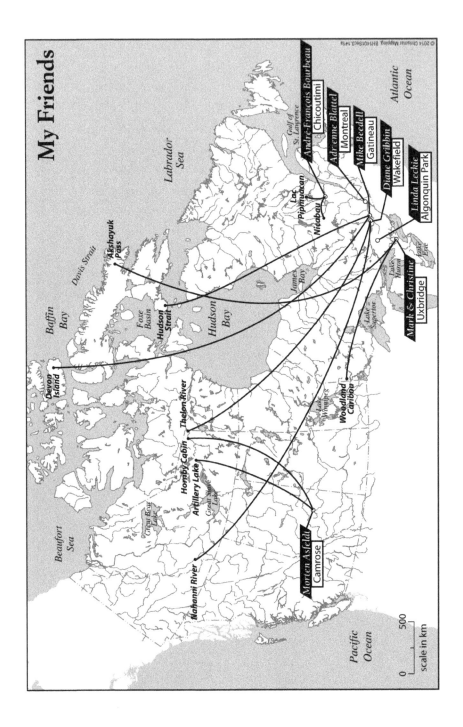

My Friends

Atlantic
Ocean

André-François Bourbeau
Chicoutimi

Adrienne Blattel
Montreal

Mike Beedell
Gatineau

Diane Gribbin
Wakefield

Linda Leckie
Algonquin Park

Mark & Christine
Uxbridge

Woodland
Caribou

Lake
Erie

Lake
Huron

Lake
Superior

Lake
Winnipeg

Gulf of
St. Lawrence

Labrador
Sea

Lac
Pipmuacan

Nicabau

Davis
Strait

Baffin
Bay

Akshayuk
Pass

Foxe
Basin

Hudson
Strait

Hudson
Bay

James
Bay

Devon
Island

Thelon River

Hornby Cabin

Artillery Lake

Great Slave
Lake

Great Bear
Lake

Nahanni River

Morten Asfeldt
Camrose

Beaufort
Sea

Pacific
Ocean

0   500
scale in km

© 2014 Chrismar Mapping. BH1401S6c3.1413

INTRODUCTION
Personalities

"Each friend represents a world in us, a world not born until they arrive, and it is only by this meeting that a new world is born."
— Anaïs Nin

My travel and my studies are mostly based on Canadian heritage themes. History, geography, anthropology, archaeology, literature: these are my main themes. I don't explore any of these alone. I learn from friends. I learn with friends. We share stories. We take turns as storytellers. Friends inspire us all. I revel in their personalities, how they approach problems, explore stories, live their lives. In a way, friends can fill the voids in life. Often you learn from friends about aspects of life that they are engaged in and you are not. I do not work with newcomers to Canada, have not had a polar bear walk into my camp, have not guided adults on river trips thirty times down the Nahanni, have not mapped many of Canada's parks, have not firmly settled into a wild place, do not practice fully in historical replica trips, have not walked over Arctic ice lakes or guided students regularly in the Canadian Arctic. But I have friends that have.

That is the aspiration for this section of *More Trails, More Tales*. My friends here will take you to places on the land and in the mind that I cannot. Yet I admit you get their story, told briefly, from my perspective and from an orientation in keeping with exploring in Canada's past. I am proud to be their friend and pleased to include their stories here. Like all good friends, their stories become my stories. I often tell their stories in conversation. Now I have enjoyed writing of them with the added bonus of the deep satisfaction of sharing the stories of good life practices. I am reminded of a powerful quote by Anais Nin that fits well for this collection of friends: "each friend represents a world in us, a world not born until they arrive, and it is only by this meeting that a new world is born."

There is rich variety here, or at least variety within the orientation of this book. There is a canoe travel guide, a map-maker, a place specialist, an educator, a photographer and adventurer, a historical replica and survival expert, and a community recreation leader for Canadian immigrants. They span the Canadian landscape from the Arctic islands to Montreal, from Alberta to Quebec.

10

Morten Asfeldt:
Educator

Morten and I first met in 1990 on a day canoe outing on the North Saskatchewan River where it flows through Edmonton. It is a fine way to see the city and to make a new friend. We had heard about each other for a decade before that Edmonton river run. In 1979, I had moved to Edmonton for graduate school. Morten was an undergraduate at nearby Augustana in Camrose. By 1990, I knew he was a guy I had to meet, who had worked extensively as a northern river travel guide with a solid woodsman background in hunting and fishing. I was jealous of that northern tripping for sure. Morten knew me as the graduate student coordinator for the exciting University of Alberta Explorations Program, which involved travelling with very capable senior students on historical routes in the west. This was no normal university offering. It took place over a calendar year. A small group of students studied travel topics and prepared and completed ambitious trips of some distinctive nature. It worked. I think it was ahead of its time. As a budding educator, I was excited as a newcomer to the west with a dream of participating in an experiential learning environment combining historical travel on the land and complementary research in the library.

Little did we know then that Morten would evolve this dynamic experiential learning environment of Explorations to create, in my opinion, Canada's premier capstone university course experience. Morten's program, Arctic Course, from which decades of students have benefited, is a masterpiece of experiential outdoor education connecting issues of Canadian identity, environmental and human heritage issues, regional politics, travel skills, and group dynamics.[1] More on that later.

Denmark was Morten's birthplace. He still visits scores of relatives today. But St. Anthony, on the northern tip of the north peninsula in Newfoundland, bears his lasting childhood memories. Here Morten developed early an affinity for northern isolation. "It ain't bleak!" We both share that. It is freedom, expansive and harsh, but welcoming: that's the way Morten remembers it and still lives it in the north.

Little Devils Pond is remembered as an epic journey for after-school fishing trips in grades one to three. On a return visit as an adult, he was surprised to learn Little Devils Pond was a mere twenty minutes from home. I am reminded of the line in a folk song by the American singer/songwriter David Wilcox: "It may look to you like nothing much to see, but you should see the way it feels to me." In winter, the boys, Morten and his older brother, were allowed to explore the landscape on the skidoo once they proved that they could lift the back end out of a snow jam. Hmmm, there might be a few more rules today. Suffice it to say, there was a certain northern freedom that brought Morten into his high school days.

First in the Yukon (Morten's father was a family doctor) where he learned hunting skills from local Native guys in the Whitehorse area, and later in Camrose, Alberta, Morten's high school time wasn't a scholastic, athletic, or social standout. Many share that one. He credits teacher Gary Gibson for his first big break. It was the chance to finish high school with a three-credit university outdoor leadership course that included paddling and hiking in the Canadian Rockies. Soon Morten joined Camrose friend and Augustana alumni Neil Hartling on the Nahanni River. Nahanni River Adventures was born in the mid-1980s. Morten would guide trips for Neil: twenty-plus days on the Nahanni River and new rivers like the Horton and Mara-Burnside. Friendship group trips followed in the early 1990s. In 1993, with Morten's first year at Augustana, the Arctic Course was born for senior students in physical education and other disciplines across campus. Only the Université du Québec à Chicoutimi and Laurentian University could come close to matching

Augustana as a capstone senior outdoor education experience. Each year since, winter or summer, Morten has travelled in the Arctic with interdisciplinary course content. The students select the river they wish to travel and organize all aspects of the experience. The Mara-Burnside river system, which flows to the Arctic, has been selected four times. Students are particularly keen to possibly see the caribou migration and related wildlife. Other rivers include the Thelon, Horton, Ellice-Huikitak, and Hood. The Kuujjua River to the town of Ulukaktok, formerly Holman Island on Victoria Island, is the most northern river that students have selected. The winter version of Arctic Course involves a dog-sledding trip onto the barrens north of Great Slave Lake using David and Kirsten Oleson's homestead at the mouth of the Hoarfrost River as a base camp.

You might assume that from this wealth of experience as an educator on northern rivers that the odd gem of a story could be told. I have shared many enjoyable and richly educational story-sharing campfires and bug shelter sessions on several trips with Morten. Here are two favourites.

Morten Asfeldt.
Photo courtesy of Morten Asfeldt.

On June 9, 2011, while walking on the ice of Artillery Lake toward Pike's Portage and the Eastern Arm of Great Slave Lake, Morten got a bit uncomfortable.[2] The group was approaching Beaver Lodge, a prominent hill on the north side of the lake. Here Morten wanted to leave an offering in respect to the Dene legend associated with this hill. The offering is a request for safe passage. He was worried students might, in his words, "think it a hoky activity, might create a parody." He wasn't sure what to do, and the inner tension could not be ignored. "I'll set up a picture of students walking towards Beaver Lodge. That might be enough. I'll decide later about an offering," he thought. With camera ready and two students walking, the unexpected happened. A student went through the ice at a melt hole. As the water flowed from the land onto the ice it pooled, seeking any crack in the ice to drain, creating a discernible thaw/freeze zone. She simply missed the obvious change in the ice structure. She fell to her shoulders in the icy water, landing on a shelf, and was easily rescued by her nearby walking partner. Morten, with camera ready, took a few pictures and at that same moment committed to leaving an offering for safe passage. That evening, the group climbed atop Beaver Lodge, where Morten told the legend to a sombre, attentive group.[3] No more inner tension! Lesson learned. Respect the traditions on the land.

A peril of Ice travel, Artillery Lake.
Photo courtesy of Morten Asfeldt.

To close, I have a powerful, enduring thought of Morten, the outdoor educator, storyteller, and creator of special experiences with students. It is from another Augustana Arctic Course, this time on the Thelon
River. At the Hornby Cabin site, the group took a rest day and Morten
read the complete journal of Edgar Christian, written in 1926/27, to the
group.[4] Christian was the last of three men (including Harold Adlard
and John Hornby) wintering over to die of starvation at the cabin. They
had arrived too late in the season and the life-giving caribou had already
passed through the region. As Morten tells the story, the students were
huddled together for the reading beside the cabin remains. The graves
of the three men were in the foreground. There was wildlife everywhere;
just the day before, they had seen muskox, grizzly bear, moose, wolf, and
caribou. It was hard to picture a starvation site. Edgar's journal tells the
story of the three men from October 1926 in a time of great promise
for the trapping season ahead to the slow demise of each man through
June 1, 1927, carefully chronicled despite his own weakened state. Edgar
was eighteen. This was his first and only trip onto the barrens. Morten
understood that his students, similar enough in age and similarly full of
promise for their travels, would feel a hypnotic connection to the des-
titute young author hanging on for his life in the cabin beside which
the students were all closely huddled. Having read Edgar's journal and
having shared the odd northern story with students in situ myself, I can
get the shivers just thinking about the emotional energy in that huddled
group reading. Here are a few sample moments from Edgar's journal students would have heard that day, including the final entry.

April 11th — 9 a.m.

Situation is now very serious. Jack last night told both
Harold and me that he felt he was sinking fast and might
pass away at any moment, so he talked to us as to what
should be done. I promised him I can carry on for five
days on Wolverine hide, doing heavy work and hunting.
Harold took a walk after Ptarmigan last evening which
proved he can walk, so Jack has told him he must get

on to the Barrens and dig up the caribou paunch. I am myself capable but do not know even where they are and Jack says I must keep my energy in case Caribou come on the river in a day or so. Last night Jack said he could last a week if I would, but he had a bad night, legs paining and now he says that two days is the most. Harold kept fire all night while in vain I tried to rest, but how can I now under such worry?

10 a.m.

Have made some soup from bones ...

April 18th

Snowstorm terrific all day, as bad as any we have ever had in winter. Lots of odds and ends to be done but even that is too much for us both now. Cutting wood is an effort which seems incredible. Harold after doing so well in helping me yesterday fixing up is simply played out, and both of us are in a bad way of being bound up by bones which have now been in our systems for weeks. Harold fixed up syringe and performed on me, which was successful, so if we can clear ourselves like that we can get out and hunt when weather is fine again. -4 deg. F. 00 deg. F.N.E.

June 1st

At 2 a.m. went to bed feeling content and bowl full of fish by me to eat in morning.

9 a.m. Weaker than ever. Have eaten all I can. Have food on hand but heart petering? Sunshine is bright now.

See if that does any good to me if I get out and bring in
wood to make fire tonight.
Make preparations now.
Got out, too weak and all in now. Left things late.[5]

Also from Edgar Christian's journal, the appendix shares the August
1929 report of Inspector Trundle of the Royal Canadian Mounted Police
August on the findings at the Thelon cabin site. Trundle writes: "A B.C.
heater 12-24 was in the centre of the building on which was a piece of
paper and the following practically illegible letters could be discerned: -
WHO ... LOOK IN STOVE."[6]

I have not lost sight of Morten, the educator, in telling as much as
I have of the Hornby/Christian story of 1926–27 on the Thelon. Morten,
for me, is entrenched in northern stories. Stories like this one can become
a part of who one is — part of one's identity. Morten carries Arctic stories
always. They are a part of who he is.

For his students, time with the Beaver Lodge legend and the Thelon
Hornby Cabin were moving experiences of feeling an aura to and kinship
with northern events in another time. The next day, before departing the
cabin, the students climbed the hill behind the cabin as John Hornby,
Harold Adlard, and Edgar Christian would have done countless times
searching for food. A wolf ambled by. Morten instructed each student
to find whatever hiding spot they could find and sit quietly. Slowly and
decidedly, the wolf came close to each student's hiding spot, had a sniff
and a sideways glance, and moved on to the next student, visiting all. A
moving experience for each student personally delivered.

Morten, the northern educator, had just struck gold. Students can
be thankful for his wise reading of Edgar Christian's journal the day
before and the wander about for one last reflective moment. He certainly
had some help from that wolf. Education in situ indeed. Morten knows
how to create a pedagogical moment in the northern wilds.

11

Linda Leckie:
Place Dweller

Linda Leckie (Lecko) and I first met at children's camp in the 1960s, almost for sure. Perhaps it was a regatta in Wigwam Bay of Camp Ahmek or passing by on a lake as a Wapomeo girls' cabin group passed by my cabin group on Ragged or Joe lakes, Algonquin Park. There were likely many fleeting meetings. We almost had opportunities to cement a friendship in the late 1970s. We were both guiding canoe trips for Camp Wapomeo in Algonquin, Temagami, and Quetico-Superior Parks. We just didn't get a chance to guide together. In the 1980s we both went into Outdoor Education studies in university. Lecko went out west to the University of Calgary and I stayed in Ontario.

The point here is that our lives followed similar paths in youth to adulthood. So when we met, I think we both thought we'd known each other for years, certainly a decade. Once we'd certainly met — I cannot pinpoint the time and place — we were instant colleagues as educators and camp folks.

Over the decades to the present, we have travelled together in many parts of eastern Canada by canoe and kayak. We have together led many professional educators' workshops at conferences for the likes of the Council of Outdoor Educators of Ontario and the Association for Experiential Education. We share many of the same friends, affiliations, philosophies, upbringing (at camp for two months), same summer residence in Algonquin park, same activities, and in many cases same mentors. Lots of sames. But there is an essential difference that will be the focus here. While we share the same passion for our cottage/camping/ day tripping residence in Algonquin Park over all four seasons, Lecko's passion and knowledge and commitment exceeds mine in spades. And this has always been pleasing and a source of learning for me. Lecko is an Algonquin Park place dweller.[1]

Being well-grounded is a personality trait that is usually applied to mean that one is comfortably surrounded by a familiar place and good friends. Being well-grounded, I think, defines Linda Leckie. In this case childhood is important. Childhood images of that little girl at her Cache Lake cottage slamming the screen door, swimming off the dock, and waving at the canoe trips passing by; these and many more images and life expressions from that Algonquin cottage remain central to Lecko still. The little girl finally got to go to camp and go on her own camp canoe trip at age seven. She wanted it badly, and she's never looked back.

Canoe trips in Algonquin with camp would become the highlight of her year, and camp offered the teenager trip lengths that allowed her to get to know the park's interior canoe routes well. Linda took pride in coming to know the place. I know this feeling. We both had a park map with our routes marked out and the promise of adding to our knowledge next year. There were also camp trips as campers and later as staff in Temagami and the Quetico-Superior.

Roots and wings go together. As an adult, Lecko has travelled widely in Canada with friends. The Nahanni River in the Northwest Territories and the Stikine in British Columbia, the Mingan Islands in Quebec, the Eastern Shore in Nova Scotia in a sea kayak, and a winter Labrador snowshoe trip would be highlights of spreading wings. We've been on some of these friendship trips together. In fact, it was Lecko who reminded all that my 2005 book, *Every Trail Has a Story*, could be called *Every Trail Has Another Story*. We joke of the time I confused the dish soap with cooking oil and after a few attempted cleanings blurted out in frustration, "That's it, no more bacon on trips!" Trips generate new stories. Lecko has a knack of always remembering these.

Linda Leckie.
Photo courtesy of Don Standfield.

The lifestyle of an outdoor educator is hectic in and out of the classroom. I am reminded of the line in the Beatles' *Abbey Road* song "The End" where they say you give and take equal amounts of love. And Lecko shares the love, particularly of Algonquin. She will retire in 2014 from Bishop Strachan School in Toronto, where she has run a vibrant outdoor education program (among other responsibilities). No surprise her students would have experienced fall, spring, and winter seasons in Algonquin, canoeing, hiking, and dog sledding. They'd also have these experiences while told the tales of park rangers, Tom Thomson, the early 1900s lodges, camps, and loggers — colourful folk of the park.

For Lecko, this educator's lifestyle also involved, and presumably will continue to involve, contributions to professional organizations.[2] There was also time and likely more time in the years ahead for stewardship initiatives. Linda is active on the Board of Algonquin Eco Watch. I have joined her and fellow Algonquin enthusiasts to clear bush and generally restore and maintain the graves at the Opeongo Lake John Dennison farm site. This is good work. I have joined in on a quest to discover the sketching site of artist Tom Thomson's 1914 *Northern River* painting. We had a good theory to pursue.[3] As Lecko settles into more time in her home in Huntsville and Algonquin, I have no doubt there will be more purposeful Algonquin explorations.

One could argue that folks who spread their wings best do so from a well-grounded position. One understands new places best when one dwells well in a place. The relationship of person to place is a complex one. Human geographer E.C. Relph has made a significant contribution toward unpacking this relationship. His insideness-outsideness continuum attempts to describe an individual's feelings for a place in seven levels from outside to inside. This involves indices of increasing knowledge, comfort, and involvement. As the theory goes, a person's relationship to a place at a given point in time may start somewhere along the seven-level continuum. The most outside level is that of "existential outsideness" (involving self-conscious and reflective uninvolvement with place), but may advance to level three "incidental outsideness" (place is experienced as only a background for human activity — it's the activity that matters most). From here a person's relationship to a place shifts to "insideness." Level four is "vicarious insideness" (which involves feelings of deep involvement with a place without actually visiting or being in it — for many Canadians, this is our relationship with the North). This may advance to level six "empathetic insideness" (involving getting beyond the simple awareness of the qualities of a place, which is level five, "behavioural insideness," to having empathetic involvement).

Level seven is "existential insideness." Here one experiences feelings of deep belonging to a place. Relph suggests this final insideness level seven is almost impossible, in our modern times, to achieve. The forces of our modern influences of "placelessness practices" are an overriding presence in our lives.[4] Well, tell that to Lecko — and her students — and the friends like myself that she has influenced and those that have influenced her. She is a level seven as a place dweller in Algonquin. I know this in my heart because I am not. As roots and wings go, I've got too much of the wings thing going on, and Relph, I think, would agree that a level can easily appreciate the next levels backwards into outsideness and forwards into insideness. Hmm, maybe that is me theorizing, not Relph. No matter, Lecko inspires me toward being rooted in place.

Lecko is aware of place-responsive work, bucking the modern trend whereby technology can only mean handheld devices and screens. She teaches that technology is also the brilliant, simple efficiency of a reflector oven for baking bannock, not to mention the snowshoe, canoe, and dog harness. Lecko, the place dweller educator, knows the value of presenting the land as teacher with the important related role of storytelling, particularly from the area elders. She wisely elevates the traditional (when still most efficient) technologies for travel and dwelling on the land so that students and friends appreciate an inherent time proven wisdom. Progress is under scrutiny with Lecko. There is an old-timer Algonquin "smarts," like "street smarts" that one would be wise to pay homage to.

C.A. Bowers refers to low- and high-status learning in today's schooling. High status worships progress and relies on experts and global perspectives. Lecko teaches what Bowers calls low-status knowledge. This knowledge is land-based and honours the local folk and story and tradition. We need more low-status knowledge to help return people to place.[5]

Australian writer Tim Winton has said, "But in an age when a culture looks first to politics and ideology to examine itself perhaps my forgetting something so basic [as the role landscape exerts] should come as no surprise … our creaturely existence is registered, measured, discussed and represented in increasingly abstract terms."[6] This is a problem for the outdoor educator and place dweller. Put as simply as I can, Lecko doesn't fit into the above culture. Lecko lives with the forces landscape exerts lovingly. Her central inheritance through childhood experiences of cottage, camp, friends, mentors, and teaching is "place" — Algonquin.[7] In not fitting in, Linda Leckie is a superb example and mentor for many a student and friend who sense something is wrong with too much politics and ideology and too much creaturely existence separate from the primacy of place/landscape/nature (too much outsideness and high-status knowledge). Margaret Atwood in a convocation speech at the University of Waterloo in the 1980s said, "Nature used to surround us. Now we surround Nature and the change isn't necessarily for the better."[8] Well, the nature of Algonquin surrounds Lecko (no matter where she is) and the result, for all to see, is for the better.

12

André-François Bourbeau:
Scientist and Historical Re-Enactor

A ndré once called me into the Camp Ahmek kitchen on Canoe Lake in
Algonquin Park to test chocolate pudding. He was experimenting with
recipes, determined to perfect his craft. I was to return on the hour three or
four times that afternoon to product test different batches of pudding. Now
that's a friend. We were both in our early twenties. I was back from guiding summer camp canoe trips and he was head chef for over 450 campers
and staff. Many things are on a big scale for André. Looking back, I think
I thought he was in his thirties, not because he looked it but because of the
job. Big responsibility for a peer my age. Later that summer, I followed him
as he went into the nearby woods foraging for edible plants for his lunch. It
didn't go unacknowledged by me that one might question his preference for
wild foods in spite of the great fare freely available in the kitchen.

Both these inspired moments for me are likely long forgotten for
André. He's had a multitude of such experiments. Me, I make the pudding in the package and eat in the dining hall. Not André! He is a scientist, his lab is nature, and he has a strange and wonderful commitment
to perfection and experimentation, be it with gear (modern and historical), technique (anything), or living comfortably in nature (primarily the
boreal forest circa 1720–1850 in survival mode).

André grew up the oldest son in a large family. He lived in Spragge,
Sudbury, and Toronto as a child with ample time to explore the bush around

the neighbourhood. By the age of thirteen, he had an early calling as magician "The Great André." Individual sports, like wrestling and bicycle racing, dominated high school life. In university André had another calling. This time it was the engineer Cyril Smith from the Jules Verne novel *The Mysterious Island*. The character Smith could solve problems independent of modern society's consumer fixations. Smith could live comfortable in nature with his wits and a spirit of trial and error. As André puts it, following in Cyril Smith's footsteps became a life's aspiration to "discover nature's magic secrets."[1] Indeed, this became a lifelong obsession. Obsessed! That's the word survivor man Les Stroud uses to describe André. I concur, and add scientist, re-enactor, and adventurer. You see, André has made many 100-percent commitments to the blending of adventure, historical re-enactments, and research. Here are a few examples.

Still in our twenties, I watched André obsess over and thus revive our camp's water boiling contest. This is a fire making speed event. The object is to bring to a boil a small amount of water (with some soap flakes to dramatize the boil over) as quickly as possible. It is all about a choice piece of pitch pine (with ample flammable pitch) and a quick fire starting process. You have to be good with an axe or knife. You get one match. André also revived a fire by friction challenge that ebbs and flows as a camp tradition. André is a master of this and not because it is a good stunt and fun to share (as was my aspiration on this front) but because he needs this skill given a collection of survival experiences he had engaged in. Bigger challenges would incorporate such finely honed skills.

We both headed to graduate schools, he to the University of Northern Colorado to study survival technique. We both ended up as young university teachers and now have both retired, affording more time for outdoor travels and, in André's case, continued research. Recently, we shared our passion for exploration literature. I wrote up the general outline of the Franklin 1818–1820 overland expedition and its torturous survival march, and André experimented with making a watercraft capable of floating men across a rapid with the same sorts of meagre materials that Franklin's man Pierre St. Germain had at his disposal. Same interests: different questions. Let's get back to the past and André's experiments.

There is the "must-mention" Survivathon: a thirty-one-day voluntary late summer survival immersion into the boreal forest with the clothes on one's back and a wallet and two cookies.[2] Cyril Smith would be so proud. André coined the expression "the charcoaled commandos" for him and survival partner Jacques Montminy. But any light-hearted muse was certainly tempered with the genuine struggles and experiments in maintaining a degree of comfort and ... oh yeah ... survival.

Yes, they were out in the forest without any gear (no matches, no knife, no bug dope), nor had they brought food for thirty-one days. A grand success. Weight was lost but certainly no pride was tampered with and a resolve was set for more experimentation on the grand scale.

Only a few years later, in 1988, André, in pursuit of a funding grant and a challenge to celebrate 150 years of the colonization to the Saguenay–Lac-Saint-Jean region, hatched a plan to retrace Louis Normandin's 1732 first survey of the region.[3] The route was an ambitious canoe trip in the Lac-Saint-Jean region. The group of four in two birch-bark canoes borrowed from the Kanawa Canoe Museum[4] would travel upriver on the Ashuapmushuan, Chigoubiche, Licorne, and Normandin rivers to Nicabau. Here, at the site of a former fur trade post, the crew would return with bales of fur roughly on the same route downstream. On the Chicoutimi River mouth at the Saguenay fjord they would board an early nineteenth-century replica sailing vessel for three days and finish after a total of forty days at Tadoussac on the St. Lawrence River.

So, from charcoaled commandos to coureurs de bois re-enactors, the authentic right-down-to-the-underwear group had made a variety of gear. This included a pig-bristle toothbrush (presumably they shared), bars of soap made from fat and ashes, cow gut sacs to store gunpowder (for flintlock muskets), bear grease, hand-forged needles, and spruce pitch for canoe repair. They carried rum too. The project was nicknamed Retro-Propulsion — back paddling in rapids and into another time. André had found another outlet for research through historical re-enactments. He would learn to pole a canoe upriver as Normandin's men certainly had. He would study the breaking strength of five-millimetre spruce root. Certainly there would be many more historically focussed projects, usually involving students at the University of Quebec

André-François Bourbeau in a spruce bark canoe.
Photo courtesy of Billy Rioux.

at Chicoutimi, where the outdoor lab would see experiments in various natural materials and techniques for survival and historical exploration like no other lab in the country and perhaps the world.

A final and quite recent story (2012–2013) involves the scientist trial and error guy André with historical adventurer Billy Rioux heading into James Bay country for two weeks in two spruce back canoes. André says of historical re-enactments, you must have a specific time period in mind and stick to it, and you must find or create a scenario that makes sense historically. André and Billy created a plausible story. It was the 1870s (pre-matches) and they had to warn a community about logging that was to be initiated in their region. They had no canoes and a sudden need, so as the history books tell us, readily available materials in this region for a quick canoe construction meant spruce. They had many questions about the spruce bark canoe. This was the true passion.

In 2012, they made a white spruce bark canoe as a trial run. It didn't hold up well to storage. This was an early discovery. In 2013, they took eight days to build two spruce bark canoes. André had made birchbark canoes before and knew from Adney and Chapelle's classic *The Bark Canoes and*

Skin Boats of North America that not only was it common practice to build spruce bark canoes, but that wood rib spacings could be much wider than the usual one to two inches.[5] André had also seen a spruce bark canoe at the Prince of Wales Museum in Yellowknife. In fact, this had served as the original impetus. André had also remembered an Eastern Cree story of a trapping family needing an extra canoe given their exceptional success one winter on the trapline. Seems all the fur and all the family couldn't fit in their one birchbark boat. The solution was to send the family and half of the fur back downriver. The trapper stayed behind and built a "quick-fit" spruce canoe and joined the family later with the rest of the furs. This was all he needed to launch a new summer's project.

He also found a gem of a reference, "Making a Spruce Bark Canoe" by Barbara Winter. He sent me the following passages, as if I was a non-believer, about the possibility of spruce bark. Honestly, I do find it hard to believe:

> ... the Dogrib, Mountain, and Slavery Tribes [of the NWT] used them. Temporary spruce bark canoes were used to traverse lakes and rivers, and to gain access to remote hunting areas. Being small, they were easily portaged and carried into the mountains ... Johnny Klondike of Fort Liard said that when he was younger he could build a canoe in two days, taking the first day to gather the material, and the second to assemble the canoe.[6]

André and Billy took a week for the same. Impressive? I think so.

What did they learn? Well, first off their planned route was too hard, and not because they were dressed and fed circa 1870. By 2013, this was old hat to André and Billy. The issue was the canoes. They leaked badly. They could only touch water or air. Hitting a rock in the water or tree branch on a portage meant a lengthwise tear (along the route of travel, so to speak) which required a stop to sew and pitch the split. Later in the two-week trip André realized there were new "holes" in the bark. He discovered spruce worms (like maggots) had entered the bark via the spruce pitch used for repairs. In all, at trip's end, André counted 110 patches. The spruce bark canoes were too fragile. They might do better next time, but just as likely, these temporary, quickly needed canoes were never meant for much serious work.

André was satisfied. The experiment was more about the canoes than the route. He had learned much about building and travelling in such a historical replica water craft, and not many people had done this. Classic André, the scientist, reflects, "as I paddle along, I suddenly realize I am floating on materials that surround us: wood, bark, roots, and pitch made from gum, animal fat and charcoal." It should go without saying, but André states the simple and profound: "Reliving the past by canoe tripping with traditional gear and garb sure provides a preciously unique understanding of history."[7]

I liken the above spruce bark canoe experiment to that early chocolate pudding experiment. Curiosity, experimentation, and striving for success: André is an obsessive seeker of knowledge and technique. Just yesterday, with power out throughout our neighbourhood, friends and I who know André joked about how much André would have enjoyed our mild predicament. We cracked jokes about what André would be doing as our house got colder. Where was André when we needed him? He would certainly have a plan for this predicament or would hatch one. Umm, suspend bedsheets as a shelter around the fireplace! Now I am thinking like André. I like that.

13
Adrienne Blattel:
Community Worker

I first met Adrienne in 1989. She was a big smile and big ideas student in McMaster University's Arts and Science program. The course we shared (you don't so much teach in this program as co-investigate) was Environmental Inquiry. I was confident Adrienne was going to be a lifer with the themes of this course. Her undergraduate thesis, under my constantly amazed supervision, was on water. That's right, water! She explored water deities, water and toxins, tsunamis, and flood control. It was sweeping and great. I remember hoping we would stay in touch, and we have.

Adrienne explored environmental and social justice issues (specifically politics of heritage interpretation) in the Environmental Studies department at York University for her master's degree and walked seamlessly into a great job with the Quebec-Labrador Foundation (QLF): one of those "hire the bright intern" jobs. She thrived in rural economic renewal work helping establish local community museums in the northern peninsula of Newfoundland and the Lower North Shore of Quebec.

I joined her, but I think she would say she joined me, for a sea kayak trip on the Lower North Shore of Quebec where she had done field work. We moved onto Newfoundland, where she had just helped the Irish community of Conche on the French Shore of the Northern Peninsula establish links to their region's early French heritage. *What great work. What a great job*, I thought.

Adrienne Blattel.
Photo courtesy of Adrienne Blattel.

So I was surprised when I got a call one day in 2009 seeking my input. Adrienne would soon leave QLF for a venture that has now become Plein Air Interculturel. I'm not sure either of us was sure what it was at that early formative stage. I thought it was a wonderful brave, determined move to leave a good choice job in her field of training. She was ready for new challenges.

This too would be good work, and certainly self-directed. Adrienne would help newcomers to Montreal/Quebec/Canada experience our brand of outdoor recreation. Why? It would help people come to feel at home here. It would be good for newcomers who wanted to move past that label. And in Adrienne's words, "it was such a waste of good snow" that folks who wanted outdoor winter (and summer) experience had a hard time entering the outdoor culture. This is entirely different than 1970s Premier Henri Bourassa saying, "such a waste of water" when seeking support for his dream project, the James Bay Power Project, that would dam rivers for hydro power.

Adrienne points out that immigrants in Canada represent nearly 20 percent of our total population. She adds, "Some amount of adjusting is inevitable and necessary for everyone as demographics shift and cultures evolve. We need to create inviting spaces where people of different backgrounds can get to know each other."[1] It really is a simple premise. Adrienne would share her love of outdoor recreation with newcomers, often low-income newcomers. All would benefit. Since that first new camping outing, Adrienne has developed outdoor programming in all four seasons. She organizes approximately seventy-five outings per year, with five hundred participants yearly hailing from fifty different countries. Some have been here only two weeks, others for thirty years. In total, that is over fifteen hundred people, including refugee claimants, international students, permanent residents, citizens, and people who were born in Montreal and elsewhere in Canada.

Soon funding came from private supporters and various companies (Mountain Equipment Co-op is a big fan) and from kind donations. People in Montreal saw the light and wanted success for Plein Air Interculturel.[2] Adrienne had supporters who helped it all happen and has built relationships in Montreal. She runs Thursday night snowshoe walks on Mount Royal, sort of like the Montreal Snow Shoe Club (Tuque Bleue) did in the late 1800s, although their excursions usually finished at the local tavern.[3] She runs short (three-day affordable and accessible) canoe trips in north Montreal locations. Outdoor French-English language exchanges are popular. Here, a mixed linguistic group simply goes for a walk in a local park, splitting their time speaking each other's primary language. This activity is called Urban Hiking and Conversation. She is now living her vision for Plein Air. I am thrilled to be one of her promoters. Keen to spread the word, I have encouraged her to write in outdoor education journals and have had her share her work as a conference keynote speaker. She writes and speaks about the joy and challenges of the work.[4] The keen folks that sign up for her outings often have no necessary equipment, such as warm winter clothing or a summer raincoat. Specific religious practices and food arrangements provide some challenges beyond the obvious gear, logistics, and skill levels. She takes all these barriers in stride, making them seem minor. She focuses on the joys of participation, of being a provider connecting keen folks to Canadian outdoor life. "I've learned too that simple inner-city outings can be as meaningful as longer trips. Here in the city, people get to experience all sorts of surprising things for the first time, including raccoons and birch trees, a breathtaking view of the city or even taking the subway for the first time to get to a meeting point." Lovely! We might all learn to be re-enchanted with our home through the eyes of newcomers. There is nothing worse than the "enthusiasm killer" seasoned outdoors type, who, when a newcomer spots their first moose, responds, "Heck, I've seen hundreds of them, bigger than that, too." Adrienne is at the other end of the continuum. I trust she would inspire many of the seasoned outdoors folk to see the land through new eyes. But Adrienne is not just an inspiration for others, she is much inspired by her own work. Better in her words, she writes,

> What a delight for me in particular to get to travel around the world without leaving my city, to hike and paddle and snowshoe with friendly folks from every corner of the earth. And while it would be impossible to offer this programming to all of the several million newcomers living here in Canada right now, I hope that by sharing this experience that others will feel encouraged to organize something along these lines elsewhere in the world, and will have the privilege of being outside in such an inspiring context.[5]

I asked Adrienne for a heritage or philosophical quote that provides meaning for her work. Adrienne is charting new ground in outdoor education in Canada. She is totally looking forward, and she is inspiring young educators to follow her. I saw this prominently in my last years of teaching university. Together we arrived at "Mon Pays/My Country," a song by Gilles Vigneault. The song was commissioned by the National Film Board of Canada for a 1965 film, *La neige a fondu sur la Manicouagan*. Quebecers know this song. Newcomers to Quebec should know it, but more importantly they should be able to feel it walking snowy trails of Mount Royal, Montreal. They should begin to feel welcomed by the seasons, feel at home.

A Plein Air Interculturel outing in Montreal.
Photo courtesy of Adrienne Blattel.

Adrienne is close to forty now. (In 2009 I taught the daughter of one of my 1984 class students — time to retire). Adrienne has years to develop Plein Air Interculturel. She is a self-proclaimed ambassador for Canadian winters. She will happily point out that people have to learn to enjoy winter and it doesn't always come easy. For the newcomers that ask, "How?" Adrienne is there! And so, from humble beginnings at Ontario's Camp Oconto (I wonder just how important children's summer camps are for advancing later outdoor health) and a crystallizing experience at a hiking club in Europe's Montenegro that wisely integrated culture, language, and outdoor activity,[6] Adrienne is creating a culture of coming together in an outdoor setting, helping people to feel at home in their new place in nature. Over lunch one lovely spring day in Old Montreal, Adrienne told me stories such as that of an Algerian woman catching fat snowflakes falling from the sky in pure delight. All she could say was, "I am so grateful."

14
Mark Smith and Christine Kennedy: Map-Makers

M ark Smith and I can share in a fond memory from our university days together. We were on a McMaster University credited winter camping course that we and others had lobbied to create. It was a five-day camp just west of the Algonquin Park border. It was a cold camp but eventful for both of us for in the learning and camaraderie experienced. On our return down the No. 11 Highway we stopped at a public works station (likely not an approved activity). We both remember it the same way, which is remarkable because it was over thirty-five years ago. We couldn't bear the reality of returning to urban Hamilton with little snow. So on seeing the high mounds of snow-covered sand (presumably meant for road work) we strapped on our skis for one more ski outing, a rather silly one at that. It was a hilarious frolic with steep side step up and silly stressfully fun downhill. Once exhausted and rejuvenated with outdoor fun after too much car time, we returned to Hamilton. Perhaps in that moment, we bonded as friends for life.

Friendship continued via the sport of orienteering. Christine Kennedy was also at McMaster (though later than Mark and I) and into orienteering. We all competed with different techniques: Mark with a calm, steady, precise mind and me with an overzealous recklessness I couldn't seem to manage. It is no surprise, therefore, that Mark soon ventured into the calm, steady, precise activity of map-making and I continued to run wild in the woods at events. I've always thought orienteering is a good way to meet a life partner. Lots of terrain to navigate in starting a relationship and in any orienteering competition. Mark and Christine got off to a good start … as did Mark and I.

Mark and Christine's second date was at a map-making project at Lake Erie's Rondeau Park. Doesn't sound very romantic to me, but an offer for that long car ride home did the trick. Mark had offered to drive Chris home from Clairemont Environmental Education Centre to York University (twenty minutes away) but they drove on together to Rondeau (two and half hours away). That part *does* start to sound romantic. Together they competed in orienteering events and took up map-making initially for orienteering. Branching out to mapping outdoor education centres and summer camps, they created a business — successful, but poverty ridden at times. Map-making back in the 1980s involved intense field work. Compass, pencil, pacing to denote and record features on a base map, but that is too simple; a trained eye and attention to detail are paramount skill sets. Together Mark and Christine were inseparable honing this craft.

Chrismar Mapping Services Inc., a small map-making business, grew out of their early orienteering and map-making clinics. Chrismar celebrated thirty years in 2013! It was a small business: a sub-culture within a sub-culture. The map-making fraternity with the orienteering group was a special group. Due to a life changing attack on Christine's life (before she met Mark), she was to have eleven surgeries in their first five years together. A traditional work environment wasn't a sound idea for the young couple. They started working together and have continued together as a staff of two since early 1983. Canada is a huge country, and our maps, generally speaking, were not up the standard set in Europe. Amazingly, Mark and Christine set out to map the darn place for anyone who asked, and sometimes when they didn't: a modern day David Thompson experience, you might say.[1] People thought they were crazy. I thought they were crazy. "You will never make a living making maps," they said. I said the same when I received a phone call asking for my opinion on starting an adventure map series of provincial and national parks. Yup, I gave them my opinion. "You're crazy! These places you mentioned already have maps. Stick with camps." Yup, I was crazy wrong.[2]

Mark Smith and Christine Kennedy in Iceland.
Photo courtesy of Mark Smith.

What fun they have had with the adventure maps series. Among their first in the series were Point Pelee and Lake O'Hara. Algonquin Park, in a collection of choice small, detailed maps, has been a grand success. Auyuittuq National Park in Baffin Islands was completed after fourteen days doing detailed fieldwork under the likes of Mount Thor with Mount Asgard visible from lovely Summit Lake. Soon parks were calling them. The Pinery, Bon Echo, Temagami, Quetico, and Rogers Pass: you guessed it, all Chrismar. Just completed is the ambitious Woodland Caribou Provincial Park map in northwestern Ontario. Also in the works are maps of Frontenac, Kawartha Highland Provincial Parks, and Lake Louise. These folks are active in lovely places. On this front, they knew what they were getting into. That is, a life of self-propelled detailed travel in Canada's most beautiful places.

But while one would be right to think of maps first, Chrismar's "small is a beautiful" business also does custom work by way of books (including this one), banners, brochures, city trail guides, and kiosk signage. Let me just indulge in a quick list of Chrismar's eclectic mix of custom map-making or cartography projects over the last thirty years:

World Cup and World Championship mountain bike course maps and profiles; Cuba Economic Development Study maps; Metro Toronto Zoo grounds map; Atlanta Olympics Visitor's Map and Guide; guides to New York City, Veradero Cuba, Tampa, Winnipeg, Vancouver, Ottawa, Chicago, etc.; Pukaskwa Coast historic map poster; Riding Mountain National Park Ski Trails map and brochure; City of Waterloo Cycling Trail Map guide; City of Cambridge downtown map signs; magazine maps as consultant/cartographer (eg. *Birders Journal*, *Kanawa*, etc.). In Mark's words, "I make as many as five hundred to a thousand unique maps a year. Many for long-term clients."

It is fun to consider, I think, the pleasure in getting to know the places and people involved in these projects, and in knowing that it is a very limited number of businesses that could do all this kind of work. Chrismar have carved a special niche. Being small (still a staff of two) means it is possible to be easily overwhelmed. They do not advertise. All work comes from referrals. They work out of their home. It is efficient, simple, and clean, just like their maps. Best of all, they travel this country on foot and by canoe with a solid purpose. Forthcoming field work includes time on Lake Superior for a Pukaswka South map and the White Otter Lake–Turtle River region of northwestern Ontario. "Ahhh, what a country," they would say. Pause to consider all the places mentioned here.

There are stories aplenty when you seek the details on the landscape as they do. The nooks and crannies of a landscape must be mapped. Christine was aglow telling me about bison encounters in Elk Island Provincial Park, Alberta. Mark enjoyed discussing Grey Owl walking the streets of Biscotasing, Ontario, and Tom Thomson almost drowning on the Mississagi River. Together Mark and Christine are exploring chunks of Canada, mapping its details and generalities, often working in the off-season when most of us never see these places. In thoughtful, abbreviated fashion, on the back of their adventure map series they share the natural and human heritage of the region in fine form. In short, they really get into the place. In Mark's words, "You might think it is capturing data, but to map a landscape, you must see the land as art, or we do, anyway."

I asked the Chrismar staff to offer up a defining passage that encapsulates their work. They selected the well-known final lines from the Robert Frost poem "The Road Not Taken."

Two roads diverged in a wood, and I —
I took the one less travelled by,
And that has made all the difference.[3]

Together, they described some of the forks in their own roads. There was Christine's attack and follow up health issues that necessitated lifestyle decisions. Here they took the road less travelled. Creating a mapping business despite the "you're crazy" advice is a road less travelled which led to early poverty and later success financially. Keeping the Chrismar brand at a high quality and keeping the business small — small is beautiful — is another decided road diverging in a unknown wood. Of course, for map-makers the forks in the trail/the less travelled by are critical to the printed product as well. It should be noted that the challenges that Mark and Christine faced in their early years together with health issues and struggling business start-up bespeaks challenges a bit more severe than most of us face as a young couple. This, along with fieldwork mapping, forges a powerful life partner bond that one easily sees now in their life together.

To close, Mark and Christine emphasized to me that they are map-makers as well as map drawers. The distinction demands attention. As map-makers, Mark Smith and Christine Kennedy travel the landscape slowly in a self-propelled, thoughtful manner. They create a map.[4] They capture the land and water nuances as data for the page, but they see the land as art. It is a creative/artful business, a rewarding contribution to the overall preservation mandate (if you don't map it — people don't go there), and a beautiful active life.

15
Mike Beedell:
Photographer and Adventurer

Mike Beedell and I go back to grade six. Smacking each other in the shoulder and eliciting a yelp when the teacher was not looking was our favourite game. It was great fun. Hey, it was grade six. At age sixteen, we convinced our respective parents that we were old and wise enough to travel to Banff, Alberta, for a downhill ski trip. We learned the importance of correctly setting an alarm clock when we almost missed that all-important bus trip back to the airport. Hey, we were only sixteen. It was our first grand adventure on our own. We also learned the excitement of a travel adventure with a good friend.

I moved to Hamilton for university. Mike went to the University of Ottawa, but university time was dominated by an opportunity to work with a fledgling business called Blackfeather Wilderness Adventures under the umbrella of Trailhead with Wally Schaber and Chris Harris.[1] Mike got in on the ground floor and paddled the Coppermine River in 1977, Blackfeather's first offering on this classic river. This started an annual northern pilgrimage for Mike guiding trips on Arctic rivers. Mike started to document his journeys in pictures. They were good in part because of the places themselves but mostly because Mike had the patience and energy to do what it takes to capture the essence of a place and reveal unique wildlife behaviour. By 1980, his photographs had attracted some attention. Parks Canada commissioned Mike to document a climb of

Mount Logan, Canada's highest peak at 19,850 feet. It was Mike's first serious assignment as a photographer, and soon after he was given a book contract by Oxford University Press to produce a work on the Arctic.

In 1983, Mike's book, *Magnetic North*, was released by Oxford University Press. Many a door now opened for the acknowledged Arctic photographer and adventurer. I was thrilled for Mike and happy our first big adventure downhill skiing in Banff at sixteen would lead to some trips together, like Baffin Island (See Chapter 5) and Tasmania and on horseback returning in the Banff area.

Mike Beedell.
Photo courtesy of Mike Beedell.

Mike and I joke particularly about that Tasmania hike with inflatable canoes into a river run trip, the Denison River next to the more famous Franklin River. We remember hysteria shared when the temperate jungle meant we found ourselves, to our surprise, elevated while hiking, six feet off the ground. We had climbed a mass of horizontal forest trunks, limbs, and general forest debris. We expected a two day-hike into the river; it turned out to be eight days of hiking. While on the hike, Mike woke me from a sound slumber to tell me his eye was sore. We were sleeping under tarps to lighten our loads and so were exposed a bit more to the elements. Well, he had a Tasmanian devil of a leech on his eyeball. It brushed off, but there was a moment of confused terror for both us. He had one red eyeball — I mean scarlet red — for about ten days.

For that Baffin Island ski tour, Mike had been hired to create images for the Canadian Office of Tourism. I was a model (it was a short career). He had been to Auyuittuq National Park before for solo ski trips on photo assignments with Travel Arctic. Now he needed skiers. It was a dream come true for two friends who'd first headed west as teens for mountain skiing. Here we were on Baffin glaciers. No lift lines, clean fall lines, and endless terrain (as long as you avoid high-risk crevasse areas and anything too vertical). I learned that the globe can be your playground from Mike. Don't settle for the Rockies, you can ski Baffin Island. Don't just go to a beach in the Caribbean, go there to swim with humpback whales.

Photography and adventures go hand-in-hand for Mike. Over the 1980s and 90s, Mike was involved in Hobie Cat sailing trips that culminated in crossing the Arctic Ocean Northwest Passage; retracing by dog team the Qitdlarssuaq expedition from Igloolik on Baffin Island into Ellesmere Island to finish at Qaanaaq, Greenland, a distance of 2,500 kilometres over four months (two summers), then four hours back by aircraft; and a sea kayak circumnavigation of Bylot Island (north of Baffin Island).[2]

More recently, Mike has developed photographic tours for specific clients and tour groups. This yearly cycle of trips involves the British Columbia coast to see the spirit bear, trips to Antarctic with Students-on-Ice, Mike as interpretive guide for Adventure Canada Tours of Arctic coastlines, ski tours somewhere on the Arctic Archipelago (in 2012 to the Devon Island Icecap), Polar Bear tours out of Hudson Bay, and a "swimming" with humpback whales trip off the coast of the Dominican Republic. If half of great photography is being in the right place at the right time, then Mike's clients would all be well regarded photographers. For great photography one has to add, I think, an evolving relationship with the animal/the species and the land. One has to develop knowledge of the patterns of the land and the wildlife. One has to develop a tacit knowledge — a sixth sense — for wildlife and habitat that amounts to respect, care, astonishment, even love. To get the best images, one has to be there with all the right reasons. Mike is the total package.

I asked Mike for a few choice stories to share. I realized over the years with phone calls and visits to his home in Gatineau, Quebec, that I had heard these stories before, but that is the joy in it. Mike's stories are exotic as adventure and art: fun and, at times, terrifying. He can tell them over and over with an obvious passion for the subject that sets him apart. I am conscious of being along for the ride, glowing in the enthusiasm he generates. If time or place allows, he will pull out the maps and show a selection of images. It is like Gil Grosvenor (former editor of *National Geographic*) once said to Mike: "A map is the greatest of all epic poems. Its lines and colours show the realization of great dreams." And so a Mike Beedell story or two.

Mike spent a week solo on the Baffin Island shore at the shortest distance between southwestern Baffin Island and Ungava-Arctic Quebec. He was photographing an ancient Inuit site that was the put-in and take-out for a serious water crossing of Hudson Strait in umiaks (skin-covered large boats). Here there are a wealth of *inuksuit* (stone sentinels) one would imagine served both as beacons (early lighthouses) but perhaps mostly as a way to appease the gods for safe passage. He felt energy in this ancient launching site, and with time he began to hear voices of elders and children playing. He could rationalize these feelings as being the strong winds. Imagine him mostly looking out to sea waiting for the best light to capture *inuksuit* presence on the land. He is hundreds of kilometres from the nearest other human, but he discovered, as he walked backwards, he had been within four metres of a very large polar bear. The tracks told the story of the bear he never saw. So enthralled with the land and light, he had let his guard down. A polar bear had collapsed his tent, pulled out his sleeping bag, and approached him only to stop at close range. One could refer to this as the secretive bear story. For Mike it is a true Arctic account. All the players are involved: the ancient presence of stone and spirit, the light, the sea, the wildlife, and human culture past and present.

Another story takes us further north to Devon Island, north of Ellesmere Island. In 2012, Mike and two European clients were dropped by Twin Otter aircraft from Resolute Bay onto the high Devon Ice Cap, for a high Arctic May ski tour. A week later they would descend the Sverdrup Glacier to the sea ice for a skidoo pickup from an Inuit friend living in Grise Fiord. Only problem was, the glacier descent (a gentle ski-able slope on the maps) had become a thirty-metre drop due to the rapid recession of the three-kilometre-wide toe of the glacier and a calving off of the end of the ice mass creating an iceberg still just offshore.[3] A problem! Mike spent a day searching for a safe descent and eventually found a spot where they could rappel down off the toe. At sea level, where the descent forced them to go, there were also polar bear tracks everywhere, including many going in circles, which indicated recent mating activity. At an *aglu* (seal hole) there were bright bloodstains of the recent kills on the ice. This was not a prudent place to spend much time lingering.

An ancient Inuit Inukshuk site to mark Umiak boat crossings on the Hudson Strait.
Photo courtesy of Mike Beedell.

While rappelling off the glacier, they succeeded in alarming the bear, who then, to their amazement, ran up the vertical iceberg immediately across from them. Claws as crampons: very functional they learned. Now they had a stressed and chuffing polar bear parallel to them staring at them eye to eye from across the hundred-metre gap from the glacier to the iceberg.

The bear relaxed and lay down atop the beautiful berg and finally went to sleep after many a portrait was taken by the skiers. Mike and his friends decided to stay on the glacier for the night, and after the bear awoke he watched them pull up their tents and finally felt safe enough to descend the glacier and hurry off into the white vastness of sea ice.

Mike Beedell has hundreds of stories. I'm proud to say I have listened to many of them over the years (and have even been involved in a few). Common to the stories, I've come to realize, is remoteness and wildlife and humour, perhaps a chilling humour mind you. Embedded in the stories and therefore embedded in Mike's life is a respect and passion for the land and wildlife and a burning desire to be among both. Mike is fond of quoting a Mongolian elder: "It is far better to experience a place just once than to hear about it a thousand times." I can't help but think that Mike experiences the North the way the North is best experienced. I think this takes years to learn — to bring to your life. I'm certain I don't have it, as it pertains to the Arctic, but with each story Mike shares I gain a bit more of that "becoming" insight. Still, one can't just hear about it, one has to experience a place. Mike continues to experience places wisely. Certainly, the Canadian Arctic is his realized great dream.

Mike says, "The richness of an extended journey for me often comes with the rythym & repetition of a self-propelled exploration. Where — by paddle, on skis or by foot — the body becomes a musical instrument played by the natural forces of wind, waves or snow. It is a communion with the landscape & its creatures coupled with the joy of shared experience which inspires my journeys."[4]

Mike is now applying his photographic skills toward issues of conservation and dwindling habitat for many creatures. He is spending time with them on the land and in the sea. He feels that there are far too many humans on the planet and that there is a great urgency to keep natural spaces protected for those creatures that undertake annual migrations as part of their life cycle. This includes whales, caribou, sockeye salmon, Arctic terns, and monarch butterflies. For they all need places to rest, feed, and rejuvenate themselves as they travel thousands of kilometres every year.

Be it on foot, on skis, by canoe, or by ship, sailing above or scuba diving below, Mike Beedell has a knack of communicating with the land and many of its creatures. He has a special affinity for migratory creatures. Friends might think this is in part because he appears to be a migratory creature himself. It seems he is always on the go between (mostly) the Arctic north and his Gatineau home. He returns with compelling stories of wildlife encounters and images that inspire us to celebrate those dwindling habitants. Thanks to Mike, our worlds are larger and more alive and we are better for this.

16
Diane Gribbin:
River Guide

In 1998, Diane Gribbin walked into my office, looked around, and blurted out, "Wait, you are not the cardiac rehab guy!"

"No, he's down the other hall," I said. Doesn't sound like much, does it, but that was the start of a great friendship. You see, I had been teaching outdoor education for almost two decades at McMaster University by then. I had accumulated lots of stuff. My office was adorned in images of outdoor experiences and student projects. "Adorned" is code for "happy mess." Diane was a fourth-year student in the fall term. That she didn't know of the Outdoor Education option within the Physical Education program bespeaks either its general importance within the program offerings and/or Diane's narrow focus at the time toward the health science profession.

She was outgoing, and we got talking with her still standing in the doorway. I learned she was a darn good soccer player (she still plays) and itching to find a home in health care. She had learned that despite just missing the nine-day canoe field trip, she could register for an Outdoor Environmental Education theory course in the winter term. We also discussed the connections of health and nature and activity, which seemed obvious in life but not necessarily as an avenue of study, even in Physical Education. I think she liked the pictures on the wall. It was the first and only time I am aware of all those pictures of past trips with students serving as a recruitment strategy.

Diane was a star student in that course. In April, I got a phone call from Neil Hartling of Nahanni River Adventures. He was seeking new, young, dynamic outdoor education students to join his river guiding staff. Despite Diane having missed our program's canoe trip, I had the feeling that she would be that special guide despite having little canoeing experience. Neil trusted my judgment. He said, something to the effect of: "Heck, I can teach the hard skills. I need interns — no pay — but a great introduction to river guiding support." From such entry opportunities Neil hoped to secure future staff. Diane was keen and spent the spring learning and helping at Hela Adventures out of Rocky Mountain House, Alberta. She graduated to the Nahanni River in the Northwest Territories by August, got her Parks Canada license to guide on the Nahanni River, and returned for over a decade. She became a premier guide for the successful northern rivers canoe guiding operation.

Beyond her summers guiding, which of course I will return to, Diane also completed an innovative master's graduate program in environmental education, through the Audubon Expedition Institute. In this program she travelled by bus in Alaska, the desert of southwest Mexico, Eastern Canada, and the United States, with fellow students visiting sites and people appropriate to students' collective and individual studies, camping along the way. She figures, with her summer's river guiding, she spent more than three hundred days sleeping outside during those years. She studied sustainable dwellings, the healing arts, and ecological education. This was just what she needed — a personal exploration on how to dwell well, cultivating ecological consciousness. Before this, she completed a three-year program in Homeopathic Medicine at the Canadian College of Homeopathic Medicine in Toronto. In the mix of time of these two alternative education programs, she studied Indigenous ways of knowing while also working on a homeopathic internship in England and volunteered at Fort Simpson, NWT, working with youth for a winter running on land healing and on-land literacy trips. This led to funding to guide a summer trip for three years with local Fort Simpson Dene youth down the Nahanni River. Diane also did some dog sledding in the Yukon. Her most memorable expedition was eighteen days with a ten-dog team travelling from Dawson to Whitehorse following the trail of the Yukon Quest. She also had a stint in East Timor, studying medicinal plants with her partner, Sean Collins, pack horsing to remote mountain grass hut villages to meet with community healers. In Ottawa, Diane worked for Health Canada in natural alternatives to pesticides and also in homeopathic and traditional medicine. There is a common thread here. In Diane's words, that thread is "health betterment and being embedded in Nature."

The house, oh yeah, the house — Diane and Sean bought property in the hills (they are atop of the hills) just northeast of Wakefield, Quebec. There, they set up a yurt to live in while they built, over three years, a circular home and studio of stacked cordwood that is off the grid and made largely from recycled materials. They learned everything necessary along the way; it's a marvellous project in environmentally sound practice and experiential learning. Sean (they met that first summer on the Nahanni River) now works for the Northern Region of Health Canada as a policy analyst for the territories (Yukon and NWT) on health issues in the North. Diane "holds down the fort." The home business is called the HeartWood Centre for Ecological Education and Healing Arts. She is immersed in seasonal practices of growing vegetables and herbs (on the Canadian Shield) and canning.

Diane Gribbin.
Photo courtesy of Diane Gribbin.

Diane tells me I had a role in all this. She remembers the teachings of Acclimatization Ecological Educator Steve Van Matre from that McMaster class years ago: if you go to the swamp, be the swamp.[1] Apparently, I fed Diane articles and was a sounding board along her path. Perhaps I anticipated needing lots of healing arts from friends along my path. These days Diane runs Tai Chi and Qigong classes (meditative and therapeutic movement) and when possible felting craft and sustainable building and living workshops. When I say "when possible," it is because there is a Jolly Jumper hanging in a white pine, and the canoe is just right for those Gatineau River paddles with the two kids.

Diane in 2006–07 had a seven-trip summer with Nahanni River Adventures on Arctic rivers. These rivers include the Nahanni (three times), the Burnside, the Soper (Baffin Island), and the Thelon. That's not much turnaround time between trips. It is over fifty days on Arctic rivers in a full summer into the fall season. She tells me that by the end of that summer, her close encounters with Arctic wildlife remain an experience into the mystical. She describes a beaver in crystal waters circling closer and closer to her till they were inches apart, so close she could see into the beaver's eyes and see the detailed lines of the webbed feet doing figure-eight motions in order to stay in place against a strong river current. Then the beaver climbed up on the bank and sat right next to her and chewed a stick. Then, at the end of the summer on the Thelon River, she had a wolf encounter. In the rainbow colours of the ground cover on the barrens in their autumn prime, Diane and a white Arctic wolf had a standoff and a shared howl at close range. The next day, the same wolf came into Diane and Sean's camp and lay down as if to join them for breakfast. In Diane's words, "By then in the late summer, I felt so embedded in the Arctic landscape that such intimate wildlife encounters seemed natural." Other trips with commercial outfitters included sea kayaking at Ellesmere Island coastline and other rivers including the Wind, Mountain, Big Salmon, and South Macmillan to name a few.

River guiding holds personal moments such as the above, but the art of guiding is ultimately a people-oriented affair. Diane shared a story of a man who had grown up loving the outdoors but for years was secure in an urban office job and deep into a busy family life with kids. Well into his Nahanni River trip he began remembering his youth. He described to Diane many powerful moments of reconnecting to the land as he came to remember his "heart song." Months after the trip he wrote a beautiful letter to Diane sharing how she had helped him realize his connections with the land and his desire now to be a similar guide for his own children. I think good river guides can receive this sort of swell of emotion over directing someone's life story. Good river guides model a way of being in good manners with the land, being comfortable and being at home. Diane has learned to "be the bog."

River guiding for so many summers involving so much of the summer has taught Diane to embrace wildlife encounters and celebrate special moments with fellow river travellers under her care. She has also learned to appreciate the delicate ecology of the Arctic landscape, her second home. She has learned about the changing North, a North more and more infiltrated by resource extraction industries, which she has seen firsthand. She has noted wildlife rhythms in disarray, particularly polar bears travelling inland up the Sopher River and unfamiliar caribou migration timing and location on the Burnside River.[2] Diane writes:

> I noticed, in this past season above all else, the differences to years past. I am concerned for the north, these places I have come to know and love, places that are woven deeply throughout me. I have shared these rivers with so many people, these powerful landscapes I've observed to deeply move and transform individuals, my own family included. I know that ultimately I have to be the change I wish to see in the world. I continue to write letters and join the campaigns to protect these places. But perhaps what has even more meaning is the empowered action I am taking in my own life on a daily basis. I am acting locally to create global change.

From that fateful day of walking into the wrong office in 1998[3] to guiding years up North and on one of the last McMaster canoe trips in

2010 (she finally got on that trip she missed as a student in 1998), Diane has had the special courage to pursue her own path interweaving health, sustainable and ecological living, and nature-based practices. She shared one of the important quotes that serve as a reference point in her life. From Aldo Leopold: "We can be ethical only in relation to something we can see, feel, understand, love or otherwise have faith in."[4]

The path that lies ahead for Diane certainly involves sharing her own heart song with others. The name of her home studio and workshop space, HeartWood Centre for Ecological Education and Healing Arts, speaks volumes to her work. As simply as I can put it, I think Diane, the river guide, healer, and educator, is on the right path for her and the planet. I am thrilled to be a part of this pathway, like others, like that beaver, wolf, and trip participant: all creatures that understand they are in the presence of something very genuine and well grounded, something that is good for person-planet relations.

EPILOGUE

Interviewer: Why did you start climbing?
Arne Naess: Why did you stop?[1]

This is a book about curiosity and exploration tied to a love of self-propelled travel, storytelling, and friendship. These activities were ones that I never started. Rather, as I see it, I never stopped.

For me, there was hide-and-seek in the neighbourhood, tearing around on bicycles over a bigger neighbourhood still, and then teachers and camp counsellors taking me to regional parks and wild lands, a still bigger place to know. There were always small groups of friends, largely free to wander and wonder. In so many ways, nothing's changed. Now trips are organized months in advance, be they three to six days away from home but still in a "home" environment or two weeks or more in a faraway "being-in-becoming"–inspired landscape. I am usually very conscious of learning with eyes wide, all senses firing in new settings that I am coming to know. One can be conscious of being in a supercharged fashion, and it follows that one is conscious of becoming ever anew.

This book opens with the epigraph, "The many become one and are increased by one." It should close with that too. It is a noble aspiration. There is always the desire to understand what it is to dwell well. It is important to have good manners and curiosity for the place, becoming comfortable and knowledgeable. One can ever expand one's notion of home, being a small person in a big landscape. That just feels really good to me. For this, one nurtures curiosity and exploration with places now and beyond. One is likely unabashedly enthusiastic and receptive to new stories in places. And one has a desire for storytelling and friendship. That is to say, to have a venue for sharing all that enthusiasm.

It feels fitting to close with thoughts from the last trip I was on before starting the final process of putting this book together. So I turn to my March 2013 field notes from a winter snowshoeing and wall tent camping trip in the Lac La Biche region of Alberta.

I love these four-day trips. It is a short, happy, liminal space, a space in between regular life events. More so, the short trip can be a happening. I was helping friend and outdoor colleague Morten Asfeldt and his travel buddy Craig Ferguson learn the ways of travelling with hand-held toboggans hauling snowshoes and wall tent and wood stove camping gear. Often, folks call it warm winter camping. But while it doesn't feel survival driven, it certainly isn't always warm.

Simply put, it is a style of winter living in keeping with the way woodland peoples have endured winter for centuries. An enclosed external heat source — a wood stove — is important to winter living. Morten takes students primarily to the nearby Rocky Mountains and the Arctic (see Chapter 10). As a teacher with integrity, he wants his students to experience a wider sample of Canadian and certainly Albertan ecosystems. Hence a four-day outing with new camping gear and a travel style well-suited to this Aspen Parkland/Lakeland environment. This camping and travel style is about the only realm of outdoor travel where I could help Morten. My number of nights in a wall tent (I estimate it's about 120, ballpark figure) matches his, plus twenty-plus day trips summer and winter. It felt good to realize one can amass a collection of the nuances of travel and camping so as to be helpful to others. One example: lay down a spruce bough inside the tent doorway so that moccasin-covered feet do not slip on the snow once it hardens and ices up. This was the stuff Morten was after.[2]

A trip like this is so many things. When I say it can be a "happening," I mean there is so much more than the obvious fun and friendship. The trip is anthropological. We get into another time and space away

Lakeland Park, Alberta.

from our regular lives. One creates, even in four days, a subculture in a small group on the land. Falling asleep to the crackling wood stove creates a rapport with another time. In this there is a restoration. You get better at the satisfying feeling, I think, with repeat awareness or, as some might say, performance.

The trip is sociological. It isn't just a friendship group. We are exploring ourselves together and relying on one another for the work, the entertainment, the act of living well. This has been called "taking on the role of the generalized other — the attitude of the whole community." Similarly, educator Simon Beames wisely notes, this "primary group" inter-reliance may occur at a deeper level on a group travel experience than in one's regular day-to-day life. It is a grand way to be and settle in for a while.[3]

The trip is geography and history. We intend to learn about this place. The Beaver River we crossed by car just before the Lac La Biche town site frames this region in the continental fur trade of the late 1700s. I was excited to photograph the river. Just east of where I stood on the road was the portage from the Beaver River to Lac La Biche to the Athabasca River system. This is a related portage, as an Athabasca watershed link connecting northern and southern watersheds with the Methye Portage and the Wollaston Lake and Fond du Lac land connections. It is an abstract feeling, but being in this region close to the portage helps put me in touch with this massive story of Canadian geography and history.[4] Certainly the Lakeland Park we travelled in was once a prime hunting ground for Cree and Chipewyan peoples living on this important headwater area.

The trip is psychological. There is a connection in moments to that primal latent spiritual impulse with nature one can feel with those first or last snowshoe strides. Heading out on that open expanse of sunny, glistening, snow-covered lake is more than just a feel-good moment. I think this has a lot to do with a complexity of humanity's connection to nature. Ahhh, the stillness, the cleanliness, that is the aura of winter. This ecopsychology conceptualization has merits to explain the highs of out-door travel and living. For folks who do it a lot, it is as natural an impulse as morning coffee and just as addictive. For folks new to, or foreign to, camping, it helps explain the confused question: Why?[5]

Too often, all folks hear and read are stories of epic proportion and scale. Magazines and films tend to report on the epic. The closer-to-home outing, as in the outing I mention above, seems to hardly exist. The epic, to a great extent, is recorded, its techniques reviewed, its

A traditional snowshoe binding setup.

A wall tent drying system. Thank goodness hot air rises.

stories the ones told. For example, here is an antic Erling Kagge, a polar and Everest adventurer, shares: "I had shaved my backside laboriously to be sure that I could perform my ablations as speedily as possible, using the minimum number of sheets of toilet paper. Altogether I'd worked out I'd use three-and-a-half sheets a day."[6]

This is epic planning for an epic outing. I respect this sort of thing, but here I am celebrating the more accessible adventure of the spirit. I want to avoid what Norwegian educator Borge Dahle said when thinking about his concerns over the North American magazine *Outside*: "looks like a bunch of nature acrobats and narcissistic journalists."[7] I also want to avoid the overly goofy, entertaining, albeit likely fabricated account of outdoor travel that is just too aware of the camera and audience, just too aware of itself. I want to celebrate the wisdom to be gained in the open air. The travel experience with an echoing attention to the then and now, with the curiosity to study the mysteries and offbeat storylines of history and land, and with the desire to celebrate amassing an inspiring friendship circle of like-minded individuals to share in a good story that does Canada proud. It strikes me as a good way to advance in years. It strikes me as a good way to advance our culture.

I find myself this snowy November day staring at a completed collection of chapters in draft form. More or less, I'm done. Yet today I will follow a lead and visit a meeting tree well known to locals. Yesterday in the library I came upon two gems while looking for another would-be gem I didn't find. "I just have to include these stories," I thought. But wait, I'm done. I realize sitting here I am never done. I can't stop. The curiosity and exploration — tied to a love of self-propelled travel, storytelling, and friendship gained — just has no end game. So I will close with a new story and site I will follow up on in the years ahead; and, if so, why not a series rather than a sequel? I realize that if I'm done, but I can't stop fitting the themes of this book centrally into my life, then perhaps this *is* my life, or a big part of it, a part I can't seem to get away from even if I try. So here is a story I will tell better once I have been there in the follow-up to *More Trails, More Tales* (if all goes well).

On Lake Windermere in southeast British Columbia there are two very old Douglas fir stumps. I hope. It seems David Thompson, the great map-maker and explorer, camped at this site by these trees 206 years ago. He and his men built a fire at the base of one Douglas fir. A significant axe cut was made deep into another nearby fir. Later he moved the campsite to a more sheltered site where he built Kootenay House. The two trees healed from their wounds over time, showing significant weeping pitch, a healing agent. When both trees died and were felled for safety (they are on cottage properties now) their annual growth rings were counted to the year Thompson and his party were on Lake Windermere. There are other tree physiology factors in play here. This evidence is supported by Thompson's detail reporting on his locations. In the 1950s, a simple plaque was erected to explain the significance of the campfire-scarred tree stump.[8]

There you go: yet another Canadian heritage site to visit by canoe, I hope. It makes sense to finish with one more tale on one more trail that explores Canada's travel heritage.

NOTES

Introduction: Following Blazed Trails

1. Alfred North Whitehead, *Process and Reality* (Cambridge, MA: Cambridge University press, 1926), 32.

2. For a history of Skoki Lodge see Kathryn Manry, *Skoki: Beyond the Passes* (Calgary: Rocky Mountain Books, 2001). To learn more about Ken Jones and Lizzie Rummel, see Lorne Tetarenko and Kim Tetarenko, *Ken Jones; Mountain Man* (Calgary: Rocky Mountain Books, 1996) and Ruth Oltmann, *Lizzie Rummel: Baroness of the Canadian Rockies* (Upshaw, AB: Ribbon Creek, 1983).

3. A fine overview of John Livingston's philosophy is found in David Cayley, *The Age of Ecology* (Toronto: James Lorimer, 1991). See page 11 for the "greater enterprise" passage.

4. Personal interaction with Professor Peter Higgins in Haeverstolen, Norway, at the Deep Environmental Education practice conference, January 2000.

5. Bob Henderson, *Every Trail Has a Story: Heritage Travel in Canada* (Toronto: Natural Heritage/Dundurn, 2005).

6. I am grateful to Nordic colleagues Nils Faarlund, Aage Jensen, and Jakob Thorsteinsson for regularly introducing me to Nordic words that help me understand human-nature relations.

7. Dave Oleson, "North of Reliance," in *Pike's Portage: Stories of a Distinguished Place,* edited by Morten Asfeldt and Bob Henderson (Toronto: Natural Heritage/Dundurn, 2010), 241. Also see Dave Oleson, *North of Reliance* (Minocaqua, WI: Northward Press, 1994).

8. Lawrence Durrell, *Spirit of Place: Letters and Essays of Travel* (Open Road Publishing, 2012).

PART ONE

Introduction: Peregrinations

1. I have never read Tolkien, but the first thing I read when I opened the exciting book by my friends Jim and Sue Waddington titled *In the Footsteps of the Group of Seven* (Fredericton: Goose Lane Editions, 2013) was, "Not all those who wander are lost." Here are kindred spirits, following a passion, wandering with purpose as a way to curb that special appetite for wondering.

2. Thomas King, *The Truth about Stories: A Native Narrative* (Toronto: Anansi Press, 2003), 152.

Chapter 1

1. Elizabeth Bradfield, "Why Shackleton's Stories Are Being Retold in Book and Film" in *Approaching Ice/Poems* (New York: Persea Books, 2010), 88.

2. In 2009, the Ibsen celebration on the border of Norway and Sweden was a hiking conference for sixty hikers/delegates travelling hut to hut with planned sessions along the trail and at huts. It was an inspiration for the Canadian Mara-Burnside conference in 2010.

3. Most of these treatments, all eminently worthy reads for outdoor travellers, can be found in a special theme issue of *Pathways: The Ontario Journal of Outdoor Education*, Vol. 24, No. 4 (Summer 2012). Of particular note are "Conference as Journey: Honouring our Pedagogical Roots" and "Learning from a Distressed Loon." In the former, Morten Asfeldt and Simon Beames expand on the wilderness expedition conference idea. In the latter, Swedish outdoor educator Hans Gelter describes an off-putting encounter with a nesting Arctic loon that led our group to relocate our camp after a five-kilometre portage. This issue can be retrieved from *www.coeo.org*. Go to *Pathways* back issues.

4. Bruce Hodgins and Gwyneth Hoyle, *Canoeing North into the Unknown: A Record of River Travel: 1874–1974* (Toronto: Natural Heritage, 1994).

5. See the four journals from the first Franklin Arctic land expedition, 1819–22. John Richardson, *Arctic Ordeal: The Journal of John Richardson, Surgeon-Naturalist with Franklin, 1820–1822*, edited by C.S. Houston and I.S. MacLaren (Montreal: McGill-Queen's University Press; 1984); George Back, *Arctic Artist:*

The Journal and Painting of George Back Midshipman with Franklin, 1819–1822, edited by C.S. Houston and I.S. MacLaren, (Montreal: McGill-Queen's University Press, 1994); Robert Hood, *To The Arctic by Canoe 1819–1821: The Journal and Painting of Robert Hood,* edited by C.A. Houston (Montreal: McGill-Queen's University Press, 1974); Sir John Franklin, *Thirty Years in the Arctic Regions* (Lincoln, NB: University of Nebraska Press, 1988).

6. Hood, *To The Arctic by Canoe,* 159–61.

7. Samuel Hearne, *A Journey from Prince of Wales's Fort in Hudson's Bay to the Northern Ocean in the Years 1769–1770, 1771–1772* (London: A. Strahan and T. Cadell, 1795).

8. The contrasts of then and now are exacting on the imagination. American poet and polar traveller Elizabeth Bradfield writes this contrast from an unusual perspective: "How do the trials of our lives compare? What would Shackleton have done when the baby didn't stop crying? What would he have done if his credit cards were all denied or his girlfriend slept with his brother or if he was downsized?" A rarely thought-of perspective. See note #1 for the third verse.

9. Brian Wattchow and Michael Brown, *Pedagogy of Place: Outdoor Education for a Changing World* (Melbourne, Montash University Press, 2011), 81.

10. William Godfrey-Smith, "Value of Wilderness," *Environmental Ethics,* Vol. 1, No. 4 (Winter 1979).

11. Warwick Fox, *Toward a Transpersonal Ecology* (Boston: Shambhala, 1990).

12. Randy Freeman, "The Beaulieu Clan: Unlettered People" in *Pike's Portage: Stories of a Distinguished Place,* edited by Morten Asfeldt and Bob Henderson (Toronto: Natural Heritage Books/Dundurn, 2010), 149–57.

13. Back, *Arctic Artist,* 60.

14. Richardson, *Arctic Ordeal.*

15. For André's replica construction efforts, see Bob Henderson and André-François Bourbeau, "Pierre St. Germain's Miracle Canoe" in *Nastawgan: the Quarterly Journal of the Wilderness Canoe Association* (Spring 2013), 9.

16. Franklin, *Thirty Years in the Arctic Regions,* 127–28.

17. Back, *Arctic Artist,* 81.

18. Warburton Pike, *The Barren Ground of Northern Canada* (London: Macmillan, 1892). This book is recommended for a vivid description of barren grounds and treeline transition zone practices of the Chipewyan with whom Pike travelled, wisely following their lead.

19. Richardson, *Arctic Ordeal,* XXIX.

20. Back, *Arctic Artist,* 129.

21. Wentzel in Back, *Arctic Artist*, 225.

22. Wallace Stevens, *Necessary Angels: Essays on Realty and the Imagination* (New York: Vintage Books, 1942), 138–50.

23. James David Duncan, *The River Why* (New York: Bantam Books, 1985), 53–54.

24. David Orr, *Ecological Literacy: Education and the Transition to a Post Modern World* (New York: State University, 1992), 130.

Chapter 2

1. This quote by Aldo Leopold has been a touchstone in my life since my first summer guiding years in the mid 1970s. Thanks to Tom Hawks for the kind gesture of purchasing Leopold's *Sand Country Almanac* for me. Aldo Leopold, *Sand Country Almanac* (New York: Ballantine Books, 1977). See "A Man's Leisure Time," 181–88.

2. When the Quetico Provincial Park and Boundary Waters Canoe Area (almost 2 million acres) was my stomping ground for four summers between 1972–79, I always pursued the less travelled waterways north of the border and missed the experience of a root beer and chat with the "Root Beer Lady," Dorothy Molter (1907–86). I feel compelled to tell a bit of her story here. Dorothy sold homemade root beer to passing canoe trippers. Her home from 1934 till her death was first a resort, the Isle of Pines Resort, and later her private residence. In the 1970s and '80s she would have up to four thousand visitors sign her guest book in the summer months. Fewer visited in the other seasons, but she averaged six thousand visitors per year. She maintained an ice house, cutting the ice to last through August so that the root beer would be cold. There was no electricity or phone, and the nearest road was fifteen miles away, involving five portages. She was once described as "the loneliest woman in America" and among the most isolated — just yards from the Canadian border in 2 million acres of canoe country. Dorothy's cabins were dismantled and moved to Ely, Minnesota, where they are now part of the Dorothy Molter Museum. See Sarah Guy-Levar and Terry Schocke, *Dorothy Molter: The Root Beer Lady* (Cambridge, MN: Adventure Publications, 2011). Alex Mathius lives on the Obabika River in Temagami. He returned to his home terrain more than twenty years ago, living alone. Like Dorothy Molter and Wendell Beckwith, he welcomes canoe-tripping folk regularly in the summer.

3. Alice Casselman was a regular visitor to Best Island during the start-up years of Outward Bound. Alice was an Outward Bound staffer, but beyond the summer visits with students, Alice visited Wendell at Best Island in the winter. No easy feat. Her insight was invaluable.

4. *Globe and Mail*, 2005.

5. Darrell Makin and Zack Kruzins, *A Paddler's Guide to the Lake Superior National Marine Conservation Area* (Thunder Bay: River Rocks Publication, 2012).

6. During a phone interview Jim Stevens reminded me that St. Ignace is no ordinary island. First off, it is Lake Superior's largest island on the Canadian side. Isle Royale on the American side is larger. But St. Ignace is arguably more distinctive. There are twenty-three different drainage patterns, over one hundred lakes and ponds (the largest lake is seven miles long), and Mount St. Ignace is among the highest points of land in Ontario.

7. In 2014, there will be a piece on Nirivia in *Cottage Life* magazine. It is wonderful to know that Nirivia is still a worthy story for mainstream publications. I suppose my assumption inherent in the above is that readers of this book are less mainstream and more ... well ... as Leopold says in the epigram of this chapter, this "tribe is inherently a minority."

8. One set of inland forested hills, The Paps, dominated the crossings of the potentially formidable Black Bay. The Paps were named by the French voyageurs after women's breasts; a small comfort for the voyageurs' paddling trials on Superior's open seas. We talked about these trials as we made two calm open water crossings. The Paps kept the past alive for us for several days.

9. See Conor Mihell, *The Greatest Lake: Stories from Lake Superior's North Shore* (Toronto: Dundurn, 2012), 104–14, to learn more about Superior's North Shore, friends, groups, and sauna culture.

10. "Of Nirivia, Oh Nirivia," *Lake Superior Magazine* (June/July 1999).

Chapter 3

1. Claude Lévi-Strauss (1908–2009) was a French social anthropologist and ethnologist. He is often considered among the fathers of modern anthropology for transforming the way twentieth-century Western society understands so-called primitive society. He argues, "tribal mythologies display remarkable subtle systems of logic showing rational mental qualities as sophisticated as those of western societies." From Edward Rothstein, "Claude Lévi-Strauss, 100, Dies: Altered Western Views of the Primitive," *New York Times*, November 4, 2009.

2. Vilhjalmur Stefansson, *My Life with the Eskimo* (New York: MacMillan Co., 1921); Raymond M. Patterson, *The Dangerous River* (Toronto: Stoddart Publishing, 1989); R.M. Patterson, *Nahanni Journals: R.M. Patterson's 1927–1929 Journals*, edited by Richard C. Davis (Edmonton: The University

of Alberta Press, 2008); George M. Douglas, *Lands Forlorn: The Story of an Expedition to Hearne's Coppermine River* (New York: G.P. Putnam's Sons, 1914); Enid L. Mallory, *Coppermine: The Far North of George M. Douglas* (Peterborough: Broadview Press, 1989).

3. Stefansson, *My Life with the Eskimo*, 43.

4. John W. Lentz, "Stalking Stef on Grizzly Shores," *Che-Mun*, Outfit 108 (Spring, 2002): 6–8.

5. Stefansson, *My Life with the Eskimo*, 5.

6. Ibid., 346.

7. Raymond M. Patterson, *The Dangerous River* (Toronto: Stoddart Publishing, 1989). Dangerous River was written when Patterson was in his fifties. Three years after our family trip on the Nahanni, Patterson's field notes were published. We could learn more about the Wheatsheaf Creek cabin. See R.M. Patterson, *Nahanni Journals*. These two texts complement each other brilliantly. *The Dangerous River* is a hero-driven adventure story, while the journals show the novice canoe tripper at the time of travel. Editor Richard Davis of *Nahanni Journals* notes, "The choice, then, of what to retain and what to omit was a very conscious one, not a mere accident of memory." (LXVI) The Patterson of the *Journals* is more like us, dear readers. Davis adds, "Patterson's journals from the 1920s better capture the ethos of childlike play and spiritual rejuvenation befitting today's traveller." (LXXXIII)

8. Patterson, *The Dangerous River*.

9. Ibid.

10. C.K. Chesterton, "A thing worth doing…," The American Chesterton Society, *www.chesterton.org*. Originally from C.K. Chesterton, *What's Wrong with the World*, published in 1910.

11. The infamous Figure 8 Rapids on the Nahanni River were washed out by high water levels in 2006. I will always remember my daughter Meghan and nephew Stuart Henderson dropping out of sight in current haystacks at the right angle bend at the end of the rapid.

12. Patterson, *The Dangerous River*.

13. Patterson, *Nahanni Journals*, 133–38.

14. Patterson, *The Dangerous River*.

15. Ian Tamblyn, "River of Gold," on *Angel's Share* (Ottawa: See Lynx Music, 2003).

16. Douglas, *Lands Forlorn*.

17. "Experiential Learning Opportunities," *The Grove News* (Summer 2013): 14.

Chapter 4

1. John Boyko, in "The Unlikely Historian," *The Alumni Review: Queen's University*, Vol. 87, No. 4 (2013): 30.

2. The following is a recommended collection of Canadian sources that deal with Canada, the canoe, and decolonization. It is interesting to note that the Council of Outdoor Educators of Ontario in their 2006 annual conference explored the themes of Outdoor Education and Decolonization. See Bruce Erickson, *Canoe Nation: Nature Race and the Making of a Canadian Icon* (Vancouver: University of British Columbia Press, 2013); Misao Dean, *Inheriting a Canoe Paddle: The Canoe in Discourses of English-Canadian Nationalism* (Toronto: University of Toronto Press, 2013); Emily Root, "The Land Is Our Land? This Land Is Your Land: The Decolonizing Journeys of White Outdoor Environmental Educators," *Canadian Journal of Environmental Education*, Vol. 13 (2010): 103–19; Jonathon Bordo, "Jack Pine — Wilderness Sublime or the Erasure of the Aboriginal Presence from the Landscape," *Journal of Canadian Studies*, Vol. 27, No. 4 (Winter 1992): 98–129.

3. Eric Morse, *Fur Trade Routes: Then and Now* (Ottawa: National and Historical Parks Branch, 1971). Also see Carolyn Podruchny, *Making the Voyageur World: Travellers and Traders in the North American Fur Trade* (Toronto: University of Toronto Press, 2006).

4. John Jeremiah Bigsby, *The Shoe and the Canoe, or Pictures of Travel in Canada*, 2 Vols. (London: Chapman and Hall, 1850).

5. Frances Simpson, "Journey for Frances, Part 1," *The Beaver*, Vol. 50 (December 1953).

6. Walt Whitman in Wade Davis, *The Wayfarers: Why Ancient Wisdom Matters in the Modern World* (Toronto: Anansi Press, 2009), 43.

7. To pursue these explorers' accounts first-hand, all you need is a good library and a long winter. Sir John Franklin's journals are available but often are found only in rare book areas of libraries. For information on the Franklin expedition, Paul Nanton's *Arctic Breakthrough* is an excellent blend of journal narrative and author commentary concerning Franklin's three Arctic voyages. Recommended for the first Franklin expeditions is John Richardson, *Arctic Ordeal: The Journal of John Richardson*, edited by C. Stuart Houston (Kingston, ON: McGill-Queen's University Press, 1984). J.W. Tyrrell's *Across the Sub-Arctic of Canada* (Toronto: William Briggs, 1908) is readily available in libraries, and in paperback copy by Coles Publishing. Thierry Mallet describes his travels in *The Beaver* (March 1950), and has a collection of barrens travel reflections titled *Glimpse of the Barrens* (New York: Revillon

Freres, 1930). For George Back's story, see George Back, *Narrative of the Arctic Land Expedition* (Boston, MA: Adamant Media Corporation, 2005), originally published in 1836 by John Murray, London. A favourite Arctic travel read with lengthy ice travel passages is George M. Douglas, *Lands Forlorn: The Story of an Expedition to Hearne's Coppermine River* (New York: G.P. Putnam's sons, 1914), 236–249. For a trip largely devoted to ice walking travel with canoes, see Morten Asfeldt, "Artillery Lake Ice Walk," *Nastawgan: The Quarterly Journal of the Wilderness Canoe Association,* Vol. 40, No. 2 (Summer 2012). In the same issue Morten also discusses the performance of Pakboats — folding frame boats — and the sledding material used to pull them on the ice.

8. A very accessible read concerning Canada and nation building is Daniel Francis, *National Dreams* (Vancouver: Arsenal Pulp Press, 1997). Also see references provided in Endnote #2.

9. Marianne Hirsch coined the phrase "post memory" to describe the effects of the Holocaust on those who had never experienced it. I wonder if, for some people, this might apply to the canoeist in thinking of the oppression of Indigenous peoples in Canada. Does the canoe then become "undermined and destabilized," as Misao Dean suggests in *Inheriting a Canoe Paddle*? See Marianne Hirsch, *Family Frames; Photography, Narrative and Post Memory* (Cambridge, MA: Harvard University, 1997).

10. Emily Root, "This Land Is Our Land?" 2010.

11. Thomas Gray, "Ode on a Distant Prospect of Eton College," 1923. Retrieved from Wikipedia, November 29, 2013.

Chapter 5

1. Barry Lopez, *Arctic Dreams: Imagination and Desire in a Northern Landscape* (New York: Charles Scribners Sons, 1986).

2. See Norman Henderson, *Rediscovering the Great Plains: Journeys by Dog, Canoe and Horse* (Baltimore, ML: The Johns Hopkins University Press, 2001). Thanks to Joe Milligan for sharing this particularly solid travel narrative. I love passages from this book. Here are a few simple and beautiful gems like the Prairie landscape itself, gems that are in keeping with this chapter's theme of deep time: "The Plains are not an easy landscape. It is a natural reflex to be awed by mountains; huge and overpowering; they are a beginner's landscape. Here the old grass, the prairie wool, is still bound tight to the soil, thick and springy underfoot, impervious to drought."

3. *The Land That Never Melts: Auyuittuq National Park*, edited by Roger Wilson

(Toronto: Peter Martin Associates, 1975), 10. In recent years, the major hiking trails between Pangnirtung and Qikiqtarjung/Broughton Island have been significantly altered from their conception as the showcase of the national park because of melting glacial ice in the higher country. Fording streams is becoming increasing difficult. Certainly the 1970s guidebook may need a new title with subsequent editions. Indeed the land is melting. Also see Auyuittuq National Park, Adventure Maps Series, produced by Chrismar Mapping Services.

4. Playfair, John, "Hutton's Unconformity," *Transactions of the Royal Society of Edinburgh* (1805). McPhee, John, "Basin and Range," Annals of the Former World (New York: Farrar, Straus and Giroux, 1998).

5. For a report on the ice2sea findings, see "Greenland's Grand Canyon found beneath ice," *The Toronto Star*, August 31, 2013, A15. The two studies mentioned are meant, in part, to explore draining melt-water from beneath ice sheets. This will advance knowledge of global warming.

6. Jamie Bastedo, *Shield Country: Life and Times of the Oldest Piece of the Planet* (Calgary: Arctic Institute of North America, 1994), 14.

7. Henderson, *Rediscovering the Great Plains*, 10–11.

8. Steve Simpson, "Speaking for the Trees: The Use of Literature to Convey Outdoor Education Themes," *Journal of Environmental Education* (Spring 1988).

9. Janet Pivnick, "A Piece of Forgotten Song: Recalling Environmental Connections," *Holistic Educational Review*, Vol. 10, No. 4 (Winter 1998): 58–63. Also see Theodore Roszak, "Ecopsychology Since 1992: As long as there is Prozac, who needs environmental sanity?" *Wild Earth* (Summer 2002): 39–43.

10. Mary Northway, "Going on Camping Trips," in *Light from a Thousand Campfires* (Martinsville, IN: American Camping Association, 1960).

11. Halldór Laxness, *Independent People* (New York: Vintage Books, 1997), 178–79.

12. Elliott Merrick, *True North* (New York: Scribners, 1943). Also see a lovely tribute to Elliott Merrick in George Luste, "Elliott Merrick 1905–1977," *Them Days: Stories of Early Labrador*, Vol. 22, No. 4 (Summer 1997): 28–30. Merrick was a master at capturing the highs and lows of the trail. The idea that one enhances the other was a central trail philosophy of Herb Pohl. Indeed, Herb, I dare say, would have fully supported Northway's "why go camping" adage. See Herb Pohl, *The Lure of Faraway Places: Reflections on Wilderness and Solitude* (Toronto: Natural Heritage/Dundurn, 2007).

13. Allison Mitcham, *The Northern Imagination: A Study of Northern Canadian Literature* (Moonbeam, ON: Penumera Press, 1993), 85.

14. Nicolas Carr, *The Shallows: What the Internet Is Doing to Our Brains* (New York: W.W. Norton, 2010). Sherry Turkle, *Alone Together: Why We Expect*

More From Technology and Less from Each Other (New York: Basic Books, 2011), also approaches this topic of losing contemplative skills, but more from a socio-cultural perspective.

15. Bob Henderson and Nicole Parisien, "Dandelions or Database: Putting Nature Words Back into the Children's Dictionary," *Pathways: The Ontario Journal of Outdoor Education.* Vol. 23, No. 1 (Fall 2010): 34–35.

16. Carr, *The Shallows*, 91.

17. Ibid., 31

Part Two

Introduction: Perspectives

1. Wade Davis, *Shadows in the Sun: Travels to Landscapes of Spirit and Desire* (New York: Broadway Books, 2010).

2. *The North Forest Canoe Trail Guide*, edited by Beth Kuksi (The Appalachian Club of America, 2010).

Chapter 6

1. Alice Beck Kehoe, *The Kensington Runestone: Approaching a Research Question Holistically* (Long Grove, IL: Waveland Press, 2005), 2.

2. Ibid., 39.

3. Ibid., 20.

4. Barry Fell, *America B.C.: Ancient Settler of the New World* (New York: Demeter Press, 1976), 26–29 and *Bronze Age America* (Boston: Little Brown and Company, 1982). For a review of Barry Fell's work, see David H. Kelley, "Proto-Tifinagh and Proto-Ogham in the Americas," *The Review of Archaeology*, Vol. 11, No. 1 (Spring 1990): 1–10. Kelley, a professor of archaeology known as an epigrapher (from the University of Calgary) concluded, "I have no personal doubts that some of the inscriptions which have been reported are genuine Celtic Ogham … We need to ask not only what Fell has done wrong in his epigraphy, but also where we have gone wrong as archaeologists in not recognizing such an extensive European presence in the New World."

5. I vividly remember the fervour of the conviction shared when I probed deeper into the story with one of the Sinclair clansmen. I was hooked, but the enthusiasm did not feel objective to me. Little did I know I would begin a long-term inquiry into all this on my own terms.

6. Frederick J. Pohl, *Prince Henry Sinclair: His Expedition to the New World in 1398* (Halifax: Nimbus, 1995) and Andrea di Robilant, *Irresistible North: From Venice to Greenland on the Trail of the Zeno Brothers* (New York: Alfred A. Knopf, 2011). Gérard Leduc and Paul Falardeau have written an unpublished paper titled, "Prince Henry Sinclair: A Legend or a True Voyage?" They conclude that Sinclair may well have travelled to the northeast from the Orkney Islands but there is not enough evidence to place him in Nova Scotia in 1398. Indeed, the Zeno map reads 1380. I do believe that their speculation that Sinclair has become an "allegorical figure representing a whole segment of an untold, secret history" of Knights Templar sympathizers migrating to North America is most plausible given the evidence found in eastern Canada.

7. John Keats, negative capability letter. See *www.poetryfoundation.org*, selections from Keat's letters (1817).

8. Farley Mowat, *The Farfarers: Before the Norse* (Toronto, ON: Key Porter Books, 1998). Gérard Leduc, "The Knights Templar in Nouvelle-France: Destination Montreal and Lake Memphremagog," *Neara Journal*, Vol. 40, No. 2 (Winter 2006): 24–35. Gérard Leduc, "No! Gladden and Royer didn't build these stone mounds in Potton," *Neara Journal*, Vol. 25, No. 3 and 4. (Winter/Spring 1991): 50–60. Michael Bradley, *Grail Knight of North America: On the Trail of the Grail Legacy in Canada and the United States.* (Toronto: Hounslow Press, 1998). Gavin Menzies and Ian Hudson, *Who Discovered America? The Untold History of the Peopling of the Americas* (New York: HarperCollins, 2013). Gavin Menzies, *The Lost Empire of Atlantis* (New York: HarperCollins, 2011). Patricia D. Sutherland, "The Norse in Native North Americas," in *Vikings: the North America Saga*, edited by William W. Fitzhugh and Elisabeth I. Ward (Washington: Smithsonian Institution Press, 2000), 238–47. James Robert Enterline, *Erikson, Eskimos and Columbus: Medieval European Knowledge of America* (Baltimore: The Johns Hopkins University Press, 2002).

9. Michael A. Cremo, "Forbidden Archeology" in *You are Still Being Lied To: The New Disinformation Guide to Media Distortion, Historical White Washes and Cultural Myths* (Disinformation Company, 2009).

10. Leduc, "The Knights Templar in Nouvelle-France."

11. *The Northern Forest Canoe Trail: The Official Guidebook*, edited by Jane Crosen (Seattle: The Mountaineers Books, 2010), 126–39.

12. Jane Armstrong, "A Twist in Time: A researcher says she's found evidence that Vikings may have settled in Canada's Arctic. Others aren't so sure," *MacLean's* (November 26, 2012): 26–27.

13. Randy Boswell, "First to the New World? Pre-Viking find on Faroes renews talk about St. Brendan's discovering Canada," *Vancouver Sun*, August 21, 2013.

14. Ibid.

15. Henry Bugbee, "Education and the Style of Our Lives," *Profiles*, Vol. 6, No. 4 (May 1974).

16. Susan Sontag, "Introduction," in Halldór Laxness, *Under the Glacier* (New York: Vintage Books, 2004): vii.

17. Robert Burcher, *The Leather Boat* (Eugenia, ON: The Battered Silicon Dispatch Box, 2012).

18. Jonathan Clements, *A Brief History of the Vikings: The Last Pagans or the First Modern Europeans?* (London: Constable and Robinson, 2005): 98–115.

19. See *www.michigan.gov/sanilacpetroglyphs*. Also see "The Sanilac Petroglyphs Historical State Park 2010 Pamphlet" (Cass City: Michigan Government, 2010).

20. Michael Bradley, *Grail Knights of North America*, 375–76.

21. I recommend the two books by Gavin Menzies mentioned in this chapter directly related to this subject of Lake Superior copper. Also see Gavin Menzies, *1421: The Year China Discovered America* (London: Bantam Press, 2002) and Paul Chiasson, *The Island of Seven Cities: Where the Chinese Settled When They Discovered North America* (Random House Canada, 2006).

22. Rob Gowan, "Amateur Archeologists' theories gaining support," *Globe and Mail* (October 19, 2012). This is a good summation on Robert Burcher's work in Newfoundland.

23. Menzies, *The Lost Empire of Atlantis*, 243–99.

24. Ibid., 276. Also see Andre Zarowny, *America Unearthered — Great Lakes Copper Heist*, *www.rightpundits.com/?p=10858*, 6–7.

25. Farley Mowat, *Westviking: The Ancient Norse in Greenland and North America* (Minerva Press, 1965) 420–38. Also see Peter Schledermann, "Ellesmere: Vikings in the Far North," in *Vikings: The North America Saga*, edited by William W. Fitzhugh and Elisabeth I. Ward (Washington: Smithsonian Institution Press, 2000), 248–56, and Alexandra Paul, "Seeking Out Ancient Norse Traders," *Winnipeg Free Press* (March 17, 2012). Also see *www.faraheim.com*. Here is a curious item connecting to shoreline stones. A Winnipeg team in summer 2013 travelled to Gimli, Hecla Island, and Berens River on Lake Winnipeg in search of discarded Viking ballast stones or mooring stones. There is a place on the lake that Indigenous peoples referred to as "White Men's Writing on a Rock." Mooring stones were apparently first identified on the lake's shore in 1950.

26. Kehoe, *The Kensington Runestone*, 86–87.

27. John Geddes, "Written by the Victors," *Maclean's* (August 12, 2013), 18–20. Johnathon Gatehouse, "When Science Goes Silent," *Maclean's* (May 13, 2013), 16–19. See *www.scienceuncensored.ca*. I understand the Canadian

government's desire to control the release of new science as it pertains to global warming. I question the wisdom of the act, but I can understand it. I find it harder to understand the control of history and archaeology.

Chapter 7

1. Sigurd F. Olson, *Of Time and Place* (New York: Alfred A. Knopf, 1982), 19.

2. Thomas Berry, *The Great Work: Our Way Into the Future* (New York: Bell Tower, 1999), 15. As an outdoor educator throughout my career, I have always worked from a premise of the cultural importance of outdoor environmental education (despite it often being marginalized in university settings). I adhere to Berry's note on page 79: "my generation has been an autistic generation in its inability to establish any intimate rapport with the natural world." Local trail sharing with heritage and nature interpretation is one way educators work to curb this quality. It is rewarding. When outdoors, walking with students, drawing out of folks some recessed rapport with nature, this result is in your face. It is inspirational. Outdoor educators who work with students in the field tend not to burn out over the years.

3. Ron Brown, *Ontario's Ghost Town Heritage* (Erin, ON: Boston Mills Press, 2007) and *Ghost Towns of Ontario, Vol. 2* (Northern Ontario, Toronto: Polar Bear Press, 1999).

4. Ibid.

5. Scott Cameron presentation. "John Muir in Grey" South Grey Museum, September 18, 2013, Flesherton, ON. Also see *www.johnmuir.org/canada*.

6. Heather Robertson, *Walking into Wilderness: The Toronto Carrying Place and Nine Mile Portage* (Winnipeg: Heartland Associates, 2010).

7. Ibid.

8. Grant Karcich, *Scugog Carrying Place: A Frontier Pathway* (Toronto: Dundurn, 2013).

9. Craig Macdonald's research in northeastern Ontario is extensive. When I asked him about the connection from Lake Simcoe north to Halliburton/Algonquin, he told me about the Big Canoe family from Georgina Island, Lake Simcoe. Their traditional hunting grounds were western Algonquin Park centring at Canoe Lake. Certainly, from Lake Simcoe canoeing north via the Gull and Burnt Rivers took travellers well north into what is now Algonquin Park.

10. Karcich, *Scugog Carrying Place*, 23.

11. Ibid., 33.

12. *The Glen Major Angling Club Handbook* (Uxbridge, ON: Glen Major Angling Club, 2012).

13. Allan McGillivray, *Tales from the Uxbridge Valley: Historical Highlights* (Uxbridge: The Uxbridge Millennium Committee, 2000). Plus personal correspondence.

14. Chris Mills, "Laura Secord Beats Paul Revere Hands Down," *Niagara Escarpment Views* (Autumn 2013): 16–19, 34–37.

15. This overview of Ridge Road history is taken from Heather Quipp, "The Old Mountain Lodge at Kingsmere," *Up the Gatineau!* Vol. 29 (2003): 22–26. Also see Charles Hodgson, "The Colourful Past of Ski Lodges and Trails in Gatineau Park," *Up the Gatineau!* Vol. 39 (2013): 31–43. It is fun to add that the Burma Road ski trail is named from the film *The Bridge on the River Kwai* because the work involved in building the trail was jokingly suggested to match the toil of prisoners of war in the popular movie of the time.

16. The Chelsea poet Arthur Stanley Bourinot is featured in "Chelsea Poems: Arthur Stanley Bourinot 1893–1969," *Up the Gatineau!* Vol. 39 (2013). It's one to share next time I am on the Ridge Road. It applies to many settings and certainly works for me!

17. I am indebted to Kathy Hooks and William Gastle for sharing their knowledge of George Douglas, the Northcote property, and its trails.

18. 18. Thanks to Cameron Deeth, local ski historian and operator of the Dagmar Cross Country Trails, for sharing his archives with me. See Les Scott, "Dagmar," *The Ski Runner: Official Publication of the Toronto Ski Club*, Vol. 12, No. 1 (December 1938).

19. Grey Owl, *The Men of the Last Frontier* (London: Country Life, 1931). The full quote is worth sharing here. I had students, each year, recite this with me at our last portage on a summer's end canoe trip (1982–2011). "Each succeeding generation takes up the work that is laid down by those who pass along, leaving behind them traditions and a standard of achievement that must be lived up to by those who would claim a membership in the brotherhood of the Keepers of the Trail."

Chapter 8

1. First, an example of an early reference is Raymond E. Janssen, "Living Guide — Posts of the Past," *Scientific Monthly*. Two contemporary references are Dennis Downes, *Native American Trail Marker Trees: Marking Paths Through the Wilderness* (Chicago: Chicago's Books Press, 2011) and Don and Diane Wells, *Mystery of the Trees: Native American Markers of a Cultural Way of Life That Soon May Be Gone* (Jasper, GA: Mountain Stewards, 2011). Finally, for Paul O'Hara's explorations, see Paul

O'Hara, "A Call Down the Path: Trail Markers in Ontario," *Field Botanist of Ontario Newsletter*, Vol. 23, No. 3 (Fall 2011): 6–8; "Call Return: Indian Marker Trees in Southern Ontario (Part Two)," *Field Botanists of Ontario Newsletter*, Vol. 24, No. 3 (Fall 2012):8–11. Also see David Lea, "Following the Oakville Trails of First Nations," *Oakville Beaver* (May 10, 2012).

2. Lea, "Following the Oakville Trails of First Nations."

3. Arthur Pegg, *Fur Trade to Farmstead: A History of Renewable Resources in the Essex Region 1750–1900* (Essex, ON: Essex Regional Conservation Authority, 1985) figures 13, 28.

4. Robert Terence Carter, *Stories of Newmarket: An Old Ontario Town* (Toronto: Dundurn, 2011), 25–26. The Whitechurch History Book Committee, *Whitechurch Township* (Erin, ON: A Boston Mills Press, 1993), 9.

5. The Paisley Centennial Book Committee, *An Historical Album of Paisley* (Paisley, ON: Paisley Town Council, 1974), 38.

6. John Vaillant, *The Golden Spruce: A True Story of Myth, Madness and Greed* (Toronto: Vintage Books, 2006), 83.

7. Ibid., 140.

8. W.H. Williams, "A Terrible Trip to Edmonton," *Alberta Historical Review* (Autumn 1974): 5.

9. Ibid., 5.

10. William E. Moreau, *Writing of David Thompson,* Vol. 1, *The Travels, 1850 Version* (Kingston: McGill-Queen's University Press, 2009).

11. See "Bruce Trail Heritage Trees," Tree site 13, *http://brucetrail.org/pages/ scavenger-hunt/trees.*

12. Downes, *Native American Trail Marker Trees*, 148.

13. R.M. Ballantyne, "An Account of a Journey from York Factor to Norway House in 1845," *Manitoba Pageant*, Vol. 14, No. 3 (Spring 1969). In the endnotes to the journal excerpts, the editor notes the following: "Lobsticks has been corrupted … into lobsticks, but the root is lop from the Middle English loppe, which as a verb means to cut off the branches or twigs of a tree."

14. See David Pelly, "J.W. Tyrell: The Man Who Named Pike's portage," in *Pike's Portage: Stories of A Distinguished Place*, edited by Morten Asfeldt and Bob Henderson (Toronto: Natural Heritage Books/Dundurn, 2010): 77, 133–64.

15. Merle Massie, "The Lobstick: Our Next National Symbol," *The Globe and Mail*, October 25, 2012.

16. Personal communication with Tyler Baker (Waskesin Golf Course). See *www.waskesiu.org/ heritage_museum.html.*

17. Peter E. Kelly and Douglas W. Larson, *The Last Stand: A Journey Through the Ancient Cliff-Face Forest of the Niagara Escarpment* (Toronto: Dundurn, 2007), 115–39.

18. Vaillant, *The Golden Spruce*.

19. Ibid., 213.

20. Grace Lee Nute, *The Voyageur* (St. Paul, MN: Minnesota Historical Society Press, 1987), 209.

Chapter 9

1. Jamie Benidickson, *Idleness, Water and Canoe: Reflections on Paddling for Pleasure* (Toronto: University of Toronto Press, 1977), 1.

2. See *www.dragonboathistory.com/history* and *www.reginadragonboat.com/index*.

3. James Raffan, *Deep Waters: Courage, Character and the Lake Temiskaming Canoe Tragedy* (Toronto: Harper Flamingo Books, 2002), 107–13.

4. I am grateful to Dave Standfield for many conversations in the canoe shop at camp about the canoes, Stan, and, somehow, always a life lesson.

5. Naturally Superior, an outdoor travel commercial business at the mouth of the Michepicoten, near Wawa, Ontario, on Lake Superior, runs voyageur *canot de maître* guided canoe trips. With friends and family, I enjoyed learning the many lessons of these canoes on a Lake Superior coastline trip in the 1990s. See Bob Henderson, *Every Trail Has a Story: Heritage Travel in Canada* (Toronto: Natural Heritage/Dundurn Books, 2005), 175–79.

6. Much of this treatment of Svend Ulstrup was originally published in Bob Henderson and Zabe MacEachren, "Svend Ulstrup: A Boat Builder/Educator for Our Time," *Nastawgan* (Fall 2012): 25–27.

7. The term "the worm" had something to do with the translation for this boat in what is known of the Bronze Age Viking age language, so when the boat flexed it helped reinforce where this term originated — the Bronze Age before the Vikings. Many anthropologists also do not agree that the boat was built with rawhide (which enabled the worm-like flex in waves) versus the rigid form of the wooden Viking era boats. Svend's work here is "experimental archeology." He is testing theories on the water, in the field.

8. Steven Heigthon, *Afterlands* (Toronto: Random House of Canada, 2006), 403.

9. John Tanner, *A Narrative of the Captivity and Adventures of John Tanner,* edited by Edwin James (New York: Garland Publishing, 1975).

10. See Edwin Tappan Adney and Howard I. Chapelle, *The Bark Canoes and Skin Boats of North America* (Washington, D.C.: Smithsonian Institute, 1964), 135–36.

11. I am indebted to the generous time I had to talk over all these details with Shawn Patterson, the Fort William, Ontario, Historical Site Collections Curator, who suggested I pursue the work of Timothy Kent. See *www. timothypkent.com/pubs.htm.*

12. James Barry, *Georgian Bay: The Sixth Great Lake* (Erin, ON: Boston Mills Press, 1995), 26.

13. "World's largest birch bark canoe will return to its birthplace," *Leader,* Eganville, ON, April 13, 2011, 22.

14. John Vaillant, *The Golden Spruce: A Time Story of Myth, Madness and Greed* (Toronto, Vintage Canada, 2006), 52.

15. Ibid., Vaillant reports on the speculation that the Haida in the 1800s could have travelled in their dugouts as far as Hawaii.

16. Misao Dean, *Inheriting a Canoe Paddle: the Canoe in Discourses of English-Canadian Nationalism* (Toronto: University of Toronto Press), 2013.

17. Ibid., 173.

18. George M. Douglas, *Lands Forlorn: The Story of an Expedition to Hearne's Coppermine River* (New York: G.P. Putnam, 1914), 295–60.

19. Mark Hume, "Totem Pole Raising in Haida Gwaii: An Ancient Tradition a Distinctive Message," *Globe and Mail,* August 17, 2013, A10–A11.

PART THREE

Chapter 10

1. For an overview of Arctic courses, see Glen Hvenegaard and Morten Asfeldt, "Embracing Friluftsliv's Joys: Teaching the Canadian North through the Canadian Wilderness Travel Experience," in *Nature First: Outdoor Life the Friluftsliv Way,* edited by Bob Henderson and Nils Vikander (Toronto: Natural Heritage/Dundurn, 2007), 168–78. For details of the program and research on educational outcomes see Morten Asfeldt and Glen Hvenegaard, "Perceived Learning, Critical Elements and Lasting Impacts on University. Based Wilderness Educational Expeditions," *Journal of Adventure Education and Outdoor Learning,* Vol. 13, No. 2 (May 2013).

2. Morten and I edited a book telling some of the main stories associated with this central link to northern travel. See Morten Asfeldt and Bob Henderson, *Pike's Portage: Stories of a Distinguished Place* (Toronto: Dundurn Press, 2010).

3. Morten tells the story of Beaver and Rat Lodge adding specific phrases from Maufelly, a guide and Native interpreter on the George Back Expedition of

1833–34, in *Pike's Portage: Stories of a Distinguished Place* (Toronto: Dundurn Press, 2010).

> The story goes that there once lived a beaver — the size of a buffalo — in this lodge [Beaver's Lodge], who roamed the neighbouring countryside, committing acts of nuisance and disturbance against the local people, often in partnership with his ally, the rat, who lived on the opposite shore in Rat's Lodge. However, wanting to put an end to the beaver's harassment, the local Aboriginal people set out to slay the beast. The beaver escaped, seeking refuge in the Rat's Lodge but was turned away by his collaborator who told him to swim "to some rocks to the south, where he would be safe from his enemies." Angry over the rat's lack of hospitality, the beaver began to pummel the rat, but quickly abandoned the fight as the local people continued their pursuit. The beaver turned and fled south "down the cataracts and rapids" of the Lockhart River and into Great Slave Lake, where the "exhausted animal yielded its life." Nevertheless, says Maufelly, "its spirit … still lingers about its old haunt, the waters of which obey its will; and ill fares the person who attempts to pass it in his canoe, without muttering a prayer for safety; many have perished; some bold men have escaped; but none have been found so rash as to venture a second time within its power." As was Maufelly's practice of muttering a prayer, today the Dene continue to leave "an offering of thanks for safe passage on the land" as they pass Beaver's Lodge.

Also see, Richard Galaburri, "The Rat Lodge Revisited," *Arctic*, Vol. 44, No. 3 (September 1991): 257–58 and James Raffan, "The Lessons of Old Woman Falls," *Up Here* (April 2005): 24–26, 61. Morten tells me Richard Galaburri has the story right but the location wrong. See *Pike's Portage: Stories of a Distinguished Place*, 273. For a report on this June 2001 trip, see Morten Asfeldt and Glen Hvenegaard, "Artillery Lake Ice Walk," *Nastawgan: Quarterly Journal of the Wilderness Canoe Association*, Vol. 40, No. 2 (Summer 2012): 1–9.

4. See Edgar Christian, *Unflinching: A Diary of Tragic Adventure* (London: William Clowes and Sons, 1937).

5. Ibid., 101, 107, 129.

6. Ibid., 154.

Chapter 11

1. Linda has written a personal treatment of her connection to Algonquin Park as landscape and people as a statement on place-based learning. See Linda Leckie, "The Spirit of Algonquin," in *Algonquin Park: The Human Impact*, edited by David Euler and Mike Wilton (Sault Ste. Marie, ON: Algonquin Eco Watch, 2009), 314–32.

2. Professional affiliations have involved workshop presenting, conference organizing, and general involvements in The Council of Outdoor Educators of Ontario, The Association for Experiential Education, and The Ontario Recreation Canoe and Kayak Association.

3. See Bob Henderson, *Every Trail Has a Story: Heritage Travel in Canada* (Toronto: Natural Heritage/Dundurn Press, 2005), 226–29 for a search for Tom Thomson's *Northern Lights* sketching site. For the story of John Dennison, see Audrey Saunders, *Algonquin Story* (Toronto: Department of Lands and Forest, 1963), 56–60.

4. E.C. Relph, *Place and Placelessness* (London: Pion, 1976). I am grateful to Ryan Howard, a Ph.D. candidate in 2014 at Brock University, for discussions and writings concerning Relph's work and helping me unpack the place-based education literature. His forthcoming Ph.D. thesis is called *The Conceptualization and Exploration of Place Allegiance: Towards a Unified Model of Person-Place Relationship within Outdoor Recreation*.

5. C.A. Bower, *The Culture of Denial: Why the Environmental Movement Needs a Strategy for Reforming Universities and Public Schools* (Albany: State University of New York, 1997).

6. Tim Winton, "Wild Brown Land," *The Weekend Australian*, December 14–15, 2013. Edited transcript of *The Island Seen and Felt: Some Thoughts About Landscape.* Speech to the Royal Academy, London, November 14, 2013.

7. I would be remiss to not mention the important role of Ester Keyser as elder and spiritual mentor for Linda. See, Esther Keyser and John Keyser, *Paddling My Own Canoe: The Story of Algonquin Park's First Female Guide* (Whitney, ON: the Friends of Algonquin Park, 2003). Also her partner Don Standfield shares in so much of the idea of place-dwelling presented here. His bond to Algonquin is the stuff of inspiration expressed through an artist's sensibility. See Don Standfield and Liz Lundell, *Algonquin: A Park and Its People* (Toronto: McClelland and Stewart, 1993).

8. Margaret Atwood used this phrase in a convocation address at the University of Waterloo in the 1980s. I have been sharing the quote ever since. I suppose it, for me, is one of those life defining passages: but it became so, in part, by the friends with whom one chooses to associate.

Chapter 12

1. André-François Bourbeau, *Wilderness Secrets Revealed: Adventures of a Survivor* (Toronto: Dundurn Press, 2013), 26. This is André's life story peppered with many a life lesson. Also recommended is André's bestseller Le *Surviethon: Vingt-cinq ans plus tard*. Here André reprinted and revisited his 1984 voluntary wilderness survival experience of thirty-one days with his friend Jacques Montminy. Twenty-five years later André explored the mistakes made — what he would do differently now — from the young spirited man to the older, more experienced, more thoughtful man. For survival specialists, this is a significant contribution to the literature. I should add that this mid-1980s experiment in boreal forest survival remains a Guinness World Record for the longest voluntary wilderness survival. The book is a Quebec bestseller.

2. Bourbeau, *Wilderness Secrets Revealed*, 143–206.

3. Ibid., 209–21.

4. The Kanawa Canoe Museum at Camp Kandalore was the precursor to the Canadian Canoe Museum at Peterborough, Ontario. Both house a collection largely generated by Kirk Wipper, one-time director of Camp Kandalore and long-time professor of Physical Education at the University of Toronto. André counts Kirk Wipper as a mentor and early inspiration. Kirk was not in the habit of lending out large birchbark canoes from the Kanawa collection. Clearly Kirk thought much of André as well.

5. See Edwin Tappan Adney and Howard I. Chapelle, *The Bark Canoe and Skin Boats of North America* (Washington, D.C.: Smithsonian Institution, 1964), 73, 132–33. André has studied this book and referred me to it for spruce bark canoe details. "Birch bark was often poor or scarce in the territory of the western Cree, as in that of their eastern brothers. As a substitute, they employed spruce bark and in general seem to have achieved better results, for their spruce-bark canoes had a neater appearance. When spruce bark was employed, its greater stiffness made it possible to space the ribs as much as ten inches on centres, but with birch the spacing was about one inch, edge to edge. The sheathing was in short splints and the inside of the canoe was 'shingled' or covered irregularly without regard to lining off the strakes …" These are among the sparse building references André and Billy had to work from. André laid down ash and spruce saplings as ribs and some spruce boughs for planking. André placed his spare paddle on the bottom of the canoe for safe foot placement.

6. Barbara Winter, "Making a Spruce Bark Canoe" in *A Way of Life*, edited by Ed Hall (Yellowknife: Department of Renewable Resources, 1986).

7. Email correspondence with André, December 26, 2013.

Chapter 13

1. See Adrienne Blattel, "New Country, New Home, New Nature," *Green Teacher*, Issue 100 (Summer 2013): 10–13. Here Adrienne notes that according to the Government of Canada, 19.8 percent of the Canadian population was born outside of the country as of 2006. *Human Resources and Skills Development Canada*, "Canadian in Context: Immigration," *www.hrsdc.gc.ca/.3ndic.1t.4r@-eng.jsp?iid=38*, consulted April 3, 2013.

2. Central among sponsors is the Milton Park Recreation Association in Montreal. Many of Plein Air Interculturel programs in the summer run through this already established association. As Adrienne put it, "it is a great platform" for all this work. I'm now actually an employee of MPRA.

3. Rosemary Lunardini, "Tuque Bleue," *The Beaver* (Winter 1976): 41–45. The Tuque Bleue was a snowshoe club founded in 1840s, Montreal. Members would gather for evening and weekend snowshoe tramps. Sherbrooke Street was a gathering spot for Mount Royal tramps. Races were also hosted. In the 1870s club members began to wear blue toques, hence the "tuque bleue" nickname. Before Confederation in 1867, the Indian Race of four miles was a major city event centered at the Priests' farm on Sherbrooke Street. The races were well recorded. In 1856, Ignace, who had been selected by Sir George Simpson to travel to the Arctic on an expedition in search of Sir John Franklin, had a first-place time of twenty-nine and a half minutes. Montreal businessmen were no match for Native northern travellers. It is pleasing to think of Adrienne and new immigrants to Canada re-enacting, in part, some of this fine Montreal "tramping" tradition. Here's hoping they might revive an old song or two of the 1950s Montrealers: "We ask no better kind of fun than on the swift snowshoe. With fellows who never shirk a tramp, who wear the bright Tuque Bleue!"

4. Beyond the *Green Teacher* article, see Adrienne Blattel, "Using Outdoor Recreation to Foster Intercultural Understanding and the Integration of New Immigrants in Montreal," *Pathways: The Ontario Journal of Outdoor Education*, Vol. 23, No. 4 (Summer 2011): 10–13.

5. Blattel, *Green Teacher*, 12–13.

6. Travelling in ex-Yugoslavia, while working with the Quebec-Labrador Foundation, exposed Adrienne to a hiking club there which offered a variety of culturally enriching and welcoming programs. This experience in 2009 served as an initial spark for Plein Air Interculturel. To learn more, see *www.pleinairinterculturel.com*.

Chapter 14

1. For a review on David Thompson, the great geographer and map-maker of Canada, see J.B. Tyrrell (ed.), *David Thompson's Narrative* (New York: Greenwood Press. Facsimile edition, 1968, 1916). Also see a road/driving and hiking based travel guide for David Thompson in the west, Joyce and Peter McCart, *On the Road with David Thompson* (Calgary: Fifth House, 2000). In the east, see David Thompson, *Even the Owl is Not Heard: David Thompson's 1834 Journals in the Eastern Townships of Quebec*, edited by Barbara Verity and Gilles Péloguin (Sherbrooke, QC: Township Cantons Publications, 2011). David Thompson is a hero figure for map-makers Mark and Christine. In December 2013, Chrismar completed the very ambitious map of Woodland Caribou Provincial Park in Northwestern Ontario. The map covers 4,862 square kilometres of provincial park, which includes a portion of the Canadian Heritage System's Bloodvein River. This map includes more than 2,000 kilometres of canoe routes, 5,200 lakes, and 2,200 campsites. Mark estimates the production of this map and related area writeup took 910 hours over a two-year period. They wouldn't say this, but I think they are in a league with David Thompson as map makers.

2. See *www.chrismar.com* or *www.theadventuremap.com* for the complete list of the Adventure Map Series.

3. The complete "The Road Not Taken" poem is rarely shared, while many know the last lines. Here is the full poem. See Wikipedia, "The Road Not Taken" for an interpretation of this Robert Frost poem.

> The road not taken
> Two roads diverged in a yellow wood,
> And sorry I could not travel both
> And be one traveller, long I stood
> And looked down one as far as I could
> To where it bent in the undergrowth;
>
> Then took the other, as just as fair
> And having perhaps the better claim,
> Because it was grassy and wanted wear;
> Though as for that the passing there
> Had worn them really about the same,
>
>
> And both that morning equally lay
> In leaves no step had trodden black.

Oh, I kept the first for another day!
Yet knowing how way leads on to way,
I doubted if I should ever come back.

I shall be telling this with a sigh
Somewhere ages and ages hence:
Two roads diverged in a wood, and I —
I took the one less travelled by,
And that has made all the difference.

4. It is an important distinction that Mark and Christine are map makers as well as map drawers. In Mark's words, "Map drawings or cartography is only one aspect of mapmaking. Mapmaking involves actually creating from scratch the data that makes up the map. That's what we do through photogrammetry and field survey — the capture of lake shores, rivers, edges of wet lands, clearings, trails, roads, even contours and the shape of the ground. Typical cartography or map-drawing, by comparison, is 'just' taking existing information 'usually other maps' and drawing it in a different way for a particular purpose. That's why my heroes are people like David Thompson, who not only drew his own maps but also captured all the information that he needed in order to draw them by surveying the land (and he didn't have aerial photos to make the job a lot easier either!) Also, David Thompson and I walked the Camp Ahmek beach on Canoe Lake making a map there centuries apart. We were the ones out in the field gathering/creating/capturing the original data."

Chapter 15

1. In Ottawa, Wally Schaber and Chris Harris started both an outfitters' store and guiding business (Blackfeather) under the Trailhead banner. Both are still operating today.

2. Guy Mary-Rousselière, *Qitdlarssuaq: The Story of a Polar Migration* (Winnipeg: Wuery, 1991). This is a story of an Inuit leader, Qitdlarssuaq, detaching himself and a group of followers from their parent community in search of new land and a new life. For the 1991 re-enactment of the mid-1800s migration, see Renee Wissink, "Qitdlarssuaq Chronicles," *Equinox Magazine* (Nov/Dec, 1987). For the Hobie Cat sailing trips on the Arctic Coast, see, Jeff MacInnis, "Braving the Northwest Passage," *National Geographic* (May 1989). As you would expect, these magazines treatments feature Mike's images. To see Mike's work from many of the experiences mentioned here, go to *www.MikeBeedellphoto.ca*. Mike is also a contract photographer, having produced images for government agencies and corporations (Parks Canada,

Environment Canada, the Canadian Museum of Civilization, Canadian Broadcasting Corporation, CanWest Global, Sports Canada) and publishers (*Canadian Geographic, National Geographic, Maclean's, Times*). His photo library has over five hundred thousand images from across the globe but with a speciality for the Canadian Arctic.

3. Mike recommends the documentary film *Chasing Ice*, a film by director/producer Jeff Orlowski. This film was recipient of the Renewable Natural Resources Foundation's 2013 Outstanding Achievement Award.

4. Mike shared this quote in an email correspondence in February 2014.

Chapter 16

1. For the environmental philosophy of Steve Van Matre, see *Acclimatization* (1972) and *Acclimatizing* (1974), published by the American Camping Association in Bradford, Indiana. These books centred on an approach of immersion with nature that so appealed to Diane and has been the cornerstone of her personal philosophy.

2. Diane Gribbin, "The Changing North," *Nastawgan: Quarterly Journal of the Wilderness Canoe Association*, Vol. 34, No. 3 (Fall 2007), 8–12.

3. Diane tells me she remembers a slightly more embarrassing version. "I walked right in, realized it was the wrong office but thought I was alone … taken in by the photos I couldn't help but come in and start looking around … turns out you were behind the opened door doing something and said, 'Can I help you?' Caught me snooping! Scared the heck out of me, so embarrassed but couldn't help but have to ask about all those great photos that drew me in … you offered me a seat and what a great long talk! What a great lifelong result to a wrong turn!"

4. Aldo Leopold, *A Sand County Almanac* (New York: Oxford University Press, 1949), 230–31.

Epilogue

1. Arne Naess has been a guiding philosophical light for me through four decades. See Arne Naess, *Ecology, Community and Lifestyle* (Cambridge: Cambridge University Press, 1989). For this specific reference, see Erling Kagge, *Philosophy for Polar Explorers: What They Don't Teach You in School* (London: Pushkin Press, 2005), 104.

2. To learn more about University of Alberta's Augustana Campus Outdoor Education program, see Morten Asfeldt, Glen Hvenegaard, and Ingrid Urberg, "Expeditions and Liberal Arts University Education" in *Understanding*

Educational Expeditions, edited by Simon Beames (Rotterdam: Sense Publishers, 2010), 67–78.

3. See Simon Beames, "Interactionism and Expeditions," in *Understanding Educational Expeditions*, edited by Simon Beames (Rotterdam: Sense Publishers, 2010), 25–32. It is G.H. Mead who introduced the phrase "generalized other." In Beames, 27.

4. Edward J. McCullough and Michael MacCagno, *Lac La Biche and the Early Fur Traders* (Edmonton: Canadian Circumpolar Institute, 1991).

5. Mary Northway, "Why Go Camping," in *Light from a Thousand Campfires*, edited by K.B. Webb (Martinsville, IN: American Camping Association, 1960). This is, in my opinion, one of the truly exceptional treatments on the psychology of camping. For ecopsychology, see Theodore Roszak, Mary E. Gomes, and Allen D. Kamer (editors), *Ecopsychology: Restoring the Earth/ Healing the Mind* (San Francisco: Sierra Club Books, 1995).

6. Kagge, *Philosophy for Polar Explorers*, 61.

7. Borge Dahle, "Norwegian Friluftsliv: A Lifelong Communal Process," in *Nature First: Outdoor Life the Friluftsliv Way*, edited by Bob Henderson and Nils Vikander (Toronto: Nature Heritage Books/Dundurn, 2007), 31.

8. Winifred A. Weir, "David Thompson Camped Here," *The Beaver* (September 1954). A fun read about David Thompson west of the Rockies is Jack Nisbet, *Sources of the River: Tracking David Thompson across Western North America* (Seattle: Sasquatch Books, 1994). Nisbet reports, "Thompson arrived by canoe to Lake Windermere July 18, perhaps to the campsite in question. Here nine men from the Kootenay band brought them a deer, enough to feed the group of ten. It was a rare full meal since they had arrived over Howse Pass, over the Height of Land-Continental Divide into the Upper Columbia River. Was that most important feed of deer cooked against a backdrop of that Douglas fir. Thompson moved camp to select a site for Kootenay House soon after this and then was encouraged to select yet another site which was just downstream but more sheltered." I look forward to travelling to Lake Windermere with David Thompson's journals in hand to find this fire-scarred Douglas fir stump, the campsite, and the fur trade post location. For an interesting tribute to David Thompson at the 1927 unveiling of a memorial over his Mount Royal Cemetery gravesite, see Sir Frederick Williams-Taylor and J.B. Tyrrell, "Report of the Management Committee — David Thompson Monument, Annual Report," *The Canadian Historical Association* (May 1927): 8–16. Here J.B. Tyrrell, himself a surveyor, comments: "For instance, one can travel in a canoe on the Kootenay River … and know every feature of the stream, its banks and the surrounding country before coming to them by using Thompson's maps."

ALSO BY BOB HENDERSON

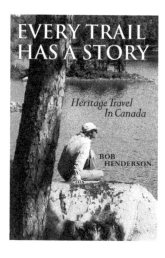

Every Trail Has a Story
Heritage Travel in Canada

Canada is packed with intriguing places for travel where heritage and landscape interact to create stories that fire our imagination. Scattered across the land are incredible tales of human life over the centuries. From the Majorville rock formation (dated as being older than Stonehenge), through the systems of walking trails developed by pre-contact Native Peoples, and the fur trade routes, to the more recent grand stories of the Chilkoot Gold Rush of 1897, Bob Henderson, the traveller, captures our living history in its relationship to the land — best expressed through the Norwegian quote "nature is the true home of culture."

The diversity of fascinating content includes the ancient James Bay landmark (the "Wonderful" Stone); the mountain treks of naturalist Mary Schaffer Warren; the west coast observations of George Vancouver; practices such as dog sledding, warm winter camping and canoeing that allow for heritage insights; the trails of Dundas, Ontario; the exploits of missionary Gabriel Sagard; the recluse Louis Gamache of Anticosti Island; the abandoned gravesites along the coast of Newfoundland — to name but a few.

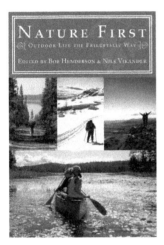

Nature First
Outdoor Life the Friluftsliv Way

Nature First combines the Scandinavian approach to creating a relationship with nature (known as *friluftsliv*) with efforts by Canadian and international educators to adapt this wisdom and apply it to everyday life experiences in the open air. The word *friluftsliv* literally refers to "free-air life" or outdoor life. A word saturated with values, the concept can permeate deeply and playfully into one's cultural being and personal psyche, thus influencing the way one perceives and interacts with nature on a daily basis.

Nature First is the first English-language anthology to bring together the perspectives and experiences of North American, Norwegian, Swedish, and other international outdoor writers, all *friluftsliv* thinkers and doers. Here, the thirty contributors' use of history, sociology, psychology, philosophy and outdoor education writings blend to provide an understanding of how *friluftsliv* applies to everyday life.

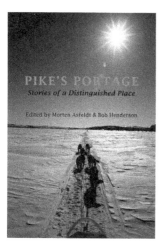

Pike's Portage
Stories of a Distinguished Place
edited by Morten Asfeldt and Bob Henderson

"Pike's Portage plays a very special role in the landscape of Canada's Far North and its human history. It is both an ancient gateway and the funnel for early travel from the boreal forest of the Mackenzie River watershed to the vast open spaces of the subarctic taiga, better known as the 'Barren Lands' of Canada.

"This book is a rich and wonderful compendium of stories about this area and the early white explorers, the Dene guides, the adventurers, the trappers, the misguided wanderers (like John Hornby), as well as the modern-day canoeists who passed this way. For the reader, it provides an absorbing escape into the past and the endless solitude of the northern wilderness."

— *George Luste, wilderness canoeist, physics professor (University of Toronto), and founder-organizer of the annual Wilderness Canoeing Symposium*

ALSO AVAILABLE FROM DUNDURN

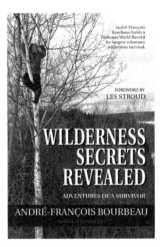

Wilderness Secrets Revealed
Adventures of a Survivor
by André-François Bourbeau

"Fire! Wake up! The shelter is on fire!"
    His students affectionately call him "Doc Survival." He's Quebec's Indiana Jones in a forest setting. Searching for the treasures of the wilderness has been his life-long quest; with passion as his only guide, he has dared to penetrate the forest on its own terms, facing increasingly difficult challenges in the hope of becoming nature's confidant, of learning her secrets.

Professor emeritus André-François Bourbeau holds a Guinness World Record for voluntary wilderness survival in the boreal forest. Herein lies his path and his stories, unadulterated: gritty and often comical mistakes punctuated by inspiring successes. What remains of this lifetime of experimentation is one man's everlasting love of the wilderness and its intricacies, a rousing reflection on our own human priorities, and need for deep connection with the environment and other fellow beings.

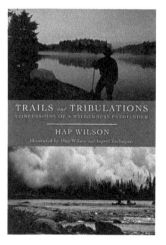

Trails and Tribulations
Confessions of a Wilderness Pathfinder
by Hap Wilson

In an age when "survival" shows permeate the media, noted northern traveller Hap Wilson shares accounts of his lifelong involvement with wilderness living within the Canadian Shield. Wilson knows better than most how to live in the woods. As park ranger, canoe guide, outfitter, trail builder, and environmental activist, he learned from firsthand experience that nature can neither be beaten or tamed.

Trails and Tribulations takes the reader on a journey with the author through natural settings ranging from austere to mysterious and breathtaking. Contents include animal attacks, bush fires, the threat of hypothermia, and vision-quest sites, to name but a few.

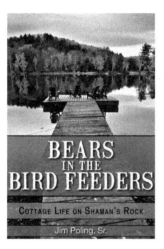

Bears in the Bird Feeders
Cottage Life on Shaman's Rock
by Jim Poling, Sr.

Listen carefully and you will hear cottage country whispering lessons that can make our lives less frenetic, less complicated. The mournful call of the loon, the wind sighing in the trees, the hammering of the pileated woodpecker remind us that we are a part of a more natural world too often lost in our urban societies.

Reflections from a still lake and a flickering campfire help us to realize that things might go easier for humankind if more issues were examined in softer, reflective light and without heated debate. People gathered at campfires, soothed by nature's tranquility, tend to listen and be more thoughtful before they speak.

This book will bring you on a journey through four seasons of cottaging and show you that nature has a remarkable power to heal — it just needs the human race to give it a helping hand. Along the way it will introduce you to some tips and tricks for making cottage life more comfortable and enjoyable.

Available at your favourite bookseller

 **DUNDURN**

Visit us at
Dundurn.com
@dundurnpress
Facebook.com/dundurnpress
Pinterest.com/dundurnpress